6·20·11   56467   73.35
                                  YBP

D1212080

Collective Action for Social Change

Collective Action for Social Change

An Introduction to Community Organizing

Aaron Schutz and Marie G. Sandy

First published in 2011 by
PALGRAVE MACMILLAN®
in the United States—a division of St. Martin's Press LLC,
175 Fifth Avenue, New York, NY 10010.

Where this book is distributed in the UK, Europe and the rest of the World,
this is by Palgrave Macmillan, a division of Macmillan Publishers Limited,
registered in England, company number 785998, of Houndmills,
Basingstoke, Hampshire RG21 6XS.

Palgrave Macmillan is the global academic imprint of the above
companies and has companies and representatives throughout the world.

Palgrave® and Macmillan® are registered trademarks in the United
States, the United Kingdom, Europe and other countries.

ISBN: 978–0–230–10537–9

Library of Congress Cataloging-in-Publication Data

Schutz, Aaron.
    Collective action for social change : an introduction to community
    organizing / Aaron Schutz and Marie G. Sandy.
        p.   cm.
    ISBN–13: 978–0–230–10537–9 (hardback)
    ISBN–10: 0–230–10537–8
    1. Community organization—United States.   2. Social change—
    United States.   3. Community organization—United States—
    Case studies.   4. Social change—United States—Case studies.
    I. Sandy, Marie G., 1968–   II. Title.
    HN65.S4294 2011
    361.8—dc22   2010041384

A catalogue record of the book is available from the British Library.

Design by Integra Software Services

First edition: April 2011

10 9 8 7 6 5 4 3 2 1

Printed in the United States of America.

To my daughters, Hiwot and Sheta, who have taught me a great deal about protest and resistance. Here's hoping they channel their great energy, creativity, and poise into a life that helps make our world a better place.

And to my wife, Jessica, from whom I have learned a great deal about compassion and tolerance. Without her support, this book could not have been written.

—Aaron Schutz

To the members of the Ontario Grassroots Thinktank and to Libreria del Pueblo's Calpulli Collective. Working with all of you has been one of the greatest gifts of my life. Thanks especially to Dr. Lourdes Arguelles for connecting me to the practice, theory, and spirit of this work, and to Cindy Marano, who first nurtured in me the capacity to do community organizing. While Cindy has been gone for several years, her work lives on through the policy changes she fought for, the organizations she inspired, and the organizers she taught.

Thanks also to my family, especially to my beloved Zeno, who I met during my years working with the Grassroots Thinktank, and he joined right in.

—Marie G. Sandy

The only way for communities to build long-term power is by organizing people and money around a common vision. . . . [Community] organizing teaches as nothing else does the beauty and strength of everyday people.
—President Barack Obama, *Dreams from My Father*

Contents

Acknowledgments

I would like to thank the range of organizers I have had the pleasure of working with, befriending, or even having in my courses. All of these people helped me understand what organizing is, including Larry Marx, David Liners, Chris Boston, James Logan, and Johnnie Morris. I am also deeply indebted to my co-leaders in Milwaukee Inner-City Congregations Allied for Hope and my students in Introduction to Community Organizing, who have put up with me for many years now.

—**Aaron Schutz**

I am grateful to Cindy Marano, formerly of Wider Opportunities for Women (WOW), for allowing me to apprentice with her during my time at WOW, and for introducing me to many organizers in the women's movement, especially those involved with the kind of organizing promoted by the Ms. Foundation for Women. I am particularly grateful to Rosa Martha Zarate and Father Patricio Guillen of Libreria del Pueblo for providing alternative ways of organizing in San Bernardino County and to Lily Rodriguez, Susan Gomez, Gilbert and Genevieve Miranda, Denise Palmer, Rosa Gonzales, Robert Gonzales, and other members of the Ontario Grassroots Thinktank.

—**Marie G. Sandy**

Introduction

I guess a small-town mayor is sort of like a "community organizer," except that you have actual responsibilities.
—Sarah Palin, Republican National Convention, 2008

I've had several reactions when I say I'm a community organizer. I had one person say to me, "Oh, you must have really clean closets."
—Vivian Chang, *We Make Change*

Few people in America know much of anything about community organizing. In fact, when a recent national survey asked people to say what came to mind when they heard the term "community organizing," few of the respondents understood what this meant.[1]

When Sarah Palin ridiculed Barack Obama in 2008 for having been a community organizer, it seemed like a teachable moment. Discussions about organizing filled the media for the first time in decades. But this coverage didn't seem to educate people very effectively about organizing. Certainly the pundit columns and TV roundtable discussions we saw exhibited little or no understanding of community organizing. These Washington insiders seemed unable to distinguish the organizing vision from the kind of short-term voter mobilization that they were familiar with.

This book joins a broader effort to address this ignorance about community organizing in America.

While we discuss other traditions, we focus on the approach to community organizing formulated by Saul Alinsky in the 1930s and developed by many others since then. Nearly all established organizing groups, today, remain deeply influenced by this still evolving tradition that we call "neo-Alinsky" or "Alinsky-based" community organizing.

Alinsky-Based Community Organizing: A Definition

- Community organizing creates durable institutions and builds local leadership, giving otherwise fractured communities a unified voice and the collective power necessary to resist oppression.

Accusations of revolutionary leftist socialism often arise when the name Alinsky is mentioned in right-wing political circles. But the fact is that, for good or ill, the organizing tradition has always been reformist, not revolutionary. Organizing groups want influence over, not destruction of, the social institutions that affect the lives of the oppressed. And although Alinsky embraced the metaphor of a "war" between the "haves" and the "have-nots," his work was fundamentally nonviolent. In fact, during the most radical years of the 1960s Alinsky actually became a voice for moderation, disgusted by the incoherent antics of violence-prone splinter groups like the Weathermen.

Community organizers believe that their work is grounded in the core traditions of American democracy. At the most fundamental level, they seek to nurture a more active and engaged citizenry in a nation where passive complaining and perfunctory voting often rule the day.

Learning to Be an Organizer?

This book is not, it is important to stress, a "how to" cookbook. A number of other good books exist that explain *how* to organize: how to run meetings, how to develop a governance structure, how to work with the media, and the like (we list a few of these in the Appendix). But before you can "do" organizing, we believe that you need to *think* like an organizer. And it turns out that learning how to think this way can be very challenging.

Between the two of us (Aaron and Marie) we have taught an Introduction to Community Organizing course to a diverse student body at the University of Wisconsin-Milwaukee for more than a decade. This experience has taught us that the organizing perspective is quite alien to most Americans. Learning to think like a community organizer generally involves critiquing long- and often strongly held convictions about social service and civic engagement. Many of our students are planning to pursue careers in a range of social service positions. And it is not unusual for these students to experience a crisis of confidence as they grapple with community organizing's criticisms of the "service" approach to social problems. It often takes an entire semester for most students to really internalize how organizers see the world—whether they decide they agree with this perspective or not.

Because of these challenges, we decided that attempting to engage readers in this task of "rethinking" was more than enough of a project for a single book.

Furthermore, while we both use cookbooks and technical manuals, we are also very conscious of their limitations. Can you really learn complex skills from a cookbook or a manual? Would you get in a car with someone who has memorized the driving manual but has never actually driven?

We doubt it.

Thus, while we invite those who are captivated by the organizing vision to move on to more "nuts and bolts" type books, we recommend finding an actual organizing effort to work on while you read them. "Nuts and bolts" knowledge is hard to retain if you aren't actually *using* it.

Principles vs. Rules

Saul [Alinsky's] understanding of the community organizing business was almost as nebulous as [Sarah] Palin's.

For Saul organizing varied in method, shape, and scope depending on the times and the circumstances . . . .

I doubt that Alinsky would have much use for [today's "standard" model of community organizing] in the changed society we live in. The least doctrinaire of men, he would in all likelihood be tinkering with new ways to realize the old goal of democratic self-rule.
—Nicholas von Hoffman, *Radical: A Portrait of Saul Alinsky*

Alinsky titled his second book about organizing *Rules for Radicals*. "Rules" was an unfortunate choice, because Alinsky also repeatedly emphasized that organizing was more of a mind-set than a set of established strategies or guidelines. A better title would have been *Principles for Radicals*.

Unlike a rule, a principle refers to a general tendency that can help guide one's actions. It is not a strict law of nature. In every specific situation, a principle will likely play out differently. Sometimes, a particular principle won't be relevant to a situation at all. For example, Alinsky generally recommended that organizing efforts move slowly, carefully building power over time. But at one point, during the 1960s, he realized that he was in the "whirlwind." So he threw that rule out the window and rushed organizations into large actions over very short periods of time.

This leaves us in an odd position for people writing a book about organizing. At the same time as we lay out the basic "principles" of neo-Alinsky organizing, we recommend that you don't take what we say *too* seriously. It is often the case that in real contexts some of the most basic "rules" of any discipline can be broken if you are going to succeed. But people are better equipped to intelligently break rules if they really understand them in the first place.

Overall, this book provides an abstract model of organizing written for an abstract world that, Alinsky noted, doesn't actually exist. The concepts and ideas we present, here, must be actively appropriated and sometimes rejected in actual situations of social struggle. So don't come back to us and say, "Well, that's what you told me to do." We don't *know* what to do to solve your problem. It's *your* problem. You need to figure it out.

I'm a Conservative. Should I Read Your Book?

Since the election of our first community organizer president, conservatives in America have become increasingly interested in Alinsky and organizing more broadly. In the "customers who bought this item also bought" list attached to Alinsky's *Rules for Radicals* page on amazon.com, for example, you find books written by Glenn Beck, Bill O'Reilly, and Ayn Rand and titles like *Liberal Fascism*, *Rules for Republican Radicals* and *Obama's Plan to Subvert the Constitution*.

Community organizing in America, as we define it, however, has usually staked out a fairly generic center-left political position. Alinsky was a pragmatist, and ideological purists of all kinds creeped him out. So he didn't have much interest in working with fiery-eyed leftists. Even if he had, there weren't enough of them in America to generate the collective power necessary to produce significant social change. He and the organizers who came after him have always understood that any effective organizing effort needs to attract a membership that reaches across existing political, cultural, religious, and other divides. In fact, aspects of organizing have actually become *more* moderate in recent years because of a focus on congregational organizing and a growing middle-class constituency.[2]

Because of the diversity of their membership, organizing groups generally avoid hot-button culture war issues like abortion, gay rights, or school vouchers because they would fracture their coalition. Instead, they focus on problems that a broad range of people can agree on, like improving education, confronting racial discrimination, and getting people access to good jobs. As a result, many conservatives have been able to find comfortable homes within Alinsky-based community organizations. At the same time, of course, community organizing groups tend to avoid issues that are close to the hearts of many conservative activists.

Some components of the organizing model may be of limited relevance to the top-down social action approach increasingly embraced by far right wing movements in America (and, historically, by some radical leftists). Community organizing groups don't, *can't,* embrace any discrete political or religious dogma. Instead of telling people what to think, organizers ask people what they care about. Instead of trying to convert people to particular political or social points of view, organizers champion a very general set of values about caring, equality, justice, and democracy. So if you want to convince people that you already have the answer, key aspects of the organizing approach may not be that useful to you.

The Tone of This Book

Because the goal of this book is to teach people to think like community organizers, we generally take a fairly partisan stance in favor of organizing in the text that follows. Pedagogically, we believe this is the most effective approach. It is important to note, however, that both of us are also critical of many aspects of the organizing vision. Some of these criticisms can be found in Aaron's "Core Dilemmas of Community Organizing" series on the blog Open Left. We plan to publish a follow-up volume drawing on the Core Dilemmas series that will provide a much more critical analysis of the current state of the field.[3]

Boxes, Epigraphs, and Body Text: The Logic of Our Presentation

In this brief introduction, you have already had a taste of some of the textual structure of this book. We use three different formats to provide diverse perspectives on organizing while also advancing our own argument.

What we call "body text" represents the traditional narrative that you are reading right now. We use this format for our core explanations of the organizing model. Epigraphs or quotations from a range of different scholars and practitioners often begin different sections of body text, illuminating aspects of the ongoing discussion or adding useful information. Finally, within what we call "boxes," you will find a range of stories, interviews, and advice drawn from our own experience as well as that of a diverse collection of community organizers. The material in boxes may bring in new issues or provide relevant examples or extend the discussion in perhaps unexpected directions. The language in the "box" writings and epigraphs often provide a visceral sense of the way different organizers talk and strategize.

Note that we have sometimes taken minor liberties with epigraphs and quotations—adding extra paragraph breaks, for example—to improve their readability.

The Organization of This Book

We have split this volume into six separate sections. We begin with an overview section that discusses what community organizing *is* and what community organizing *isn't*. The organizing vision diverges radically, at points, from more common ways of thinking about social action or community change in America. We have found that unless we explain how organizing is different from the visions people bring with them to our courses, they often try to fit organizing into a model that they are more familiar and more comfortable with.

The second section focuses on history and theory. A fairly long chapter summarizes the history of community organizing in America, describing the evolution of social movements and local organizing efforts, as well as the emergence of what some call the "nonprofit industrial complex." Another chapter goes into more detail about Alinsky's idiosyncratic but extremely influential
vision.

The third section provides case studies meant to give readers a rich sense of the different forms community organizing can take in America today. The first chapter describes Obama's recent presidential campaign and explains how his campaign appropriated some key organizing techniques for its voter mobilization effort. The next two chapters are written by outside authors. Mark Warren contributes a selection from his outstanding book-length study of congregational or church-based organizing within the national Industrial Areas Foundation, *Dry Bones Rattling*. And Heidi Swarts draws from her equally important in-depth research on the Association of Community Organizations for Reform Now, or ACORN (see her book *Organizing Urban America*), to provide an overview of its strategy and an explanation of its recent demise. In the final chapter in this section, Marie discusses a local organizing project she worked with that was unaffiliated with any national organization: a university-sponsored grassroots "think tank" that brought poor and middle-class people together around community problems.

The fourth and longest section of the book introduces a range of key concepts in community organizing, explaining how organizers think about leadership, "cut issues," come up with tactics, and much more.

Comments or Criticisms?

We look forward to hearing from readers. We have set up a blog where people can enter a discussion about the book at www.educationaction.org/collective-action-discussion.html. Feel free to join us there!

Notes

1. National Conference on Citizenship, *Civic Health Index 2008* (Washington, D.C.: National Conference on Citizenship, 2008).
2. Nicholas von Hoffman, *Radical: A Portrait of Saul Alinsky* (New York: Nation Books, 2010).
3. See www.educationaction.org/core-dilemmas-of-community-organizing-html, accessed April 6, 2010.

PART I

Overview

CHAPTER 1

What *Is* Community Organizing?

A People's Organization lives in a world of hard reality. It lives in the midst of smashing forces, dashing struggles, sweeping cross-currents, ripping passions, conflict, confusion, seeming chaos, the hot and the cold, the squalor and the drama, which people prosaically refer to as life and students describe as "society."

—Saul Alinsky, *Reveille for Radicals*, 1946

Community Organizing

Groups seeking social change in American history have drawn from many different sources for their strategies. In this book we introduce you to the tradition of community organizing first formulated by Saul Alinsky in the 1930s. Alinsky's tradition, as evolved by those who came after him, has become a prominent model used by less privileged groups in America to create collective power. Nearly all groups fighting for social change in the United States today are at least influenced by this approach.

The prominence of the Alinsky tradition of social action has grown over the last few years, especially after organizing became a hot-button issue during the 2008 presidential election. During the campaign, the community organizing group ACORN was often in the media and frequently attacked. The public was reminded that presidential candidate Barack Obama had been a community organizer when Sarah Palin belittled organizers during the Republican National Convention. And Obama's opponent and later Secretary of State, Hillary Clinton, was criticized because she not only wrote her college thesis on Alinsky's strategies, but was even offered a job by Alinsky after college.

Although references to community organizing have become more common in the media, few people in America really know what "organizing" is.

Most people who were asked in a recent survey what "community organizing" meant thought it was somehow related to community service, even though Alinsky developed community organizing in reaction *against* the limitations of the "service" approach.

What Is Community Organizing?

Organizers develop institutions to represent impoverished and oppressed citizens in the realms of power. Organizing groups conduct strategic campaigns, pressuring powerful individuals and groups to improve the lives of their constituencies. They bring masses of people together in actions where they make demands through their leaders in a collective voice. Successful campaigns have forced banks to support low-income housing, lobbied city councils to pass living-wage laws, and pressured legislatures to lower class sizes in public schools, among many other accomplishments.

In the most general sense, community organizing seeks to *alter the relations of power* between the groups who have traditionally controlled our society and the residents of marginalized communities. Organizing groups shift the relations of power by

- increasing their membership,
- nurturing and training leaders,
- gaining a reputation for canny strategy,
- raising money to fund their infrastructure and staff, and
- demonstrating their capacity to get large numbers of people out to public actions.

Ideally, over time, success in individual campaigns increases the public reputation of an organization so that it will increasingly be consulted on important issues *before* decisions are made.

In contrast with more cooperative approaches to community change (like "community development," discussed in Chapter 2), organizers believe that significant social change only comes through conflict with the entrenched interests of the status quo. In fact, organizing groups usually *seek out* issues that are likely to generate controversy and tension. Vigorous, nonviolent battles for change draw in, energize, and educate new participants, enhancing a group's public standing in the community.

The Invisible History of Power in America

Few of us consider how much our environment is filled with the remnants of forgotten conflicts. As we go about our daily lives, it is easy to forget that what is familiar and unremarkable today was often unusual or forbidden not long ago. The social struggles that created much of the infrastructure and many of the institutions we depend upon have become largely invisible. To note just a few examples, today:

- Women can vote because generations of "suffragists" fought for equality in the nineteenth and early twentieth centuries.
- People grow old without fear of destitution because "Townsend Plan" clubs across America agitated for social security during the 1930s.
- People with mental limitations participate in public life instead of being hidden away in asylums because of the disability rights movement.
- Children from impoverished families eat for free in public schools because of the work of antihunger activists in the 1960s.
- AIDS research and treatment receives federal funding because thousands of activists fought against discrimination in the 1980s.

We could go on.

In your own neighborhood, wherever you live, you are almost surely surrounded by the consequences of social struggles, both small and large. The location, size, and contents of your local park, for example, likely represent the power of different collective efforts in the past. Don't have a nearby park? Well, that is likely the result of your neighborhood's *lack* of collective power. Is your park clean and sparkling, or unkempt and littered? Either way, it likely reflects your neighborhood's influence with the local public works department.

It is no secret in our country that public schools in low-income areas are badly funded, or that millions lack health care. It is no secret that if your skin is dark you have a much greater chance of being convicted of a crime or ending up on death row. It is no secret that our central cities are crumbling, or that children still go hungry every day.

The problem is not that we don't *know* about social problems in America. The problem is not that no one *cares* about these problems. The problem is that most of us have no idea how to do something concrete to solve them.

Cleaning Up a Local Park

When the pastor of the congregation one of the authors attends first arrived, the land behind the church was overgrown and full of trash. He didn't realize this space was actually a park until he asked around. Of course, this church is in one of the poorest neighborhoods in the city.

He called the local alderman to complain, and nothing was done. Then he asked thirty or forty people in the congregation to call and complain. He asked them to tell the alderman that if something wasn't done they would show up at his office, next. The parks department showed up the next day to clean up the park. Today, the space behind the church is a place for children to play, not a dumping ground for neighborhood trash.

An argument didn't win the day. A plea for help didn't win the day. A demonstration of collective power won the day.

The shiny play structure and trimmed grass of the pastor's park, today, is a testament to the work of community organizing. But the struggle that produced this nice place to play is largely invisible. Few, if any, of the children and families that visit the park know why it looks the way it does today.

Civic Miseducation in America

You come to school to get the abilities to learn and to strengthen yourself, but you don't learn how to fight. In fact, you learn how *not* to fight. They teach you just the opposite. Don't make waves, don't make noises, don't take any risks.

—Dolores Huerta, *Dolores Huerta Reader*

On the first day of our "Introduction to Community Organizing" class, we often ask a simple question:

How many of you, after more than twelve years of schooling, have ever complained to a teacher or an administrator about some problem you are having and had that person say, "Well, why don't you get together with some other students and see if you can do something about it?"

Few students ever raise their hands. And those few who do invariably have pretty unique stories. With very few exceptions, what we learn every semester is that in all of our students' years of schooling, *no one* has *ever* taught them about power—how it works or how to generate it.

They have, of course, heard about some of the social struggles that occurred in American history. They may have read about abolitionists who fought slavery before the Civil War or about the struggle for women's voting rights. Most have seen black-and-white newsreels from the Civil Rights Movement: lines of black people walking to work alongside empty buses in Montgomery, or children bravely facing snarling police dogs and water cannons in Birmingham. These stories, however, have largely become part of our American mythology. Students learn that these events *happened*, but they do not learn how people *made them happen*.

Social change in America is usually explained in quite sanitized ways. Martin Luther King, for example, has become an icon of peace and reconciliation. We often hear the "I Have a Dream" speech, where he spoke of his hope that people would learn to get along with and love each other. We almost never hear King's much more typical speeches where he exhorted masses of people into often brutal (if nonviolent) confrontations with inequality. And, of course, we rarely hear about the speeches of Malcom X, Stokeley Carmichael of the Black Power Movement, or other leaders who didn't speak as much about love and compassion as King.[1]

In school we are mostly taught that *truth matters* and will win out in the end. In school we learn that, in the end, people are mostly reasonable and willing to cooperate.

Of course, there is some truth to this. Most people are not evil. Most people at least *want* to do what is right.

What is missing from these lessons, however, is the fact that if one group of people is to "get" something, in most cases another group will have to give something up. We are not taught that truth, alone, is rarely enough to produce significant change, or that cooperation usually only works between people who already respect and understand each other.

These omissions are no accident. It is simply not in the interests of people in relatively powerful positions to teach the less powerful how to resist them. This, we will argue, is a basic fact of human society, not some elaborate conspiracy. In fact, in our community organizing classes we often use the course itself and our relationship with students to make this concretely visible.

Why Teachers Don't Teach Students How to Be Powerful

"Why," Aaron asks his class at their first meeting, "would I teach you how to make my own life difficult? If *one* of you goes to the Dean and complains about me—my grading for example—that wouldn't really matter. In fact, if I wanted, I could make an example of that person, showing other students why they better not cross me. But what you probably don't realize is that if *most of you* go as a group to complain, I could have real trouble on my hands. Because the Dean doesn't want the headache. He'll put a lot of pressure on me to 'solve the problem'.

"The truth is that if you stick together, you have quite a lot of power to make my life difficult. So the last thing I want is to teach you how to act collectively. In fact, it's in my best interest to keep all of you fairly isolated from each other. Sure, I can put you in groups to chat and work together on projects. But I don't want you to start seeing yourself as a collective.

"What is the most effective thing I could do," he asks, "if one of you gets upset with me and starts getting people together to do something about what a terrible teacher I am?"

Students often make suggestions like "grade the student even harder," "threaten the student with a bad grade," or "threaten the whole class." At some point, however, someone will usually suggest the opposite, that Aaron might just "give in and raise the complaining students' grades."

At this point, Aaron jumps in with a "Yes!" While he acknowledges that some of the other approaches might work, he argues that the most effective approach is probably just to "buy the complaining student off." This is a classic strategy that powerful people use to short-circuit collective resistance. "If I ease off on the grades for anyone who might become a leader," Aaron says, "then I probably don't have to worry about the rest of you. The rest of you are sheep! I only need to worry about potential shepherds."

"In any case," Aaron emphasizes, "the last thing I want is for you to figure out that you actually do have some power. I want you to think that I am all powerful, that I can give you whatever grades I want, can make you complete whatever assignments I demand, and you don't have any choice about it. If my 'buying the student off' strategy doesn't work, then I may even preemptively eliminate a few assignments for everyone to make your lives easier and cut any organizing off at the pass. If I make things easier for you and it's *my* decision, then I haven't given up any power.

"But if you actually go to the Dean and complain, I'm not necessarily going to just give in. In fact, that may harden my resistance, even if you are asking for changes I don't really care about.

"Why?

"Because the last thing I want is for students to get the idea that they might have any power over me. At this point the key issue shifts from what you specifically want to a contest over who has the real power over this class. If I lose, who knows what you might demand next time?"

The Lack of Support for Organizing

The antiorganizing position of teachers and schools is only magnified in the world outside of schools. Corporations and the governments have no incentive to support collective empowerment that generates resistance and produces conflict. It makes a lot more sense to sponsor service activities. They'll give money to a homeless shelter or a food pantry, but not to an organization fighting for more housing or to a group seeking to increase food stamp allocations. Even philanthropic foundations generally shy away from social action. They don't want to endanger their status in the community or future contributions from donors. Giving money for service avoids controversy and makes everyone happy. It's the "feel-good" approach to social change and civic engagement.[2]

In fact, it is the exception that proves the rule. As we will discuss in more detail in Chapter 3, during a short period in the 1970s the federal government actually did fund locally controlled groups engaged in collective action that disrupted the status quo. In response, mayors and other established officials flooded federal offices with complaints. Local officials couldn't understand why the government would fund people to threaten *their* power. Not surprisingly, the democratic aspects of this program quickly ended. Today, few community organizing groups receive government funding.

When we are given opportunities for civic engagement in school, on the job, or more generally in the community, then, these are generally restricted to charity or service. We join a walk to raise money for the local children's hospital; we tutor once a week in a low-income school; we help build a home for a single mother. Of course, there is nothing wrong with these activities. On some level, however, many of us likely know that the amount of money raised by a pledge walk probably won't pay the cancer treatment bills for even a single seriously ill patient. What cancer patients really need are not small pledges, but better health insurance. On some level many of us must realize that a couple of hours of (untrained) tutoring is not what children in bad schools really need. What they need are better schools. And it seems hard to ignore the fact that spending an enormous amount of energy building a single house is a not a particularly efficient way to respond to the needs of the hundreds of thousands of homeless and ill-housed families across America.

But we don't know what else to do. At least we are doing *something*.

Sometimes, People Do Act

Sometimes an injustice strikes enough people with enough force that they get together to do something about it. It can be something as small as a plan to chop down a beloved neighborhood oak tree. Or it can be as large as a threat to close the largest employer in town, or, more broadly, a president's refusal to end an unpopular war.

But since most of us don't know much of anything about collective action and power, we end up reinventing the wheel. Without access to the strategies and tactics developed by those who came before them, groups frequently make the same greenhorn mistakes again and again.

Partly as a result, these efforts often fail. The tree gets chopped down. The employer leaves. The war doesn't end.

Highly experienced community organizing groups often fail. It is always difficult to win against the powerful. Inexperienced groups are at a greater disadvantage. This is partly why so many believe that "you can't fight City Hall." As this book will show, you can fight City Hall. But you need to know what you are doing.

Sometimes, even when an inexperienced group *seems* to win, it ends up losing in the end. The city may agree to save the tree, wait a few months until things die down and protestors go home, and then chop it down anyway when nobody is looking. An employer may agree to accept tax relief from the city, but then ship its jobs to another state the next year anyway, happily pocketing the extra tax money and leaving the community in even worse shape.

Those who can't hold decision makers accountable over the long term often find that short-term "wins" don't get them much.

In this book we introduce many of the lessons that organizers have learned in their efforts to contest inequality and injustice over the past century. We lay out the core principles that guide many of the most sophisticated groups engaged in collective struggle in America today.

We refer, as we note in the introduction, to "principles" and not "rules," because there are no certainties in our changing world. Yesterday's strategies must always be adapted and transformed to meet the needs of the unique challenges of the present. Expertise at any task always involves combining knowledge drawn from the past with insight about contingencies encountered in the present. There is no simple "textbook" for power. Anyone who tells you otherwise is living a fantasy.

Rinku Sen describes this tension another way. She calls organizing a "craft" that lies somewhere between "art" and "science." Only when you can actually put art and science together creatively amid struggle have you learned the *craft*. And you can't learn this craft from a book. You need to go learn it on the streets.

Social Service vs. Strategic Social Action

Alinsky often told versions of the following parable to help people understand the difference between the way we normally think about social problems and the way community organizers think about social problems.

The Parable of the River

One warm summer afternoon, a group of five friends gathered around a fire on the banks of a small river in the woods. Sprawled on the grass or sitting on logs, they drank cold beer from a cooler, chatting lazily amidst the sounds of rushing water, birdcalls, and the buzz of crickets.

Suddenly, one of them stood up with a cry. Dropping her beer, she skidded down the muddy bank into the river. The rest of them watched, bemused, as she waded in up to her waist, grabbed something floating there, and carried it back to them. As she came out of the water, the others heard something crying.

"Oh my God!" one of them said. She held a baby in her hands.

"It was drowning," the woman with the baby said, "I don't know if it's okay."

Then someone else in the group shouted, "There's another one!" He rushed down into the water as well, followed by the others.

As they waded in to get the second baby, one of them happened to look up the river. "Oh no," she said. As far up as she could see, babies struggled in the water.

The group began frantically rushing in and out of the river, trying to catch the babies as they went by. At first they managed to get all of them before they went by, but after a while they started getting tired. Babies started getting by them. They saw some babies go under without coming back up. Crying and shaking from the cold river water, they couldn't stop. The riverbank became littered with more and more babies, some crawling around, others not moving. But there wasn't time to check on them. There were always more in the water.

Finally one of the rescuers stopped. She stood for a moment, thinking, and then she took off running up the river, away from the group.

"Come back!" cried one of her friends.

"What are you doing?" yelled another as he struggled toward the bank with a baby in both arms.

"I'm going to find out who's throwing all these babies in the river," she shouted back, and she kept running.

The woman running up the river, Alinsky would tell his audience, was thinking like an "organizer." She realized the futility of trying to rescue an endless torrent of drowning babies. What they needed to do was prevent babies from being thrown into the river in the first place.

Alinsky often complained about social service workers who tried to solve problems "downriver" but never looked "upriver" to think about how to prevent problems from happening in the first place.

A central aspect of this story is that the woman running upriver assumed that babies are not just *accidentally* in the river. She was going to see who was *throwing* the babies in. Versions of this parable in texts for social workers and other service professions often miss this point. A textbook for public health professionals, for example, has the person running upstream say: "I'm going . . . to see why so many people keep *falling* into the river." It continues the story little farther, reporting that, "as it turns out, the bridge leading across the river up stream *has* a hole through which people are falling. The upstream rescuer realizes that fixing the hole in the bridge will prevent many people from ever falling into the river in the first place." Note the passive voice in the textbook version. The bridge just *happens* to have a hole in it. No one in particular is responsible.[3]

From the perspective of a community organizer, this textbook completely misunderstands how the world works.

Bad things, organizers argue, rarely just "happen." Most "babies" in "rivers" around the world are black babies, poor babies, babies of undocumented immigrants, and the like. This is no accident. Real people and the institutions they control are responsible for a world that allows so many of these babies to drown (or go hungry, or get a bad education, and so on). Elected officials fund bridges in their own districts and not in others. Rich voters don't want to pay money for repairs in someone "else's" community.

Unless you are individually powerful or come from a pretty privileged community, you can't just call the people "in charge," tell them that you have a problem, and expect much to change. Like the inner-city pastor with the trash-filled park, you can rarely just say "pretty please" and get the support you need. The *fact* of a crisis is not enough.

Most crises like these are not new or unknown. If people were going to do something about them, they already would have. Instead, what we usually get are excuses. "We'd love to give all babies life preservers, but we just can't afford it." "It's someone else's responsibility." "We're too busy fixing holes elsewhere." "Yes, we know, we've got a team working on that." "We're waiting for the results of a feasibility study." "We'll get to it. Just trust us."

Babies *are* in the river, today. Prison construction, for example, is often based on third-grade reading scores. By the time they reach the age of nine, then, we *already know* how many kids are likely to end up in jail. They are already in the river heading toward incarceration. And we do, in fact, know about concrete changes that would both pull many of them out of this river and prevent other kids from ever falling in. But we lack sufficient political capacity, sufficient *power*, to make them happen.

Internal Tensions and Problems with the River Parable

Alinsky wasn't under the illusion that the choice made by the woman running upstream was easy, or simple, or unproblematic. In fact, he sometimes used this story to make a further ethical point. When the woman abandoned her role as a savior on the bank, there was now one fewer person to help "those poor wretches who continue . . . to float down the river." In a world with limited resources, the woman who runs upstream is, in fact, allowing some babies to drown in the hope that she can deal with the problem in a different way. Hers is a tragic choice.[4]

Social workers and other service providers will always be necessary in our world. No matter how much power we generate for positive social change, there will always be some babies in the river. So we don't mean to denigrate service in this book. The problem is not that some people provide services. The problem is that so *few* people are organizing to reduce the need for these services. So many babies are in the river that there is no hope that we could ever rescue them all. Most will continue to float down the stream. Many will drown. Service workers, in prisons, child welfare agencies, inner-city emergency rooms, police stations, and elsewhere, face the same growing hopelessness experienced by those in the parable. They catch a few babies here and there, but watch most of them drown.

(At the same time, however, organizers note how dependent the livelihood of service workers is on a continuing stream of drowning babies. In fact, it seems at least possible that the very structure of the "service industrial complex" may play a role, however unintentional, in perpetuating this suffering. Think, for example, of the many jobs provided in rural areas by prisons filled with people of color from urban areas. There is solid evidence that the need for jobs for prison guards is part of what drives an increasing tendency to incarcerate people of color. There is the potential for a destructive cycle in many different areas, here, supported by service providers' need for jobs providing services.)

From an organizing perspective, there are also problems with the way Alinsky tended to present this parable. First of all, the people that organizers try to help are rarely "babies." Those who suffer the effects of inequality are almost always capable of acting for change if they can develop the right tools and resources. Organizing is not about doing *for* others. Instead, organizers are supposed to work *with* people to produce social change. A key tenet of organizing is that those affected by a particular social problem are usually best equipped to figure out what changes are most likely to make a real difference.

Second, the parable implies that organizers worry a lot about who has *caused* a particular problem. In fact, however, causation is frequently unimportant. The key question is not who dumped PCBs in a lake, for example – that company may be long gone. Instead, organizers try to figure out who can be *held responsible* for cleaning it up, now. From an organizing point of view we live in a world where some people have enormous privilege and resources, while others have little or nothing. Unless those with resources and decision-making power are pressured to act in different ways, the core challenges of our society cannot be addressed.

People with no boots cannot pull themselves up by their bootstraps.

How Do Organizers Think?

In this section we introduce some of the key concepts that organizers use to make sense of the world around them. We lay these out here in fairly simple form. When you get to the second half of the book, you will discover that these concepts are more complicated and challenging to apply than they may initially seem.

Every tradition of social action has a different perspective on social problems. Social service professionals, for example, look into oppressed communities and see masses of suffering people who need their help. Organizers, in contrast, see not victims but potential actors in the same communities. While service professionals learn skills for helping people in crisis, then, organizers develop strategies for helping people come together to demand change.

Building Power, Not Just Winning Campaigns

In our experience, people who are new to organizing often struggle to internalize organizing's focus on power. Novices generally understand organizing, at least initially, as a set of strategies for *winning* on particular issues. The ultimate goal, they often think, is to win things like wage increases, more low-income housing, more resources for schools, and the like. Of course, they are right to some extent. Winning is critical. An organizing group that never wins is clearly not accomplishing much, however much effort it puts into its work.

Experienced organizers, however, understand that winning specific social changes is really a *means* for achieving a more important goal: *power*. Organizing groups do not simply want to win, they want to win in ways that enhance their capacities for winning *even more* in the future. This means that *how* groups organize around particular issues is at least as important as *what* they win.

What do organizers mean by power? In a simple sense, organizers define power as:

> The capacity to influence (or affect) the actions of powerful people and institutions.

Power for a community organizing group is the product of many things:

- how many people it can bring out to key actions,
- how many leaders it has,
- how effective and savvy its leaders are,
- how much money it has, and
- how strong its reputation is.

These are the kinds of capacities and resources organizers seek to build up over time.

When you have real power, other powerful people and groups are

- more likely to keep their promises to you,
- more likely to consult you before they do something your constituency might object to, and
- less likely to make decisions that might hurt your constituency.

> The two central goals of organizing are: building collective power and developing leaders who can sustain that power over the long term.

Organizers and Leaders

Community organizers in the Alinsky tradition make a distinction between two critical roles: organizers and leaders. In more established organizations, "organizers" are usually paid staff. They do the day-to-day work necessary to keep an organization going, seek out and train leaders, and support the work of emerging or ongoing campaigns. Their focus is on enhancing the overall power of the organization and on helping leaders become more effective. Organizers may come from outside a community or emerge from within it.

"Leaders," in contrast, govern a community organizing group and decide what issues it will work on. Unlike organizers, leaders are almost always unpaid volunteers. Leaders, not organizers, speak for and provide the public "face" of an organization. Some leaders may serve on a central board that takes care of administrative issues and fund-raising, while others work on issue committees that plan and conduct campaigns. Becoming a leader does not necessarily involve taking on some formal position within the organization. Instead, due in part to a chronic lack of sufficient leadership, anyone who reliably participates in the central tasks of the organization is generally considered a "leader."

Organizing groups strive to be democratic, and important decisions are usually voted on in large public meetings attended by many members. Usually, however, these meetings ratify decisions made by fairly small groups of active leaders. Many day-to-day decisions are, of necessity, made without much broader consultation. To ensure that leaders stay connected to their constituencies, leaders run house meetings and conduct one-on-one interviews with members. These strategies help them stay in touch with the interests and desires of the larger mass of less involved participants. In the ideal, leaders develop relationships with a wide range of members, seeking to draw them into more active participation in campaigns and actions.

Given the absence of pay, competition for leadership positions is generally less of a problem than the lack of sufficient leadership to get all the work done. As a result, the core task of an organizer is identifying and developing new leaders.

While people may sometimes move between leader and staff organizer roles, the roles themselves are usually kept separate. While there are examples of organizer/leaders (e.g., Cesar Chavez, discussed in Chapter 3) usually one cannot be both a leader and an organizer at the same time.

Problems vs. Issues

Another basic distinction in community organizing is between *problems* and *issues*. Problems are broad, vague challenges in the world. *World hunger* is a problem. *Bad schools,* collectively, are a "problem." *Police harassment* is a problem. Problems are so enormous, ill defined, and overwhelming that just thinking about them can be disempowering. Nobody really knows how to deal with a problem. Instead of motivating people to act, thinking about problems can make people want to go home, pull the covers over their heads, and take a nap. Thinking about problems usually just makes people feel hopeless.

To make life more manageable, community organizers "cut issues" out of problems. When you "cut" an issue, you carve a discrete, achievable goal out of an overwhelming crisis. Here are some examples of "issues" that community organizing groups have cut out of "problems" in the past:

PROBLEM	→	ISSUE
World hunger	→	Provide 3 million dollars from the county budget for a local food pantry.
Bad schools	→	Reduce class size to 16 in grades K – 3 in high-poverty schools.
Police harassment	→	Put automatic video cameras in squad cars to record traffic stops.

What "Counts" as a Good Issue?

In a Chapter 13, we discuss how to cut a good issue in more detail. At this point it seems helpful to emphasize just a few of the most critical criteria.

First, notice how specific each issue is in the table above. Whenever you cut an issue, you should know *exactly* what you are trying to achieve (even if you may eventually have to compromise). Otherwise, you leave decisions about what should be done in the hands of your opposition. If you make a general request for "more money" to the city for a food pantry, for example, they could give you $1,000, or $100. "We gave you 'more' money," they might say, "What's your problem?"

Second, you want your demand to be crystal clear to your constituency and other potential supporters. Instead of distributing 10-page documents filled with complex specifics, you want to communicate the key aspects of your demand in brief, simple language.

Similarly, third, you want your audience to immediately grasp the injustice of your issue. They need to feel it viscerally, in their "guts." You want to show people what it is like, for example, to have 35 children in a classroom with one teacher, or what it is like for hungry families turned away from empty food pantries.

Locating a Target

A *target* is the person or, sometimes, group of persons that can make the change you want. You need to know who your target is, because you can only begin to strategize about effective actions after you understand your target's goals and motivations.

As we noted in "The Parable of the River," at the core of organizing is the conviction that inequality and injustice are not simply the product of anonymous forces in the world. Organizers believe that we are all responsible in one way or another for the fact that so many problems in the world around us have not been solved. Again, organizers are less concerned about who *caused* a problem than about who can legitimately be *made responsible* for it.

Health care is a good example of a social "problem" out of which a group could cut many different, specific "issues." Each issue would likely have a different target, and figuring out what the target should be in each case will inevitably require extensive research.

If you wanted to get a new dental clinic in your neighborhood, for example, the "target" might be the dental school in the city, or the local health department, or even some part of city government. The right "target" would depend upon what your research discovered about the kinds of responsibilities these different institutions have generally taken on in the past, whether they have the actual resources to support a new clinic, and whether you can figure out how to put enough pressure on them to win. Choosing the right target from the beginning is critical, because you don't want to spend a whole lot of effort pressuring the dental school only to find out that it's the health department that really has the resources to create a dental clinic.

It's important to remember that institutions like dental schools or health departments are always made up of people. Within or at least connected to every institution is a person or group with the power to decide what it will do. Ultimately, therefore, targets are always *persons*.

Sometimes you find that you cannot locate a target that you can put sufficient pressure on to get what you want. In these cases, you need to find a different issue.

If you don't have a target, you can go out in the streets and wave signs or hold an angry rally to raise public awareness, but you can't "organize."

No target = no organizing.

Tactics

In part because we are so uneducated (miseducated) about how power operates, when we get upset about something our first inclination—if we do anything concrete at all—is usually to put together a "protest." In the next chapter we discuss "activist" groups that "do" protests. Groups like these get together and plan out events where they wave signs on the street. Or they hold rallies where people speak passionately about the need for change—usually to other people who already agree with them. The media doesn't usually bother to come to events like these.

Organizing groups don't simply "act" for the sake of action. Instead, as the following story shows, they develop "tactics" or "actions" (we will mostly use these terms interchangeably) carefully designed to put pressure on their specific target.

Putting Pressure on a Target

A few years ago, a conservative talk show host on a local radio station referred to Latinos in our community as a bunch of "wetbacks" from across the border. Some outraged community groups responded by protesting in front of the station.

During this time, a community organizer came to talk to one of our classes. He belittled the protestors for their failure to think strategically.

"What does the radio station *really* care about?" he asked the class.

After some silence and different answers, like "audience numbers" and "reputation," someone said "Money!"

"All of the issues you mentioned are important," he said, "but the core issue is usually money. In the end, however, it's an empirical question. A good organizer always explores a range of possible motivations for the actions of his opposition. But let's assume money is the key for now."

Then he asked, "Given their core motivation, how much do you think they will care if some people walk around with signs in front of their building?"

Students thought about it for a while, and then agreed that it probably wouldn't make that much difference to the station. "Everyone already knows they are conservative," one student pointed out. Another speculated that it might actually *increase* their audience.

"Okay," the organizer said. "So let's think about this differently. Do you know who the biggest advertiser on that radio station is?" No one knew. "Well, see, you would need to do some research instead of wandering around in front of the building yelling. I happen to know that it's Durable Motors." Many students nodded. Some had heard commercials from about this dealership.

"Okay, then. Let's think about the station's motivation instead of just running off to hold another protest. Now that you have this information, what kind of action would you suggest?"

One student came up with the idea of having groups go to the dealership every day to test-drive cars without buying them, tying up the dealership's staff until the station agreed to pull its ads.

"Now you're thinking like an organizer," our visitor said. "If a radio station has to choose between a talk show host and a key financial supporter, who do you think is likely to win?"

As with "issues," there are specific criteria in the organizing tradition for what counts as a good "tactic." One basic criterion is that a tactic must be doable, something you can actually carry off. Other criteria, as in the story above, involve more strategic concerns about whether an "action" will really put significant pressure on a target. As with issues, however, the most important criteria for organizers are the ones related to *building the power of an organization.*

And as with issues, the power-building criteria for tactics can be somewhat counterintuitive. For example, actions that don't require you to bring that many people together usually don't build your power very effectively. Sometimes you can run an effective "action" simply by taking a few powerful people who are sympathetic to your position to a meeting with the target. But a tactic like this doesn't excite or activate or engage your members. Nor does it provide opportunities for a wide range of leaders to learn more about organizing by actually doing organizing. It doesn't give you a public space where you can educate your members or the larger public (through speeches at a mass event, for example). The media can't report about how effective you are at mobilizing people and putting strategic pressure on targets—you didn't *do any* mobilization.

In other words, drawing on a few powerful allies doesn't enhance your capacity to win campaigns in the future. It may "win" the day, but it doesn't build power. Experienced organizing groups, then, usually employ tactics that force them to use the range of people and resources they have at their disposal. In fact, community organizing groups sometimes even put together more expansive actions than they actually need to win.

The Real Action Is in the Reaction

Being invincible depends on oneself, but the enemy becoming vulnerable depends on himself.

—Sun Tzu, *Art of War*

The less powerful rarely have the capacity to *force* the powerful to do anything. Community organizing groups are almost never "invincible" in Sun Tzu's terms. All they can do is act and then see how the opposition responds. This is why Alinsky frequently emphasized that "the real action is in the enemy's reaction." If you are unlucky, the opposition will be smart in their reactions. They won't overreact or do something stupid that you can take advantage of. As a result, organizers often seek out targets whose reactions they think they will be able to exploit.[5]

Martin Luther King, Jr., for example, chose to organize marches against segregation in Birmingham, Alabama, precisely *because* he knew that the chief of police, Bull Connor, and the city's other leaders were virulently racist. He knew they would aggressively resist any efforts to contest segregation. If Connor had done nothing, if he had simply let the black citizens of Birmingham march where they wanted to march, maybe even handed out coffee and doughnuts, then the Birmingham administration might have contained the rebellion. In fact, something like this had happened earlier to King in Albany, Georgia, with the result that the civil rights forces largely failed to achieve their aims. Because Connor pulled out his water cannons and attack dogs, because people all across America saw vicious attacks on peacefully marching black children, the Birmingham campaign generated the horrified public response King wanted. The powerful in Birmingham *gave* power to King through their reactions to his tactics.

A good tactic, then, is based on a depth of knowledge about the opposition. Organizers and leaders need to understand what kind of people are in opposition, what their interests are, what they care about and despise, what kinds of constraints they work under, and more. This knowledge helps an organizing group understand what kinds of actions are likely to provoke a response. More generally, organizers seek to employ tactics that the opposition is not prepared for. In the example of the racist talk show host, above, the radio station knew how to deal with a picket—almost everyone knows how to deal with pickets these days. But it would likely have been thrown off guard by the disruption of one of its key sponsors.

Any tactic may suffice if it puts the opposition off guard. In fact, the truth is that most organizing actions really aren't that creative. The key is that a tactic must target an opposition's specific weaknesses; it must, in Sun Tzu's words, "attack where they are not prepared," by going "out where they do not expect." Actions like these are the ones mostly likely to provoke reactions that can be exploited.[6]

Sometimes, the opposition actually tells you it is willing to do something stupid. For example, at one point during a farm worker strike led by Cesar Chavez in California, the local sheriff told the strikers he would arrest people who shouted "huelga!" or "strike!" to the workers in the fields. Of course, the leadership of the farm worker's union immediately arranged for a large number of its supporters to shout "huelga!" in front of a large group of the media. Chavez had arranged to speak to student activists at the same time at the University of California, Berkeley, just after their successful fight for free speech on campus. The announcement of the arrests angered the students, who collected a large donation for the union. More broadly, the arrests put the growers on the defensive for their attack on basic constitutional rights. Later on, one of the growers made a similarly self-destructive move, having Chavez arrested for trespassing, after which he was shackled and strip-searched. Outraged farm workers streamed to the union after this insult.[7]

Notes

1. On the limits of the "I Have a Dream" speech, see Michael Eric Dyson, *I May Not Get There with You: The True Martin Luther King Jr.* (New York: Free Press, 2001).
2. See this webpage for more information on foundations that do support organizing: http://comm-org.wisc.edu/node/7, accessed November 30, 2010.
3. Larry Cohen, Vivian Chávez and Sana Chehimi, *Prevention Is Primary: Strategies for Community Well-Being* (Washington, D.C.: Jossey-Bass, 2007), 5.
4. M. Huxley and O. Yiftachel, "New Paradigm or Old Myopia? Unsettling the Communicative Turn in Planning Theory," *Journal of Planning Education and Research* 19, no. 4 (2000): 336.
5. Saul Alinsky, *Reveille for Radicals* (New York: Vintage, 1946).
6. Sun Tzu, *The Art of War,* trans. Thomas Huynh, *Sonshi.com* (2001), http://www.sonshi.com/sun1.html (accessed July 17, 2010).
7. Miriam Pawel, *The Union of Their Dreams: Power, Hope, and Struggle in Cesar Chavez's Farm Worker Movement* (New York: Bloomsbury Press, 2009).

CHAPTER 2

What *Isn't* Community Organizing?

In our efforts to help people understand what community organizing *is*, we have found it is useful to discuss what organizing is *not*.

In this chapter, we examine a range of different community improvement strategies that are likely much more familiar to you than organizing. Thinking like a community organizer means *not* thinking like a community developer, or a social service professional, or a lawyer, or from the perspective of any number of more standard fields of community engagement. By distinguishing between the worldviews internal to each of these models, we seek to help people new to organizing better internalize organizing's unique perspective on power, conflict, and social change. Just because these other visions of community engagement or change are not organizing, it doesn't necessarily follow that they are useless or bad, however. Many of these approaches are quite effective and important in their own way, and organizers often depend upon the skills and resources of groups like these in their work.

Legal Action Is Not Organizing

Lawyers are often quite important to those engaged in social action. Lawyers can get you out of jail, and they can help you overcome bureaucratic hurdles, among many other services. The problem comes when a social action strategy is designed primarily around a lawsuit.

Our own state of Wisconsin provides a good example. For a number of years, a major lawsuit was working its way through the courts seeking to force the state to provide more equal funding to impoverished schools. In the end, this lawsuit mostly failed in the State Supreme Court.

Over this time, people interested in state funding reform didn't do much organizing. They were basically waiting for the court case to solve their problem. By the time the court case was lost, then, not much infrastructure still existed in the state to fight for change. Those interested in funding reform essentially had to start over, and it took years to slowly build the strength necessary to even begin to confront this problem.

Lawsuits, then, can actually have a detrimental effect on organizing.

The problem is not simply that you might lose. Even if you win, it is important to have the power to hold the courts and other officials accountable for putting legal decisions into effect. Winning in a court case is usually only the *beginning* of a long campaign to produce the social changes you seek.

For example, the Supreme Court decision against school segregation in *Brown vs. Board of Education* was really the start and not the end of a long series of struggles. The victory in the Supreme Court provided important legitimacy, but it did not, by itself, desegregate schools. Many districts resisted for many years. And the approaches that school districts eventually used to "integrate" their schools often had extremely destructive effects on minority communities and students. Many schools in the black community were closed, many African American teachers were fired, black students generally carried the burden of being bussed out of their communities, and these students were usually not well treated in their new schools. Today, our schools remain deeply segregated. Integration opponents have developed new strategies and new barriers have emerged. In fact, recent court decisions have even begun to eliminate the anti-segregation protections secured decades ago. In his book *Savage Inequalities,* Jonathan Kozol similarly cites many examples of court cases that were won in the states, in this case requiring more equal funding for schools in impoverished areas, that never had much actual effect.[1]

In these and many other examples, "winning" a court case did not eliminate the need to organize for power. In fact, when legal strategies end up reducing capacity for organizing they can create real problems.

The point is not that you never want to use lawsuits as a strategy. Many important changes in America have been won at least in part through lawsuits. But you need to be careful to distinguish between organizing and lawsuits as a strategy. If you are going to pursue a lawsuit, you need to develop strategies for keeping organizing groups engaged in the issue while the case is moving through the courts. And there are, in fact, examples where those struggling for social change have effectively combined these strategies.[2]

Activism Is Not Organizing

Activists like to "do things." They get up in the morning and they go down to a main street and hold up some signs against the war. Or they march around in a picket line in front of a school. (Activists love rallies and picket lines.) One well-known activist in Los Angeles occasionally chained himself to an overpass on a major freeway during rush hour to draw attention to the problem of homelessness in the city. He usually generated a fair amount of media attention, but no lasting attention on homelessness ever resulted from it.

Activists feel very good about how they "fight the power." But in the absence of a coherent strategy, a coherent target, a process for maintaining a fight over an extended period of time, and an institutional structure for holding people together and mobilizing large numbers, they usually don't accomplish much. People in power love activists, because they burn off energy for social action without really threatening anyone.

We are exaggerating a little, here. But not as much as we wish. There are moments, of course, when enough activists get together to create a real social movement, as we note in Chapter 3, but these moments are rare.

Obama Better Watch Out!

A few months ago, we heard a story on National Public Radio (NPR) that captured some of the ways activists can fool themselves about the importance of their activities. NPR reported on a small group of people protesting the Iraq war in a town in upstate New York State. They met every Sunday beginning soon after 9/11 at the same street corner together to shout at traffic and wave antiwar signs. After Obama was elected president, after a lot of thought, this group had decided to give him the benefit of the doubt. They decided to discontinue their weekly protests.

"But if he starts backsliding," one of the lead protesters declared, "then we'll be back!"

Obama, we are certain, is trembling in fear.

Mobilizing Is Not Organizing

Mobilizers get pissed off about a particular issue or event. They bring out a lot of people who are hopping mad, and they get some change made (for better or worse). Like activists, they generally feel pretty good about what they have accomplished. But then they go back to watching TV, or playing golf, or whatever they were doing before. They accomplished what they wanted and now they're done.

The problem with mobilizing is that, as we already noted above, winning a single battle is often quite meaningless unless you are in the fight for the long term. Once the mobilized group goes home, the people they were struggling against are mostly free to do what they were doing before. In fact, mobilizers can actually make things worse without necessarily meaning to, and they can be used by those who are more sophisticated about what is really going on.

As Richard Rothstein notes, "spontaneous militancy is rare in social life. When it happens, a spontaneous movement, a mass unplanned uprising, is very powerful. It is also very short-lived.... To build lasting political force on any issue requires not spontaneity but organization. It requires a slow process of leadership development. It requires the multiplication of leaders with a long term perspective, with the ability to plan strategy and the skill of marshalling forces at the right time in the right place."[3]

Angela Davis worries that today, however, "mobilization has displaced organization." Activists seem increasingly to think that mass demonstrations, by themselves, represent "the very substance" of organizing for power. In fact, however, little is accomplished for the long term when "the millions who go home after the demonstration" don't "feel responsible to further build support for the cause." "Mobilizing," she stresses, "is not synonymous with . . . organizing."[4]

Throw the Bums Out!

A few years ago in Milwaukee, our county government passed a horrible pension payout rule that was going to cost the county an enormous amount of money. People got up in arms. They banded together to "throw the bums out" (the executive and the county supervisors who had voted for the change). They successfully recalled quite a few.

Very little thought seemed to have been given, however, to who, exactly, would replace these officials, or what larger changes people wanted in the county. In fact, the groups that "threw out the bums" dissolved pretty quickly.

On many issues the recalled county executive and supervisors were quite progressive. Partly as a result of the recall, however, an extremely conservative executive as well as some conservative supervisors were elected in this majority democratic county. (This conservative county executive later used his position as a base to win the governorship of the state.)

Whether this was good or not depends on your perspective, of course. But the mobilizers were not really seeking fundamental change in the political leanings of county government. They just wanted "those" people out.

They knew what they didn't want, but they didn't present any coherent perspective on what they *did* want.

No organization was created to allow these people to have some say about who would replace the officials they threw out. In fact, the mobilizers didn't seem to think much about the long-term impact of their action.

They generated a lot of energy for change, but they didn't generate any power to control that change.

Political Campaigning Is Not Organizing

It is not enough to just elect your candidates. You must keep the pressure on. Radicals should keep in mind Franklin D. Roosevelt's response to a reform delegation: "Okay, you've convinced me. Now go out and bring pressure on me!"

—Saul Alinsky, *Rules for Radicals*

In politics, groups work to elect particular individuals to public office. Once candidates are in office, however, the structures that helped them get elected—that helped "get out the vote" for example—are usually dismantled until the next election comes around.

Powerful people and institutions maintain their ability to influence elected officials, of course. Bank presidents, the Chamber of Commerce, big donors, and the like can all get their ear.

But regular citizens won't get much access. As with the example of the pastor who got his park cleaned up by organizing his parishioners, elected officials like legislators or mayors or governors rarely pay attention to citizens unless they come together to assert *collective* power.

Political campaigns seek to elect people who will be responsive to voters' needs. Once these people get in office, however, they usually become a part of the system. They focus their limited attention on individuals and groups with real power to affect their election.

Even elected officials who may agree with you privately on an issue can often end up voting against you in the end out of fear that they will lose their next election if they don't. The more controversial or costly an issue is, the less likely it is that elected officials will support you, regardless of their personal feelings on the matter.

Community organizing groups sometimes get involved in political campaigns. But they generally focus on efforts to influence whoever does get elected. Organizers generally work with whoever is there, pushing for changes and holding officials accountable for promises they have made. (We examine political campaigning in detail in Chapter 5.)

A core motto of community organizing is "no permanent enemies, no permanent friends." Organizing groups usually fight for specific *issues*, not particular *individuals*. If someone joins with an organizing group, then they are that group's friend, at least during that campaign. If someone opposes the group, then they become an enemy, even if they have been a friend before.

Advocacy Is Not Organizing

Advocates generally speak *for* others instead of trying to help people speak for themselves. The relatively privileged professionals that usually head up advocacy groups decide *for* the less powerful what they need and present these expert conclusions to the powerful. Similarly, self-appointed "grassroots leaders" who don't actually represent any significant collection of local people sometimes take it upon themselves to represent the point of view of "their" entire group without making much effort to find out what people in this group actually believe or want. Leader-advocates of this kind are often chosen by the powerful to serve as "legitimate" representatives of groups that otherwise might oppose them more vigorously.

Advocates usually consult in one way or another with the groups they are speaking for. They may even recruit individuals to present testimonials and perform other tasks. In the end, however, the advocates and not those they are speaking with end up making the final decisions about what needs to be done and what should be said. The advocates retain the power to decide which perspectives will be legitimized and which will not. In other words, advocates seek local "informants," not equal "participants."

Some advocates speak for groups like children and the mentally ill who (they assume, often incorrectly) cannot speak for themselves. More generally, whether intended or not, advocacy often implies that the groups they represent are not capable of representing themselves. Sometimes advocates make this point explicitly: "We can't expect uneducated people to understand what needs to be done about public health." Or, "Educational funding is too complicated for people on the street to really make sense of."

Advocacy is not always a bad thing. If I go to court, I need to have a lawyer to represent me. (In fact, another term for lawyer is "advocate.") Advocates often conduct important research and their efforts have produced many positive changes in our society.

The truth is, we live in a world in which grassroots organizing groups don't hold nearly the power they should. As we will see, getting people organized for the long haul is an enormously challenging and resource-intensive process. Powerful organizing groups are not easily created nor maintained. In a world of limited resources, then, professional advocacy groups will likely always be a necessity, serving a critical function by defending those who have not developed the capacity to protect themselves.

It is our opinion that organizing groups are most powerful when they include those who are directly impacted by the issues that the group is fighting to change. A core aspect of organizing is providing opportunities for people impacted by injustice and inequality to acquire the skills to fight for themselves and to build their own power. Not only does this reap benefits for the organizing group, the process of taking on these leadership roles may also positively impact members' lives in ways not directly related to the organizing goals. However, the truth is that most community organizing groups do not fully include those most affected by a social problem. It turns out to be very difficult to organize disempowered and fragmented groups like homeless people, returned prisoners, people working two shifts to support their family, impoverished parents, and the like. As a result, many community organizing groups are often led by and made up of people who are relatively well off in comparison to those who are suffering the full effects of inequality and oppression. In other words, many community organizing groups actually operate in a gray area between "advocacy" and "grassroots democracy."

In addition, the larger your group is, the more distant your leaders will be from individual members. On a broad, national scale, especially, the kind of direct participation valued in organizing is difficult to sustain. There may be something inevitable about the "advocacy-like" structures of huge organizations like the Sierra Club or the American Association of Retired People (AARP). As we will see in Chapter 3, the second-wave women's movement faced some of these challenges of scale, developing small, relatively egalitarian organizations on the local level and more traditional hierarchical ones like the National Organization for Women (NOW) on a much larger scale.[5]

Nonetheless, to the extent that advocacy suppresses or replaces the authentic "voices" and "power" of the people, it remains problematic. Whether organizers can always achieve it or not, full participation of those most affected by a social problem remains a key ideal in organizing.

Community Development Is Not Organizing

"Community development" seeks consensus, not conflict. In community development, leaders of local groups, directors of community agencies, and representatives of powerful institutions work together on efforts to improve local communities. They try to find solutions that everyone at the table can agree upon, drawing on the skills and resources at the table. Community development assumes that social change can happen through a collaborative "win-win" process and that significant social change can happen without struggle and contention—essentially the opposite of the perspective of community organizing.

Community development efforts often provide direct services to individuals and families through food pantries, mortgage counseling, and medical clinics. They also include broader community change projects: building new housing, beautifying blighted areas, and forming business incubators, among other similar projects.

Community development is sometimes driven by "deficit" perspectives on impoverished communities. It can treat impoverished communities as if they are largely made up of problems (often problem *people*) that need to be "fixed" by outside agencies. Efforts like these are often led by outside organizations and/or professionals with few, if any, long-term connections to the communities they are trying to assist. Private institutions like large hospitals, public school systems, and banks are involved too often in this kind of "top-down" community development. A deficit perspective also pervades many agencies in impoverished areas that represent themselves as "community based."[6]

On the other hand, an increasingly popular approach, often referred to as "asset-based community development," emphasizes that however oppressed they might seem, communities always contain many resources as well as challenges. Asset-based approaches take a "half-full" instead of "mostly empty" perspective on community institutions and individuals. They try to mobilize the resources already available in a community for its own improvement before seeking any outside resources. These resources include the skills and leadership of community members and the capacities of existing local institutions (like churches). Asset-based approaches usually at least try to follow a democratic process, seeking guidance and participation from indigenous communities or groups.[7]

Because impoverished communities do, in fact, lack sufficient financial resources to fundamentally transform themselves, however, even asset-based efforts require outside support from powerful institutions. And these outside individuals and groups inevitably hold significant power over what can and cannot be done with their money. This power is magnified by the positions, connections, and "cultural capital" of outside experts and institutional officers who usually direct asset-based efforts. In the end, therefore, individuals and groups from outside the community hold the real power in efforts like these.[8]

Direct Service Is Not Organizing

Community developers often try to improve and expand services for marginalized communities. "Service" includes a vast range of activities, ranging from child welfare work, to soup kitchens, to counseling, to education, to returned offender support projects. The common characteristic of service efforts is that they all seek to help improve the lives of struggling and suffering individuals and families. In the terms of the "Parable of the River" of the previous chapter, service efforts almost always stay focused on the "downriver" aspect of social problems. In other words, service-focused agencies seek to improve the lives of individuals and families, but rarely try to intervene in the broken systems and institutions that produced this suffering in the first place.

Community organizing groups often seek improvements in services. But they almost always avoid providing services themselves. Groups that try to provide services *and* fight power often find that their service arms quickly get targeted. For example, an organizing group in New York City decided a few years ago that it would try its hand at actually running a couple of public schools. Not surprisingly, however, the next time this group challenged district policies, one of the first things the district did was threaten to cut funding from the group's schools. This put the organizing group in the difficult position of defending what it had already won while fighting for something new.[9]

"Pulling Yourself Up by Your Own Bootstraps" or "Community Building" Is Not Organizing

Bringing people in your neighborhood together to clean up a park, creating a block club to watch out for scared children or criminals, or developing a local savings plan in your church can be wonderful things to do. Community building activities like these sometime serve as precursors to community organizing efforts. Many projects like these involve truly creative and relevant grassroots approaches to social engagement and change. Sometimes organizers themselves create local organizations like block clubs to act as components of a larger community organizing group.

On their own, however, projects like these are not community organizing. The Alinsky tradition we discuss in this book assumes that the problems facing impoverished communities result from the effects of powerful forces acting on them from outside. If you don't contest these outside forces, Alinsky and those who came after him have argued, you are unlikely to be able to maintain the kind of community you want. Cleaning up a park, for example, won't stop the police department from putting huge numbers of men in African American communities in jail.

"Bootstrap" efforts occasionally lead to organizing when they get people working together and talking together about problems that they share. But because most people lack a coherent understanding of power and how to contest it, they generally don't.

Movement Building Is Not Organizing

Mass "movements" occur when a wide range of different organizations and individuals start acting for change. Movements are often somewhat vague and amorphous, with many "leaders" of different kinds who don't completely agree with each other on a range of issues. In fact, different leaders and groups often compete with each other for control and recognition. With most movements, no individual group is really "in control."

In the Civil Rights Movement in the South, for example, while King became the most prominent leader, other important figures struggled for control over the movement's direction and core principles. Neither he nor anyone else really controlled the emergence of local struggles in different cities and towns across the South. And when King decided to participate in one of these local struggles, he did not simply take over. Instead, he entered arenas with already established local leaders and sometimes multiple organizations. For example, King came to Birmingham (where children eventually marched in the face of dogs and fire hoses) some time after the struggle had begun. While he became an important voice in this effort, he was only one of a number of different leaders negotiating behind the scenes about what should be done.

No one really knows how to start a "movement," despite a great deal of research about them in the last couple of decades. In fact, there seems to be general agreement that movements happen when the conditions for their emergence are right (whatever *that* means). One thing we do know, however, is that established community organizing groups of different kinds provide important foundations for the success of movements when they do happen. Organizing efforts train leaders, experiment with different tactics, and develop key resources that the movements depend upon.[10]

In the Civil Rights Movement, for example, sophisticated strategies of nonviolent protest were only available because these had been developed previously over time by members of an established organization, the Congress on Racial Equality (CORE). Leaders from CORE conducted the first nonviolence trainings in Montgomery during the bus boycott and elsewhere.

Further, as in the example of Birmingham, many of a movement's key protest actions are generally led or facilitated by established organizations. When researchers look closely, it usually turns out that many, if not most, seemingly spontaneous movement protests were actually catalyzed by organized groups acting in the background.

While a social movements are not the same as community organizing, then, organizing is usually a crucial aspect of successful movements. Community organizing groups are distinct from social movements in that organizing groups are discrete "organizations" with clear structures of governance, identifiable members, a shared mission, and a common understanding of how power operates. Most established organizing groups have training programs for their leaders which initiate them into a common language and shared perspectives about the practice of "organizing." While we don't know how to "make" movements happen, we do know a lot about effective strategies for forming community organizing groups.

Nonpartisan Dialogues about Community Problems Are Not Organizing

Different models have been developed for bringing people together in formally structured dialogues about community problems. One of our favorite examples is the Study Circles or Everyday Democracy model, which brings small groups of citizens together from all walks of life to discuss their different perspectives on a specific social problem. This community dialogue approach is very important and is sometimes overlooked by those focused on community organizing and fights over power.[11]

Unlike community organizing, which tends to self-select those who already mostly agree on a particular issue, nonpartisan dialogues seek to draw in a diverse range of opinions out of which some consensus may or may not be reached. While dialogue also happens inside organizing groups, of course, the ultimate aim is not getting the details of each person's opinion on the table, although organizing groups are more effective when they can hear the diverse perspectives of their members. Instead, leaders seek to generate a collective and singular "voice" and to wrest resources and power away from "others." (Organizers do have an approach for getting at each participant's unique perspectives, however, as we discuss in Chapter 10.)

In the Everyday Democracy model, after a few weeks of dialogue the small groups come together in a large meeting to see if they can agree on action items to work on together. Some dialogue efforts, then, do move from discussion to collective action. But their vision of action is ultimately grounded in the community development "consensus" model, placing its hope in the possibility that we might all get along if we could just talk honestly with each other.

In the end, while organizers might see such dialogues as useful, they believe that most of the critical challenges our society faces will not be solved through dialogue. An organizer might paraphrase Aristotle: "talk alone moves nothing. Only talk that is tied to action can do so."[12]

Lifestyle Changes Are Not Organizing

Buying a Prius may help the environment in some small way, but it is unlikely to make any real impact on pollution or climate change. (But Marie still wishes she could afford to buy a Prius.) Sometimes (mostly middle-class) lifestyle activists will say, "well, if everyone bought a Prius, then we'd change the world." From the perspective of organizing there are two key problems with this statement. First, even if everyone did buy a Prius, it probably wouldn't make much of a difference. And second, everyone is not just going to go out and buy a Prius because they see you or even a large number of people do this. Most people are not going to make costly or difficult changes even if this becomes a fad among a few.[13]

Lifestyle activism is usually a way for relatively privileged people to feel good about their actions without needing to leave their familiar comfort zone. A small, committed group of individuals that begins with lifestyle changes may sometimes provide the core for the emergence of a social movement that can fight for larger structural changes. But organizers argue that the resulting collective struggle and structural changes would make the significant difference, not the fact that a few people started buying Priuses.

We do not mean to suggest that people should start tossing their trash on the sides of highways because it doesn't matter. In fact, organizers often seek out people who have tried to contribute to the betterment of society, and this includes people who engage in lifestyle actions. While buying a Prius is not a gateway drug to organizing, lifestyle activists have at least indicated that they care about social change and have shown they are willing to do something to promote it.

Conclusion

The point of this chapter is not necessarily to critique alternate approaches to community engagement and change. Most of the strategies we examined have their place, each serving different purposes. And people working in these different traditions often provide support for organizing campaigns. By laying out the logics behind these other approaches, however, we have tried to show

how organizing serves functions and pursues goals largely missing from standard models of community engagement. As you move forward through the book, we hope the analysis in this chapter will help you to avoid conflating organizing with models that are more familiar to most Americans.

Notes

1. Gary Orfield, Susan E. Eaton and Harvard Project on School Desegregation, *Dismantling Desegregation: The Quiet Reversal of Brown v. Board of Education* (New York: New Press, 1996); Jonathan Kozol, *Savage Inequalities: Children in America's Schools* (New York: Crown Publishing, 1991).

2. The *Williams vs. California* lawsuit and the community organizing work that took place around it seems like an example of the latter. See the Web site of the Californians for Justice Education Fund at http://www.caljustice.org/cfj_live/index.php (accessed July 17, 2010).

3. Richard Rothstein, *What Is an Organizer?* (Chicago, IL: Midwest Academy, 1974), 7.

4. Angela Y. Davis and Joy James, *The Angela Y. Davis Reader* (Malden, MA: Blackwell, 1998), 122.

5. Jane Mansbridge makes this argument in a number of her works. The most condensed version can be found in Jane Mansbridge, "A Paradox of Size," in *From the Ground Up,* ed. George Bonnello (Boston, MA: South End Press, 1992), 152–176.

6. Aaron Schutz, "Home Is a Prison in the Global City: The Tragic Failure of School-Based Community Engagement Strategies," *Review of Educational Research* 76, no. 4 (2006), 691–743.

7. A key text is John P. Kretzmann and John McKnight, *Building Communities from the Inside Out: A Path toward Finding and Mobilizing a Community's Assets* (Evanstan, IL: The Asset-Based Community Development Institute, Northwestern University, 1993).

8. See Mike Miller, "A Critique of John McKnight & John Kretzmann's 'Community Organizing in the Eighties: Toward a Post-Alinsky Agenda'," *Comm-Org Papers* 15 (2009), http://comm-org.wisc.edu/papers2009/miller.htm (accessed July 17, 2010).

9. For those interested in a more sophisticated discussion of relationships between community organizing and development, see Randy Stoecker, "Community Development and Community Organizing: Apples and Oranges? Chicken and Egg?" *Comm-Org Papers* 8 (2001): 1–10, http://comm-org.wisc.edu/drafts/orgdevppr2c.htm#N_1_, accessed December 6, 2010.

10. See David A. Snow, Sarah Anne Soule and Hanspeter Kriesi, *The Blackwell Companion to Social Movements* (Malden, MA: Blackwell, 2004) for an excellent overview.

11. See the Everyday Democracy Web site at http://www.everyday-democracy.org/en/index.aspx, accessed December 6, 2010.

12. *Nichomacean* Ethics book 6, originally it was "*thought* alone."
13. See more detailed arguments about the limits of lifestyle politics along with quite contentious discussions at Aaron Schutz, "Self-Delusion and the Lie of Lifestyle Activism," Open Left Blog (2009), at http://www.openleft.com/diary/13032/ selfdelusion-and-the-lie-of-lifestyle-politics-core-dilemmas-of-community- organizing, and Aaron Schutz, "Part II: The Distortions of Lifestyle Politics," Open Left Blog (2009), at http://openleft.com/diary/14295/part-ii-the- distortions-of-lifestyle-politics-core-dilemmas-of-community-organizing (both accessed July 17, 2010).

PART II

History and Theory

CHAPTER 3

Collective Action in Twentieth-Century America: A Brief History

Introduction

We call this a history of "collective action" not "community organizing" because we include a range of the movements and even some community development efforts that we distinguished from organizing in the previous chapter. A history that attempted to limit itself more narrowly would miss many of the rich ways the organizing tradition has been deeply intertwined with these other social transformation strategies. In fact, the history of collective action in America has been one of constant cross-fertilization and debate.

By necessity this overview is oversimplified. We focus in on moments of social action that seem to best exemplify the range of social action strategies visible in the twentieth century. As a result, many movements that could have been discussed are not, either because they didn't seem as relevant to the purposes of this book, or because they seemed to repeat aspects of models already included. While the history of religious movements in the United States has much to teach us about how visions of social and personal transformation spread, for example, we decided there was not space to include them. The same could be said about the struggles of anarchists, syndicalists, and many more.

Our focus on America is also limiting, since there is much to learn from international movements and organizing in other countries, including the Zapatista movement in Mexico and landless people's movements more broadly. Finally, because we "use" different efforts to highlight particular tactics and strategies, our descriptions often downplay their full richness and complexity. Thus, you should treat this chapter as merely an entry point to the rich tapestry of collective action in our history.

Despite the inevitable limitations of such a condensed overview, we decided it would be even more problematic not to include it. Too many writings on organizing are not grounded in history. They leave readers without an understanding of the ways organizing—as a shifting bundle of approaches to social change—is related to, overlaps with, and is indebted to other traditions and visions. We worry that readers come away from such discussions without understanding that there have been a range of vibrant and often quite effective alternative approaches to social struggle employed by oppressed groups in America.

Note that the dates accompanying each section heading are approximate at best. Clear beginnings and endings can rarely be delineated with any clarity in efforts like these. The chapter as a whole also necessarily includes some aspects of traditions that preceded or continue beyond the twentieth century. The note reference at the end of each section title includes a list of key texts for further reading.

The Labor Movement (1860s–)[1]

Labor organizing in America, preceded by efforts in other countries, began long before Saul Alinsky formulated his vision of community organizing. As we note below in "Saul Alinsky and the Birth of Community Organizing," Alinsky was deeply influenced by the union organizing model. In fact, the term "community organizer" was adapted directly from "labor organizer."

Labor struggles in the United States emerged in response to these processes of industrialization which rapidly transformed the nation's economy over the later half of the 1800s. Huge populations of workers from rural areas and immigrants from overseas crowded into burgeoning cities. By 1886, 65–75 percent of the workforce was industrial, facing long hours in filthy, backbreaking jobs, ruled by "compulsion, force, and fear." Again and again unions that had been painfully created during times of prosperity dissolved in the frequent economic "panics," when widespread unemployment fractured their tenuous solidarity. Unions only began to put down durable roots at the end of the 1800s. Samuel Gompers, president of the American Federation of Labor, celebrated this development in 1883 when he proclaimed that unions had finally begun to achieve "stability and permanency," in contrast with "every previous industrial crisis" when "trade unions were literally mowed down and swept out of existence."[2]

Until the 1940s, some of the most broad-based labor organizing was led by socialists, communists, syndicalists, and the like. They generally worked through their own organizations, including the Knights of Labor and the International Workers of the World (IWW). The militancy, resourcefulness, and bravery of their organizers were legendary. Focused not simply on unions but on broad social transformation, along with some important independent groups (like the Women's Trade Union League, the International Garment Worker's Union, and the Brotherhood of Sleeping Car Porters) those working in these traditions often contested oppression outside the workplace, like attacks on free speech, as well. Those working in these traditions also represented the only significant group of organizers in these early years willing to work with women, people of color, and integrated groups of workers. At the same time, however, their focus on expansive social change could also hinder their labor efforts. Their ideologies could run counter to the traditional values that predominated among American workers, providing one of many excuses for brutal government repression.

The mainline union movement largely excluded women, people of color, and unskilled laborers. Ironically, this stance served to reduce their power by leaving a broad army of potential workers outside their control. Not until the 1930s, with the Congress of Industrial Organizations (CIO) led by John L. Lewis, did line workers and African Americans finally gain significant mainline union protection; the same did not happen for women until decades later.

During the 1930s, the pragmatic Lewis recruited communists and other radical leftists for the emerging CIO, since they included many of the most effective organizers available. But he purged them from the CIO ranks during the "Red Scare" of the 1940s, eliminating many African American leaders in the process. This ended any significant presence of communists and socialists in the leadership of mainstream unions in America.

Union organizers were (and still are) the hardy souls sent to nonunionized work sites to identify potential worker-leaders and generate the solidarity necessary to force owners and management to recognize a new union. Entering a new site, organizers develop relationships of trust with potential leaders, guide meetings, help plan strategy, negotiate between different factions, nurture solidarity during times of struggle, and more. Organizers have to overcome well-founded fears that workers will lose their jobs amid aggressive resistance from employers as well as often underhanded attempts to derail their efforts by outside "union busters."

Through the nineteenth century and into the early years of the twentieth century, labor organizers often saw community engagement as an integral part of their job. Local communities could provide crucial support to strikers: joining boycotts, conducting sympathy strikes at other firms, and walking picket lines. During and after the 1930s, however, labor legislation and judicial decisions narrowed the boundaries of what union organizers were allowed to do as a part of a larger set of compromises between labor and business. Union organizing tightened its focus on the workplace. Manuals and guide-books standardized some of the key tasks involved in the organizing process, further reducing community engagement. At the same time, the union move-ment increasingly looked away from active efforts to organize new businesses and industries, focusing instead on serving those who were already organized (a shift that left them ill-prepared when anti-union efforts intensified). Not until the last decades of the twentieth century would unions return to any significant efforts to integrate community and labor organizing.

Progressivism and the Settlement House Movement (1890s–1920s)[3]

At the turn of the twentieth century, the "progressive" movement emerged along with a new middle class in America in response to industrial chaos and class conflict. Two key branches of progressivism predominated: "admin-istrative" and "democratic." Administrative progressives pursued scientific approaches to efficiency and bureaucratic control. They were driven by a vision of a society controlled by benevolent experts. In contrast, a much smaller group of democratic or "collaborative" progressives sought to create a new society grounded in grassroots democracy.[4]

For our purposes, the most important example of the democratic pro-gressive approach took shape in the settlement house movement. In places like Jane Addams' Hull House in Chicago and Lillian Wald's Henry Street Settlement in New York City, located in impoverished neighborhoods, middle- and upper-class whites worked with recent immigrants. At their best, settlement houses were richly experimental. In touch with the desires and cultures of the local people, they developed a wide array of programs ranging from recreation to service, from clubs to worker associations, and from public showers to museums of ethnic culture. Settlement houses sought to engage with slum dwellers as fellow citizens, not "clients," helping them to become "active architects of their own destinies." The most important legacy of the settlement house movement for community organizing is likely the emphasis they placed on the importance of respecting local knowledge and culture.[5]

In direct contrast with labor unions, however, middle-class settlement house leaders generally believed that class conflict and social inequality resulted from misunderstandings and inefficient institutions—a common belief among middle-class activists throughout the twentieth century. If work-ers and owners could learn to work together, settlement leaders believed society would move toward enlightened collaboration and equality. Even Addams, who actually allowed some labor unions to work out of Hull House, opposed the labor movement's focus on mass conflict. During the nationwide Pullman railway strike of 1894, for example, Addams chided both George Pullman and his workers for their failure to be reasonable with each other. While she recognized workers' grievances, she rejected the need for class "war" in response, condemning "the fatal lack of generosity in the attitude of workmen toward the company." *Both* sides, she argued, were at fault for their lack of empathy and their inability to engage in reasonable, respectful dialogue.[6]

The settlement house movement in the vibrant democratic form envisioned by Addams and others came largely to an end in the 1920s. It was absorbed into the growing field of professionalized social service promoted by administrative progressives. With little connection to local communities, professional social workers largely jettisoned democracy in favor of scientific efficiency. The remnant of the settlement house vision, the field of "group work" within social work, was eventually absorbed by the administratives as well. This shift away from a commitment to democracy was driven by funding agencies that were increasingly controlled by administrative progressives and philanthropists who shied away from anything with even a hint of controversy.[7]

Marcus Garvey and the Universal Negro Improvement Association (UNIA) (1917–1927)[8]

The first major black freedom movement of the twentieth century in America was Marcus Garvey's Universal Negro Improvement Association (UNIA). Believing that white Americans would never accept blacks as equals, Garvey argued that "developing a separate and powerful Black society was more important than winning the right to participate in white American society." While participant numbers are hard to pin down, it was likely the largest black movement in American history, with more than a million members. The UNIA held huge marches and public meetings in support of its vision, forming hundreds of chapters. It published its own newspaper, created its own separate service organizations like the Black Cross Nurses, formed a paramilitary faction, created its own community-owned businesses (including a short-lived shipping line), and crafted its own cultural symbols including a flag, uniforms, and songs.[9]

Hopes for the UNIA were short-lived, however. Garvey's prominence and autocratic leadership, combined with the group's problematic finances, made him the target of attacks from within and outside of the organization. A Jamaican citizen, Garvey was convicted on questionable grounds, jailed, and then deported from the United States in 1927, marking the end of the UNIA in America.

56467

The UNIA, however, set the pattern for most nationalist movements to come in America. In contrast with labor and community organizing, nationalist movements like the UNIA in the United States, include the Nation of Islam and the Black Panthers (see "The Black Power Movement," below), have generally eschewed efforts at social reform, instead promoting racial or ethnic pride and the development of independent social institutions. Because of their hierarchical structure, nationalist efforts are generally dependent upon their core leaderships, with a mostly working class membership and a fairly traditional vision of gender roles. Finally, efforts to develop an independent economic base have met with little success. They have mostly proved unable to sustain themselves or compete with established capitalist businesses given the lack of capital in impoverished communities.[10]

The First Women's Movement (1848–1920)[11]

While women [in the late 1800s] were playing an ever larger role in the life of the country as wage-earners and professionals, they were still not able to make their influence felt because they were not organized. Without adequate organization in sufficient numbers, they could not hope to challenge deeply rooted prejudice and encrusted tradition in the citadels of economic and political power.
—Eleanor Flexner and Ellen Fitzpatrick, *Century of Struggle: The Woman's Rights Movement in the United States*

One of the longest struggles for social change in America, after the fight against slavery, involved the effort to secure the vote for women, what was called "women suffrage." Success required what Flexner calls "a century of struggle," with most scholars marking the 1848 Seneca Falls Convention and the emergence of key leaders like Elizabeth Cady Stanton and Susan B. Anthony as the beginning of a coherent movement. Thousands of mostly forgotten organizers worked tirelessly—traveling miles in deepest winter through snow banks or oppressive heat, giving many speeches a day, and living on little sleep—despite years of almost complete failure in numerous state-by-state efforts to win the vote.

While the movement met little concrete success in the beginning, behind the scenes these organized efforts, along with other social changes, were slowly shifting America's cultural vision of the place of women. The challenge was not simply cultural, however. Key corporate interests opposed women suffrage and often provided the funding for its defeat in different states. The liquor industry worried that enfranchising women would strengthen efforts to ban alcohol and was only removed as an obstacle with the passage of

Prohibition in 1918. A range of other industries feared that women would support more liberal labor reforms.

The movement also faced difficult questions of strategy. While many suffragists supported the temperance movement, for example, leaders generally sought to keep the voting and the liquor questions separate in an effort to dampen opposition from drinkers and alcohol producers. More problematically, throughout its history the suffrage movement was careful to distinguish itself from the struggle against racial oppression. This was not simply an issue of racism. Leaders knew that they could never achieve the two-thirds of the states necessary for ratification of a constitutional amendment without the votes of the south. Black groups were excluded from the national organizations and black women were often treated as second-class citizens. In fact, "in the South, suffragists [even] made the argument that white women would strengthen white supremacy" by "doubling the white vote."[12]

Across the years, there was often tension between more radical and more moderate wings of the movement. This was especially visible in the decade before the final ratification of the nineteenth amendment in 1920. On the moderate side, Carrie Chapman Catt led the venerable National American Women Suffrage Association (NAWSA) which stressed cooperation and persuasion. On the radical side, Alice Paul's National Women's Party (NWP) was "one of the first organizations ever to use nonviolent resistance for a political cause." Drawing on her experience with the much more contentious women's movement in England, Paul employed a wide range of creative confrontational tactics, including marches, pickets of the White House, banners insulting the president, hunger strikes in prison, and more. While each side criticized the approach of the other, it seems clear that suffrage only passed through the combined efforts of both organizations—the moderates working in individual states, the radicals keeping heat on President Woodrow Wilson and Congress throughout World War I. Catt's success in passing suffrage laws in key states made it possible to reach the two-thirds ratification. Paul's frequent accusations that the stance of the president and others was antidemocratic while America was fighting a war for democracy, and the national outrage (and respect) for women created when illegally arrested NWP picketers endured deplorable conditions and painful force-feedings eventually forced Wilson to their side.[13]

Women suffrage succeeded through a combination of perseverance, strategic savvy, and creative action. At the end, Paul was especially effective at making President Woodrow Wilson upset enough to overreach and take unwise actions that then came back to haunt him (like arresting peaceful picketers). Getting the powerful to "react" like this has become a standard organizing tactic.[14]

The vast social transformations feared or hoped for by many as a result of the women's vote never emerged. While suffrage had an impact on politics and legislation, women were largely absorbed into the existing party system. The key leaders of the movement did not enter the political realm themselves. Catt transformed the NAWSA into the nonpartisan League of Women Voters, while Paul and the NWP shifted its focus to the never-passed Equal Rights Amendment. With the loss of the issue that had held it together for so many years, the movement largely dissolved. Although an important movement of what Dorothy Sue Cobble calls "labor feminists" did begin in unions in the 1940s, women's concerns did not emerge again in such a visible way until the "second wave" of the 1970s.[15]

The Unemployed Councils and the Depression[16]

When Chicago blacks received eviction notices, it was not unusual . . .
for a mother to shout to the children, "Run quick and find the reds!"
          —Roy Rosenweig, "Organizing the Unemployed"

After the stock market crash of 1929, during the Great Depression, unemployment rose to levels not seen since the panics of the nineteenth century. At points, nearly a quarter of American workers could not find a job. In response, the Communist Party and other groups organized "unemployed councils" to coordinate resistance actions and plan mass protests. The councils organized resistance to evictions, held protests at local relief offices to increase payments, and supported large marches in many cities.

For a few years they successfully forced many local governments and officials to respond to their concerns. But a hoped-for mass movement did not arise. The involvement of the communists in many (not all) councils made them special targets of state repression, while the "revolutionary posturing" of party officials could alienate working-class Americans. Councils also struggled to retain their most effective local leadership, because the best leaders were often the first to find employment. And the cultural mores of the time weakened efforts to foster solidarity, as self-reliance in America at the time was nothing short of a religion. Despite the evidence all around, many continued to see unemployment as a personal failing.[17]

According to Francis Fox Piven and Richard Cloward, after only a few years the national leadership of the unemployed—both communist and noncommunist—was increasingly co-opted by the government. Spontaneity dropped out of the movement, and participation fell. Soon, the window of opportunity for mass action also began to close. While unemployment remained high for years to come, by 1935 business had recovered enough to go onto the offense. Redeploying the norm of individual responsibility, newspapers printed stories about "people on the dole" who "refused to work" and ran titles like "Relief Clients Refuse to Work as Corn Pickers."[18]

The concrete accomplishments of the unemployed movement were mostly local. These made a real impact on the day-to-day lives of thousands of impoverished Americans, however. Perhaps even more important, "for many," Roy Rosenzweig notes, the "movement was their first experience in any sort of mass pressure organization." "Through this affiliation many learned the power of organization as a weapon," preparing a large cadre for leadership roles in the successful union organizing campaigns in years to come.[19]

Saul Alinsky and the Birth of Modern Community Organizing (the Late 1930s)[20]

[The Back of the Yards] was the nadir of all slums in America. People were crushed and demoralized, either jobless or getting starvation wages, diseased, living in filthy, rotting unheated shanties, with barely enough food and clothing to keep alive. And it was a cesspool of hate; the Poles, Slovaks, Germans, Negroes, Mexicans and Lithuanians all hated each other and all of them hated the Irish, who returned the sentiment in spades. . . .

—Saul Alinsky, "Empowering People, Not Elites"

We the people will work out our own destiny.

—Motto of the Back of the Yards Neighborhood Council

The Back of the Yards neighborhood sprawled around the stinking slaughter-houses, stockyards, and packinghouses that gave the area its name. The stench of rotting carcasses, smoke from the packinghouses, and huge swarms of flies filled the air. Dripping, open-topped trucks carrying maggot-filled carrion to fertilizer plants rumbled through the streets. Local creeks were so polluted that they were known to catch fire. And residents earned a pittance working long hours in dangerous, filthy conditions.

Many had tried and failed to organize a union in the Back of the Yards, only to face defeat in the face of the neighborhood's vicious ethnic and religious rivalries and the deep pockets of enormous companies like Armor and Swift. In 1936, however, the CIO began yet another organizing effort that slowly began to attract support. By 1937, more than 2,000 workers attended a union meeting, and after this they began to "come in droves" to pay dues. Most of the local CIO staff, including lead organizer Herb March, were communists recruited by CIO President Lewis. They understood that winning a campaign would be extremely difficult if the community remained fractured, and worked to engage community leaders and institutions. They "raised funds for Polish orphans, sent...officials to attend neighborhood conferences on housing, and sponsored the Packingtown Youth Committee," among other projects.[21]

Into this mix, in 1938, came the brash and profane young Alinsky. A long-time University of Chicago researcher with extensive experience as a sociologist in the juvenile and criminal justice system, Alinsky came to the Yards under the auspices of the Chicago Area Project founded by Professor Clifford Shaw. Dissatisfied with the expert-client relationship that dominated the field of social work, Shaw and his colleagues looked back to the progressive vision of the settlement houses. They hoped to create spaces for democratic dialogue that would allow local communities to solve their own problems.

But Alinsky was no progressive. Earlier ethnographic work with the Chicago Mob, in poor communities, and in social institutions had taught him that power only responded to power, not dialogue. He "spent most of his time [in the Yards] with the CIO organizers...learning how to organize mass meetings, to focus attention on the issues that really bothered people, to direct and action, to raise money, and to recruit members." (While Alinsky deeply respected these communist organizers, he never had any interest in becoming a communist. The bureaucracy of the Communist Party clashed with his deep pragmatism, distaste for ideology, and open democratic inclinations.) He found a partner in Joe Meegan, director of a local park, who also felt like something more had to be done.[22]

Together, Alinsky and Meegan came up with a plan to create "a neighborhood council, patterned after the CIO's union organization." They hoped to bridge the communities' antagonisms and build the power necessary to support the union effort and address the Yards' entrenched problems. Alinsky and Meegan met with leaders large and small for months. Most important, they gained the confidence of the respected Auxiliary Bishop Bernard Shiels. With Shiel's blessing, they made inroads into the conflicting ethnic churches in the Yards, recruiting younger associate pastors who were less embedded in the long history of interethnic rivalry. Alinsky appealed to leaders' self-interests, pointing out the benefits of solidarity. If they didn't get involved, he warned, opposing groups would gain advantages.

In 1939 a broad range of local organizations came together for the founding convention of what was called the Back of the Yards Neighborhood Council. As was Alinsky's pattern going forward, organizations, not individuals, were the formal members. While the council's central agenda focused on "child welfare and health and housing," Shiel, the convention's keynote speaker, charged it to "urge Armor to avert the impending strike by negotiating a settlement" with the CIO. A day later, Alinsky convinced Shiel to speak at an enormous rally of more than 10,000 packinghouse workers, where the bishop appeared on the same stage with CIO President John L. Lewis. Their handshake shook Chicago. After the rally, just before the strike began, the packinghouses gave in, convinced "that they could not hold out against this coalition of neighborhood churches, residents, and workers."[23]

The founding of the Back of the Yards Neighborhood Council marked the beginning of modern community organizing in America. The council went on to create new services for residents, and to win a range of social changes relevant to the people in the neighborhood.

Alinsky's accomplishment came to national attention. With the help of a few wealthy supporters, he set up the Industrial Areas Foundation (IAF) as a base for expanding his strategy more broadly. In 1946 he published *Reveille for Radicals*, the "Bible" of community organizing until his second book, *Rules for Radicals*, came out in 1972.[24]

Fred Ross and the Community Service Organization: Alinsky in the 1950s[25]

It isn't hard to organize if you take it granule by granule, brick by brick.
—Fred Ross, *Axioms for Organizers*

The 1950s, the McCarthy era, were a fallow time for community organizing. As Robert Fisher notes, "in the highly centralized, conservative, Cold War economy there seemed to be little place or encouragement for neighborhood organizing.... [F]or Saul Alinsky, the anticommunism of the early 1950s made a wasteland of his community organizing."[26]

The key exception was the Community Service Organization (CSO), created in California in 1947 by Fred Ross after Saul Alinsky hired him on a tip from a friend. Ross had spent the Depression helping and advocating for migrant workers and other rural poor people. In the CSO, Ross developed an important new approach to organizing for the IAF. Because there were few established Latino organizations, Ross organized individuals, developing what he called the "house meeting" model. He and another local CSO member would go door to door, visiting promising prospects, listening to each person's concerns and stories, and educating them about the ways the CSO could help them and their community. Recruits paid dues and were asked to arrange meetings at their homes with friends and relatives, who were then treated to the same experience.

Initially, the CSO focused on voter registration, successfully electing the first Latino City Council member in more than a half-century, before moving on to a range of other issues. Ross developed new chapters across California. In 1952 he hired Cesar Chavez and Delores Huerta, who worked with and learned from Ross and Alinsky.

The Civil Rights Movement (mid-1950s–mid-1960s)

The relatively quiet acquiescence of the 1950s ended with the emergence of the Civil Rights Movement in the South, beginning with the Montgomery Bus Boycott in 1955. It is difficult to know how much Alinsky's ideas influenced the Civil Rights Movement. While *Reveille for Radicals* was almost universally read by activists, the struggle in the South drew deeply from indigenous African American resistance strategies and the traditions of the black church. Strategies of nonviolence drawn from Gandhi and elsewhere were also imported by activist groups, especially the Congress of Racial Equality (CORE).

The Southern Christian Leadership Conference[27]

Grounded in the structure of the black church, the most famous civil rights organization, the Southern Christian Leadership Conference (SCLC), was led by Martin Luther King, Jr. Middle-class pastors, supported by committees made up mostly of working-class African Americans, led mass resistance in towns and cities across the South. King led the first major action, the Montgomery Bus Boycott, and then headed the SCLC, which provided a loose umbrella for many of these local movements, with King usually coming in after an effort had begun. Masses of local people marched, attempted to vote, and engaged in other protest efforts, seeking to force the local white power structures to make concessions. In contrast with Alinsky's model, participants and leaders saw these local efforts as part of a larger *movement* for civil rights across the South. While people fought for specific changes in local areas, the real goal was nothing less than a fundamental transformation of the oppression of African Americans.

Local campaigns were rooted in African American churches—although a relatively small percentage actually participated—and they were organized around what Aldon Morris calls a "formal, non-bureaucratic" structure. Pastors led with the guidance of church elders (often reluctantly taking up the mantle in response to pressure from their congregations). An elaborate committee structure did most of the real "work" in these churches and in movement organizations. Decisions usually emerged through extended dialogue facilitated by a range of different leaders and activists. In fact, the apparent hierarchy and charismatic domination of key movement leaders, so visible to the public, obscured the extent to which these groups drew on a range of more or less democratic procedures in often loose coalitions of different groups. Participation was also not tightly organized. Large numbers of people often showed up for marches without requiring much central "organization" to get them there.[28]

The Student Nonviolent Coordinating Committee (SNCC)[29]

SNCC (pronounced "snick") drew more deeply from the democratic progressive tradition of Jane Addams and others than did the SCLC. The group's key early organizers, highly educated students from the North, including Robert Moses, were mentored by Ella Baker, herself a brilliant autodidact and experienced organizer. Under Baker's tutelage, SNCC rejected SCLC's focus on strong, charismatic leaders. "When ordinary people elevate their leaders above the crowd," Baker believed, "they devalue the power within themselves." SNCC was also influenced by Myles Horton's similar views during visits to his famous Highlander Folk School. SNCC members often referred disdainfully to King as "the lawd," resentful when King arrived as a savior in communities they had been working with.[30]

SNCC "field secretaries" did not see themselves as leaders but, instead, as facilitators of dialogue and local democracy seeking to develop what they called an egalitarian "beloved community." They worked to help individuals see themselves as citizens with the capacity to make changes in their world. Mostly unwilling to tell local people what to do or how to do it, SNCC efforts often became rich strategic hybrids, integrating progressive visions of democracy with more traditional forms of local solidarity.

SNCC made critical contributions to the movement, building cadres of committed leaders and precipitating many important struggles. During Freedom Summer in 1964, they brought privileged white college students into Mississippi to work with local blacks, an experience that influenced subsequent efforts by white students in the North. SNCC's impact was limited, however, by their discomfort with mass action and their tendency to reject the strategic benefits of strong leadership. In Birmingham, in fact, they were reduced to pleading with King to lead mass marches, fearing that otherwise the local movement would collapse. SNCC eventually dissolved in 1965, in part because of conflict between the original founders and new, working-class Southern members who demanded opportunities for more active leadership roles. But as it faded, SNCC contributed to the subsequent rise of the "black power" movement in America.[31]

Alinsky and the Civil Rights Movement (1959–1964)[32]

Despite his respect for its accomplishments, Alinsky was critical of the Civil Rights Movement's strategy in the South. He was especially concerned about its failure to develop "into a stable, disciplined, mass-power organization." "Many of the victories that have been won," he argued, "were not the result of a mass power strategy. They were caused by the impact of world political pressures, the incredibly stupid blunders of the status quo in the South and elsewhere, and the supporting climate created particularly by the churches."[33]

At the end of the 1950s, Alinsky founded two new African American organizing groups in Chicago and Rochester, which became key examples of civil rights organizing in Northern cities. He began with The Woodlawn Organization (TWO) in Chicago and then created FIGHT in Rochester (discussed in a later section). TWO was created in a poor black neighborhood in part as a response to the gentrification plans of the nearby University of Chicago. Alinsky believed, however, that single-issue organizations were dead ends, as a single issue could not draw together a broad range of participants with different interests and concerns. To rally local residents and build up a sense of power in the neighborhood, then, TWO began with a series of different campaigns. For example, TWO "organized squads of local shoppers to investigate suspected merchants." Always the pragmatist, Alinsky was careful to make sure these little campaigns didn't get too big for the capacity of his organization to handle. He constantly examined how much power TWO had and how "winnable" an effort seemed to be, pulling the plug when a campaign went too far.[34]

The early 1960s, however, was a "movement" moment in America, one of those rare times when it was possible to draw large numbers of participants to actions without necessarily intensively organizing them. After an event that turned out hundreds more people than he had expected, the lead TWO organizer, Nicholas von Hoffman, told Alinsky that "I think that we should toss out everything we are doing organizationally and work on the premise that this is the moment of the whirlwind, that we are no longer organizing but guiding a social movement." Alinsky agreed. Alinsky's response, Sanford Horwitt notes, highlighted "Alinsky's brilliance as a political tactician: he was able to shed even his most favored organizational concepts and assumptions when confronted with a new, unexpected reality." This is a lesson that many organizers who came after him have failed to learn.[35]

After this conversation, Alinsky, von Hoffman, and other TWO organizers and leaders stopped looking "only or primarily for 'specific, immediate, and realizable' issues." Instead, they organized their own "freedom ride" to city hall. After only a couple of weeks of planning, 46 buses carrying more than 2,500 African Americans headed to city hall to register to vote. Led by a convertible filled with TWO leaders and organizers, including religious figures in full regalia and a bus full of nuns (in Chicago, Alinsky believed, "you couldn't be too Catholic"), they faced down a phalanx of police. "Hey, what are you going to do," von Hoffman shouted, "machine-gun the nuns?" It ended up being "the largest single voter-registration event ever" in Chicago, fundamentally altering the city's view of its black residents and its attitude toward Woodlawn. TWO went ahead to win its fight with the University of Chicago.[36]

In this postcommunist age, the organizers Alinsky was able to recruit were a motley lot. While some came from no coherent ideological background, a large number were "ex-seminarians" with leftist Christian backgrounds. This was not a "policy decision"—they were simply the only people available who "would work until they dropped and who did not flinch at derring do." Von Hoffman notes, however, that Alinsky—who was "agnostic" but in no way anti-religious (he knew the Bible better than many pastors and held a weekly reading group with local priests)—"every so often had to administer a kick in the pants to some of these people of the faith lest they turn an organizational drive into . . . a Salvation Army soup kitchen."[37]

Students for a Democratic Society (SDS) (1960–1969)[38]

In the North, the most important social action group during this time was the almost completely white Students for a Democratic Society, or SDS. As in the early SNCC, the leaders of SDS were highly educated (in fact, key aspects of SDS were inspired by SNCC). Unlike SNCC, however, they usually came from privileged upper-middle-class families and, of course, did not face racial discrimination. SDS produced the famous "Port Huron Statement" in 1962, which attempted to envision how America could become a more open and participatory democracy, harkening back to the visions of turn-of-the-century progressives.

In 1963 SDS developed an SNCC-like organizing/popular education effort in the North to organize poor whites, called the Economic Research and Action Project or ERAP. While SDS' commitments to collaborative democracy were similar to SNCC's, ERAP projects were not as responsive to the divergent cultural norms of local working-class residents. ERAP projects often attempted to embody a truly leaderless democracy, exemplified by a motto: "freedom is an endless meeting." Partly as a result, they often had trouble making any decisions at all. At one point one group apparently spent more than a day discussing whether they should take a day off and go to the beach. An iconic picture from the time shows a key ERAP leader, Sharon Jeffries, staring determinedly at the camera, while all around her compatriots are falling asleep. One ERAP organizer "lamented how the quest for 'community—soul—whole man' had led within SDS and the ERAP projects to 'elite isolation—in-groupism.'" ERAP groups in different cities did achieve some goals, however, including laying the groundwork for the emergence of the National Welfare Rights Organization in Boston and Cleveland. By 1965 the groups began to disband. Their "utopian vision" collapsed in the face of reality.[39]

Cesar Chavez and the United Farm Workers (1962–)[40]

They come and they go, good organizers and would-be organizers. But one thing they all have in common is that all of them have failed and will fail.

—Mexican American farm worker to Chavez

Cesar Chavez's family lost its ranch in Arizona in 1938 when he was 11 years old. They became migrant farm workers in California, picking vegetables and fruit for pittance wages. After the eighth grade, Chavez quit school to support the family, but read widely under the mentorship of a local priest, including biographies of labor leaders like John L. Lewis, and Mahatma Gandhi. Fred Ross recruited him to work with the CSO in 1952.

After working with the CSO for about a decade, learning Ross' house meeting strategy and developing new tactics of his own, Chavez became executive director. At this point, he asked CSO, with the support of Ross and Alinsky, to develop a farm workers' union. When this idea was voted down, Chavez resigned, with no funding, to do it himself.

Labor unions had come and gone with little effect on the situation of migrant workers in California. Enormous strikes produced little or nothing in the end. Deeply conscious of this history, Chavez decided to slowly build an underground community-based movement that could eventually support a union. He and a few supporters, like Delores Huerta, built slowly, forming organizing committees in small towns across the San Joaquin Valley. After 6 months, they held a founding convention for what would later be called the United Farm Workers (UFW), published a newspaper, and created a credit union and a life-insurance plan.

In 1965, before Chavez thought they were ready, Filipino farm workers went on strike and the UFW decided it had to join. Thus began the famous strike against grape growers. While other unions were attempting to organize farm workers at this time, Marshall Ganz argues that the UFW succeeded because it went beyond standard labor workplace – focused organizing models by involving the entire community, by experimenting with creative tactics, and owing to its diverse democratic structure.

The UFW used a wide range of classic organizing tactics. Sensing the limits of traditional pickets and strikes, the UFW came up with the famous boycott against grapes and related products. Instead of simply appealing to the conscience of the public, however, volunteers fanned out across North

America to organize boycott support efforts. In Chicago, for example, a 21-year-old farm worker with an eighth-grade education mobilized sit-ins in stores that sold California grapes. In their final push, the union conducted a 280 mile march to Sacramento, drawing thousands of participants.

Despite many legislative and labor achievements, the UFW faded in influence in later years, in part because of Chavez's increasingly autocratic style—another lesson in the limits of dependence on charismatic leaders. Nonetheless, it still exists. Today it faces new challenges supporting undocumented immigrant workers.

The Black Power Movement (1966–1975)[41]

Informed by ideas about oppression and social change drawn especially from Malcom X and national struggles against imperialism in Africa, aspects of black power and other racial and ethnic "power" movements replaced the nonviolent Civil Rights Movement in the mid-1960s. Armed self-defense often replaced nonviolent protest.

The most important Southern group, Deacons for Defense, emerged out of local working-class fraternal organizations, reflecting working-class traditions in its "formal command structure of elected officers." "The Deacons' campaigns," Lance Hill notes, "frequently resulted in substantial and unprecedented victories at the local level, producing real power and," as Alinsky had recommended, "self-sustaining organizations." While participants in earlier efforts had mostly been women and children, Deacons was primarily a male organization.[42]

In Northern cities, young working-class leaders created the Black Panther Party, which, at different times, combined a Garvey-UNIA-like separatist nationalist vision with a more broad-based socialist vision. Their overall goal was to foment a national revolution against white oppression (later framed as "capitalist" oppression), organized around a 10-point plan for social transformation in America. Like nationalist groups before them (with the exception of later electoral efforts), they generally did not fight for specific reforms. The party provided political education courses for members in local branches across the United States, while disseminating information about the struggle, seeking to renew a sense of power and pride among African Americans. To keep members involved and ensure "survival pending revolution," they developed social service projects: serving school breakfasts for poor children, opening health centers, and creating liberation schools.

The Black Panthers participated in a broader black arts movement, which sought to transform black identity and make possible a more authentic and self-affirming "blackness" in America. The arts movement included a wide spectrum of black intellectuals, psychologists, actors, musicians, and more. Food, dress, styles of interaction, hair, music, religion: all of these became mediums for the development of a sense of common cause.

Student struggles on college and high school campuses around issues like the formation of Afro-American Studies programs and separate facilities for black students represented the most "organizing-like" aspect of the black power movement in the North. Campus conflicts often took the form of extended campaigns, involving marches, pickets, sit-ins, and the like, supplemented by student-initiated support efforts like tutorials and orientation programs.

The Panthers eventually succumbed to internal (sometimes violent) conflicts between factions combined with unpredictable shifts in aims and ideology. Intense state repression, including shoot-outs that killed many members and the imprisonment of hundreds, as well as infiltration magnified these issues. While police agencies were understandably concerned about an armed revolutionary organization, many of their actions were clearly illegal, fitting into a coordinated, ongoing effort to suppress ethnic and other freedom efforts more generally.

The example of the Panthers was replicated in different ways during these years by nationalist and/or socialist efforts among Mexican Americans, American Indians, and other ethnic groups (including whites). These efforts generally included the different components of the black power movement: collective action, nationalist tendencies, socialist aims, and efforts to foster cultural validation and transformation.

The Second-Wave Women's Movement (1963–1982)[43]

Within the different movements of the 1950s and 1960s, women increasingly resented their treatment as second-class citizens. Women did much of the "grunt work," yet were given little recognition and rarely allowed to take important formal leadership positions. These criticisms intersected with the publication of *The Feminine Mystique* by Betty Friedan in 1963. Friedan captured the suffocating life of middle-class white women, describing how a group of elite Smith College graduates were trapped in the "private" sphere of the family. Placed on a pedestal of privilege, they lacked the capacity to make real choices about a fulfilling and engaged life.

Growing discontent fed the emergence of mostly white, middle-class "consciousness-raising" groups, where women told their stories to each other, uncovering and identifying key aspects of what Friedan called the shared "problem that has no name." Out of these efforts came the famous motto of the second wave—"the personal is the political." The movement discovered that many apparently private women's concerns—including child care, domestic violence, contraception, and women's health—were in fact broadly shared social problems.[44]

The second wave was highly decentralized with many internal divisions. Van Gosse, however, argues that, paradoxically, the movement's "apparent weaknesses proved to be strengths." "Feminism succeeded," he believes, "because it was as much a cultural revolution, a new way of understanding the world, as an organized movement." Many of the movement's legislative successes were as much, if not more, the result of a broader shift in "common sense" about the place of women as they were responses to specific organizing campaigns.[45]

These changes in "common sense" were in large part produced by the willingness of many courageous women to tell stories about aspects of their lives that had previously been taboo. In "speak-outs," "take back the night" marches, and myriad forms of literature and media, women regaled the nation with stories of rape, sexual assault, domestic violence, workplace injustice, botched abortions, and more. Careful research backed up what they were saying. Speaking out was supplemented by more traditional political lobbying. As a result, politicians across the spectrum began to shift from opposition to support for reform.

As Myra Ferree and Beth Hess note, the second wave employed two relatively distinct organizational models: a more bureaucratic strategy and a loose egalitarian "collectivist" approach. In some ways the second wave echoed tensions between the earlier administrative and democratic progressives. The National Organization for Women (NOW) exemplified the administrative model, with a fairly hierarchical structure. Groups like NOW engaged in relatively traditional lobbying, but also occasionally employed mass organizing tactics. Bureaucratic groups organized around fairly clear legislative and legal goals like the never passed Equal Rights Amendment (ERA) and other successful reforms, including laws and court decisions supporting equality for women's athletics, access to credit, equal consideration in hiring, numerous state ERA amendments, and more.[46]

In contrast, the "collectivist" approach embraced new forms of "sisterhood," eschewing established leaders and nurturing individual participants. Collectivist groups came together around an enormous diversity of social problems as they contested the sexism of modern society. The fluidity of these groups facilitated broad experimentation "with attention-getting 'zap' actions such as picketing the Miss America Pageant to protest the sexual objectification of women, or . . . sit-ins at bars that served men only." Later on, collectivists created service organizations, including battered women's shelters and rape hotlines. Contesting standard professional bureaucratic approaches, they sought to develop communities of mutual support between staff, volunteers, and victims, minimizing power differentials and resisting attempts to define victims as "clients." All of this was part of a broader effort to fundamentally transform the position of women in society.[47]

Like SNCC and SDS before them, the feminist movement struggled with tensions between the constraints of bureaucratic structure and the unpredictable openness, occasional chaos, and cliquishness of "collectivist" efforts. Administrative groups worried that the collectivist approach was ineffectual, while collectivists often called bureaucrats traitors to the movement in their embrace of male-derived structures of domination and inequality. Eventually, with the help of Jo Freeman's famous essay "The Tyranny of Structurelessness," the movement became more open to a hybrid of the two approaches, developing more formal structures for accountability and more explicit roles grounded in egalitarian approaches to democratic decision making, blurring distinctions between the two sides.[48]

The second wave began to fade in the mid- to late 1970s as it achieved key aspects of its legislative, social, and cultural goals, leaving many new laws, institutions, women's studies programs, and a transformed culture in its wake. Groups like NOW became increasingly moderate in response to the backlash against all the social movements of the time. Egalitarian service organizations struggling with the requirements attached to new government funding became more professionalized and hierarchical like the settlement houses had before them. At the same time, women of color, poor women, and international women began to criticize the middle-class, white focus of the second wave. The second wave slowly dissolved with the election of Richard Nixon amidst a general backlash against the movements of the 1960s.[49]

The Environmental Movement (1962–)[50]

Scholars generally mark the beginning of the modern environmental movement with the publication of Rachel Carson's *Silent Spring* in 1962. "Prior to Carson's book," focused on the dangers of the pesticide DDT, "conservation organizations [had] limited themselves to preserving scenic outdoor amenities. After it, protecting the ecosphere and human beings from all the depredations of modern life became paramount." *Silent Spring* "drove home a moral message: that society had to alter its unthinking acceptance of technological innovation and its conceited attitude that nature was to be controlled for man's use." Over time, environmentalists embraced an increasingly broad range of concerns: from suburban sprawl, to pollution, to water quality, to demands for open space in cities, to overpopulation. As with the second wave, nearly all participants came from the middle class.[51]

The environmental movement was dominated by large organizations with mostly passive, if large, memberships like the Sierra Club and the Audubon Society, which engaged in fairly traditional political lobbying or court battles. Earth Day, begun in 1970 by Senator Gaylord Nelson, was more like a nationwide "teach-in," albeit with 20 million participants, than an effort to coerce political change. Environmentalists also organized marches and protests in support of different legislative efforts, often with a characteristic "hippie" flair. A few small groups pursued more direct conflict, including the Sea Shepherds and Earth First!, attracting media attention by blocking whale hunts, "spiking" trees to ruin expensive saws, or sabotaging equipment, with little interest in mass action. A few more focused organizing efforts emerged, including the Clamshell Alliance's 1976 occupation of the Seabrook nuclear power plant site in New Hampshire with 2,400 activists. As with the second wave, tensions emerged in the movement between organizations and grassroots "flat" democratic efforts like that of the Alliance.

Most environmental actions focused on public education and demonstrations of public support for the environment. And this educational strategy proved highly successful for these issues in the liberal and receptive climate of the 1970s. The environmental movement produced a wave of state and federal environmental legislation, including the creation of the Environmental Protection Agency and the Clean Air and Endangered Species Acts. Their efforts also produced profound and lasting shifts in the cultural values of a wide swathe of Americans.

Amid the declining economy of the mid-1970s, however, conservatives and business elites began to paint environmentalists as anti-job reactionaries and irresponsible hippies. Part of the broader reaction against the 1960s, this helped to magnify an increasingly deep, partially class-based divide in America. Nonetheless, environmentalists continued to expand their areas of concerns in the years to come. While the egalitarian aspects of the movement faded, more traditional organizations established themselves as key players in U.S. politics. Environmentalists also learned to make compromises, paying more attention to often class-based sources of division and building broader coalitions with groups like hunters and ranchers.

Organizing the Middle Class: The Last Years of Alinsky's Organizing (1964–1972)

In 1964, the second major urban riot in the United States (after Los Angeles' Watt's riot) exploded in Rochester, New York. Young blacks facing high unemployment and dismal futures lost patience with the integrationist, non-violent vision of the Civil Rights Movement. With Malcom X's assurance that even though he was white, Alinsky "knew more about organizing than anybody in the country," Alinsky's model came to Rochester.[52]

To take advantage of the ferment of the time, informed by his TWO experience, Alinsky dropped his usually slow approach to information gathering and held the convention that founded Rochester's FIGHT organization only 60 days after the formal invitation. FIGHT's key issue was increasing black hiring at Eastman Kodak, the largest employer in the city.

The struggle with Kodak eventually extended past the boundaries of Rochester, reflecting new challenges for organizing created by national and international companies. Stymied in their local actions, Alinsky collected stock proxies from sympathetic Kodak stockholders. FIGHT took 700 members to New Jersey to attend Kodak's shareholders' meeting. Entering the meeting to mutters of "throw the niggers out," FIGHT President Franklin Florence gave the company till two o'clock to meet their demands. Kodak refused. Florence told the media that "this is war," stressing that "Kodak will honor the agreement or reap the harvest."[53]

But in the days that followed, Alinsky found only limited success in his proxy effort. And Kodak attempted an end run around FIGHT by creating its own jobs program with another, more friendly Rochester organization. A little more than a month later, worried about the prospect of a stalemate that he thought FIGHT could not survive, he called Kodak to negotiate, but was only able to secure a fairly vague "agreement." Kodak agreed to recognize FIGHT as the legitimate representative of inner-city blacks, and to work together on jobs programs, but made no concrete commitments.

Alinsky's experience in Rochester reaffirmed his growing belief that there weren't enough downtrodden people in America to catalyze broad social change. "One thing I've come to realize," he said, "is that any positive action for radical social change will have to be focused on the white middle class, for the simple reason that this is where the real power lies." And he began to explore strategies for building alliances between poor and middle-class people. Around this time Alinsky also realized that he needed to develop a more focused and structured approach to training organizers, creating a new training institute within the IAF led by Chambers.[54]

As the 1960s ended, amid the fervor of the black power and other radical movements, Alinsky became an almost moderate voice for pragmatic reform, deeply critical of radical activists' lack of a coherent and pragmatic strategy for building power. In his last years, he also helped develop a broad-based regional coalition, the Citizen's Action Program in Chicago.

His plans for the future ended abruptly with a heart attack in 1972 at the age of 62. He was laid low by his ubiquitous cigarette instead of by the reactionary thugs that he had romantically hoped would complete his image as a hated enemy of oppression. Chambers followed him as head of the IAF, carrying the Alinsky legacy forward with others into the 1970s and beyond. Chambers' religious background as one of Alinsky's many ex-seminarian organizers and the similar background of many other organizers today have likely influenced the evolution of organizing toward a congregational model, with an increasing focus on relationships, and a tendency at points to downplay the need for aggressive conflict.

The Anti-Vietnam War Movement and the End of Mass Confrontation (1963–1975)[55]

There was no way to join; you simply announced or felt yourself to be a part of the movement—usually through some act like joining a protest march.

—Sarah Evans, *Personal Politics*

The effort to end American involvement in the Vietnam War was the most broad-based movement of the era, a roller coaster in which lulls of quiet despair could be followed by unpredictable explosions of mass rebellion. Waxing and waning from 1963 until the signing of a peace agreement in 1973, the movement involved nearly every left-leaning activist group and organization in the country. It became "the largest domestic opposition to a warring government in the history of modern industrial society." Although organizations helped coordinate some movement activities, they were not a central moving force. Protests did not have clear leaders; at most, "coordinators" "set the dates," "formed networks," and performed services like training marshals to try to control sometimes unruly militants. Most participants were not members of any coherent group at all. The organizations that did exist were often at odds with each other. As a result, most movement actions lacked any strategic focus, limited to generalized (if creative) demonstrations of opposition or efforts at popular education.[56]

The middle class dominated the movement. Few efforts were made to engage the working class and people of color, even though they represented the largely silent majority of opposition to the war. In fact, tactics and perspectives that made sense to alienated middle-class youth, including the occasional desecration of national symbols like the flag, the "hippie" peace symbol, the counterculture's theater of the absurd (trying to "levitate" the Pentagon or to elect a pig to the presidency), attacks on selective service offices, and scattered examples of violence, often alienated these other groups. War supporters magnified these differences, making it difficult for outsiders to separate resistance to the war from attacks on cherished symbols of patriotism and respected social institutions.

Established authorities largely controlled the narrative of the movement instead of the other way around. Until his downfall, for example, Nixon repeatedly outmaneuvered those opposed to the war by making calculated and often illusory concessions like drawing down ground forces while intensifying the air campaign, painting himself as the champion of "peace," and appealing to honor instead of failure. He used the violence and the outrageous actions of a few to paint the movement with a broad, radical, anti-American brush in the minds of the general population. "Anarchy," Nixon declared with typically calculated hyperbole: "this is the way civilizations die!" And the apparatus of the state harassed, monitored, and infiltrated movement groups, sometimes instigating the very actions war supporters later condemned.[57]

The years 1969 and 1970, the high-water marks of the movement, illuminated both its power and limitations. On October 15, 1969, a "moratorium," the largest protest in American history, was held across the United States. Millions of Americans participated in peaceful, often sober marches, memorials, rallies, teach-ins, vigils, and more. But it was not clear what this event really accomplished in political terms. A year later, National Guardsmen at Kent State University fired on a crowd of peaceful demonstrators, killing four students. Students went on strike at more than 300 universities, some clashing with police, smashing windows, and damaging buildings. The National Guard was called out to campuses in 16 states. And then two black students died in a barrage of police fire at Jackson State, a black college in the South, setting off more upheaval. But national anger was mostly directed at the protestors, not the unprovoked killing.

At this point, the movement mostly dissolved into cynicism and exhaustion, with the exception of fantastic violent actions by tiny splinter groups like the Weathermen with little apparent interest in coherent strategy.

Scholars do not agree on the movement's influence on the length or intensity of the war. Clearly it had a direct effect on Presidents Lyndon Johnson and Richard Nixon, preventing some actions and leading to others like Nixon's combined strategy of troop withdrawal and increased aerial bombardment. At the same time the movement's actions often alienated those who might otherwise have been their allies. The movement's inability to identify what, if anything, it had accomplished intensified alienation already widespread among young people, encouraging many to turn away from the public realm as the 1970s advanced, "dropping out" into a counterculture focused on self-development and the creation of utopian communities.

The Community Action Program and the Emergence of the "Nonprofit Industrial Complex" (1964–)[58]

America's vast array of nonprofit organizations, especially in the arena of social services, is a fairly new phenomenon. While private aid agencies existed prior to the 1960s, there were restrictions on who could form nonprofits. The battle for civil rights, however, convinced federal courts to allow a wider range of people to create independent institutions.

President Lyndon Johnson's War on Poverty took advantage of this new opportunity, diverting funding to nonprofits and away from local government. Most important, from an organizing perspective, was the Community Action Program (CAP) written into the 1964 Equal Economic Opportunity Act. CAP funded independent community action agencies (CAAs) across the United States and required "maximum feasible participation" of the local residents. According to Fisher, CAP was meant to "reincorporate African Americans into the political process" in response to the "urban rebellions" of the mid-1960s, and to solidify black "support for the Democratic party."[59]

But many CAAs went farther than national politicians had anticipated. CAP gave local activists a way to "bypass traditional instruments of local government" and fund local organizing. Despite doubts, even Alinsky was drawn into this federal experiment, helping to start an organizing program in Syracuse with Ross and Walter Haggstrom. Across the nation, grassroots leaders pushed many CAAs "beyond an emphasis on child and social welfare programs to [focus on] neighborhood advocacy, organizing, and development."[60]

CAAs were rarely as militant as some of the rhetoric indicated, but they did threaten the power of local elected officials. After only a couple of years, these officials successfully convinced the federal government to eliminate grassroots control. Nonetheless, in their short democratic period, CAAs provided major support to a range of movements and local organizing efforts. CAP's most important legacy may have been the new generation of local leaders it prepared. As Fisher notes, "tens of thousands of poor and black people . . . became active in local politics for the first time." They discovered that they could generate "power and could successfully pressure the political system."[61]

After the end of its democratic phase, CAP programs were taken over by professional managers and reoriented to the hierarchical staff-client relationships standard in other service programs. In this way, they replicated the pattern experienced earlier by the settlement houses. Going forward, a range of emerging pressures and requirements continued to increase the pressure on nonprofits to become more bureaucratic.

The reverberations of the CAP experience are still felt today. Most important, the CAP program sensitized elected officials to the danger of funding organizing efforts that might turn around and bite them. This led to new restrictions on political participation for nonprofits, and regulations that prevented government-funded internship programs like Volunteers in Service to America (VISTA) from engaging in organizing. At the same time, former organizing groups across the nation increasingly transformed themselves into service organizations to secure government funding, dropping any contentious activity. Well-paid service jobs co-opted many former organizers.

What is called "community development" emerged as a politically palatable replacement for contentious community organizing. John Kretzmann and John McKnight's vision of "asset-based community development" is perhaps the most prominent, today. Arguing that Alinsky's conflict-based approach is passé, Kretzmann and McKnight assert that existing community assets can be leveraged in non-threatening collaborations with outside interests. They envision newly democratic communities and cooperative enterprises that can attract investment—although organizers question the long-term payoff of this approach.[62]

In a parallel development, on a national level, as John Atlas notes, during these years "hundreds of new [top-down] public interest organizations were organized," ranging from Common Cause, to the National Abortion Rights Action League, to the Children's Defense Fund. "Staffed by lawyers, lobbyists, and policy experts, these groups sought to influence the government" without mobilizing a grassroots constituency. In fact, "most groups had no members at all." They "rarely brought individuals together across lines of income, education, and social status; and siphoned donor money away from groups that mobilized the poor," paying much higher salaries than neo-Alinsky groups. The dominance of national advocacy groups of this kind has only intensified in the years since.[63]

National Welfare Rights Organization (1966–1975)[64]

You control our lives and so far you've treated us like slaves. You're responsible for the health and welfare of our children but you're not interested in how we live. . . . It's time to treat us like human beings.
—Etta Horn, Testimony before Congress

The critique of white feminism that emerged at the end of the second wave was foreshadowed by the welfare rights movement. In the 1950s, poor black women began to come together in small groups to discuss their experiences in the degrading welfare system and explore avenues for resistance. By pooling their experience, as more privileged women would later on in consciousness-raising groups, women on welfare learned that "their problems were not exceptional" and that "abuse and arbitrary treatment . . . was designed . . . to prevent them from knowing and asserting their rights."[65]

Through the 1950s and early 1960s, the Aid to Families with Dependent Children (AFDC) program became increasingly controversial and oppressive. White, middle-class social workers reached snap judgments about who was "worthy" and who was not with little recourse, and the bureaucracy was impenetrable and rife with mistakes. Although most recipients were actually white, stereotypes of black women dominated the popular imagination. Ironically, the gross injustice of the system was a crucial impetus for mobilizing recipients. Historically, disrespect has been a much more powerful impetus to righteous anger and collective resentment than abstract questions of economic inequality. Thus, welfare bureaucracies were perfect candidates for sparking social conflict.

By the early 1960s, local welfare organizing groups began to spring up around the nation. With the support of scholars like Cloward and Piven and organizers like George Wiley (who came out of CORE and participated in Alinsky's efforts in Syracuse) and Bill Pastreich (who was also part of the Syracuse effort), groups from around the country came together at a conference, leading to the first nationwide welfare rights protest and to the National Welfare Rights Organization (NWRO) directed by Wiley. Organizers hired by CAAs were important in the emergence of strong local branches of the NWRO. The movement spread across the United States, as "welfare rights activists marched into welfare offices, . . . negotiated with caseworkers, lobbied welfare officials, held mass rallies, and took over welfare and state offices." As usual, the system slowly found ways to adjust to this new environment, bureaucrats learning to stand more firmly against protestors, and states changing regulations to meet a few key demands. But as one avenue for successful mobilizing shut down, the NWRO shifted to new issues, moving at one point from welfare office confrontations to battles with department stores for access to credit.[66]

From the beginning there were tensions in the NWRO between the mostly male, college-educated central staff and the working-class female African American leadership. Women leaders resisted the staff's Alinsky-based focus on short-term goals over long-term development and resented the idea that they lacked their own "analysis of long term social change." In fact, as Premilla Nadasen notes, the women developed a sophisticated, "multilayered analysis of their situation: combining ideology, economics, and political power." They focused "on the slow and patient work of winning people over politically and ideologically—of empowering them to take control of their lives" instead of focusing on quick wins. Although few identified with the second wave, they ultimately developed their own "full-fledged feminist agenda" focused not on individual freedom but instead on poverty, motherhood, the plight of black men, and the drudgery of low-wage work.[67]

By the mid-1970s the movement began to falter. In part, as usual, this was an almost inevitable result of the movement's successes. But larger cultural and political shifts toward more conservative perspectives on welfare were also under way. Ironically, black women leaders took control of their organization from the original staff just as it was failing. NWRO shut down in 1975, although some local organizations survived.

Association of Community Organizations for Reform Now (ACORN) (1970–)[68]

In the last years of the NWRO, conscious of declining mobilization around the welfare issue, Wiley and other staff were searching for ways to create a broader movement. In 1970, Wiley sent the young Wade Rathke to Arkansas to create a broader, multi-issue organization. Rathke planned to extend on the NWRO approach to organizing individuals one by one, combining this with alliances with existing local progressive organizations, and with an exploration of electoral politics. Instead of focusing on a limited constituency, like welfare mothers, Rathke sought to build more power by recruiting widely and appealing to issues of interest to a range of potential members. After building power in Arkansas, the organization began to expand rapidly into multiple states, supported, in part, by interns paid for by the VISTA program.

ACORN eventually coalesced into a broad-based national organization that differed in significant ways from all the other existing national organizing networks (discussed below in "The IAF and the Emergence of Congregation-Based Community Organizing"). Like the NWRO before it, ACORN organized mostly individuals and not existing organizations (like churches). Individual ACORN chapters and their staff were largely under the command of the national office, with less (but still significant) power given to local leaders. In addition, as already noted, ACORN participated in electoral politics. And, it got deeply involved in labor efforts, actually developing its own unions, while entering into innovative relationships with the local, state, and national governments, providing a range of housing and tax-related services to poor residents.

Despite many important accomplishments, described in more detail by Heidi Swarts in Chapter 5, ACORN disbanded in 2010 under attack for financial irregularities and in response to a video tape that purported to show ACORN housing staff trying to help a "pimp" lie on loan forms. While the tape was later shown to be an almost complete fabrication, the damage had been done. A number of state-level and other local ACORN groups remain, re-formed into independent organizations.

The "Backyard Revolution" (1975–1985)[69]

In the popular imagination, the conservative backlash and the emergence of the counterculture brought an abrupt end to grassroots action in the mid-1970s. There is some truth to this belief with respect to national movements, even though environmental, women's rights, and other efforts continued in less popular forms. But many grassroots activists and organizers did not simply walk away. Instead, many turned their focus to local issues. What Harry Boyte calls a "backyard revolution" emerged, representing "a groundswell of citizens" that called "for the return of political and economic power to the local level." Some of this rebirth in local organizing was supported by the IAF and other emerging national training and support groups around the nation at the time, including ACORN (formed in 1970), PICO (1972), Midwest Academy (1976), the Direct Action and Research Training Center (DART) (1982), the Gamaliel Foundation (1986), and the Center for Third World Organizing (mid-1980s). Many new local organizations grew independently as well.[70]

Throughout the mid- to late 1970s, "neighborhood activism appeared in urban communities across the nation. Rent strikes, pickets of local savings and loan associations, and school demonstrations became common features of urban life." Organizations successfully fought highways and urban renewal projects, saving parks, libraries, and firehouses. Local "environmental justice" organizations in poor areas (to be distinguished from the middle-class environmental movement) began resisting the placement and operation of power plants, toxic waste dumps, and other threats to human health in their communities.[71]

Some of these groups remain, and new groups are always forming. But in retrospect the "backyard revolution" looks more like the last hurrah of the 1960s than a hoped-for "rebirth." After their experience with the CAP, local governments and business elites became increasingly savvy at suppressing grassroots organizing. Lacking significant funding, many organizations didn't last long. Others couldn't resist the clarion call of large social service grants, which allowed them to pay competitive salaries and hire more staff, joining the growing "nonprofit industrial complex." Government-funded organizations ceased their contentious action, or lost their governmental support, becoming lessons for others. The grassroots groups that have survived generally avoid such funding, but partly as a result they remain small and few in number.

The IAF and the Emergence of Congregation-Based Community Organizing (1972–)[72]

After Alinsky's death, the IAF founded local organizations across the United States and provided this network with training and on-the-ground guidance. As Mark Warren discusses in more detail in Chapter 6, Chambers and key organizers like Ernesto Cortes evolved Alinsky's approach in a number of crucial ways, creating what is now a fairly standard neo-Alinsky model. Other networks also emerged in response to the disappearance of most indigenous neighborhood ethnic, service, and religious groups, the IAF and most other organizing networks (with the exception of ACORN) intensified their focus on one organization that remained: churches.

Organizers quickly realized that faith-based community organizing demanded a more systematic engagement with the relationships between theology and power. Priests, pastors, and organizers explored how Bible stories could provide metaphors for organizing, extending on Alinsky's earlier work. ("Paul," Alinsky would say, "now, Paul was an organizer.") In contrast with more right-wing efforts to connect religion and politics, the diversity of congregational center-left coalitions (which often include non-Christian groups like Muslims and Jews) makes agreement on strict dogma impossible. Instead, faith-based groups come together around more general values that run across their different faiths: belief in the dignity of all human beings, revulsion for poverty and inequality, and the like. There are some problems these diverse organizations cannot work on at all: abortion, for example.[73]

Congregational organizations have also developed systematic strategies for nurturing new leaders in their organizations, looking beyond leaders in formal positions into the pews. The most important strategy has been the one-on-one interview, described in Chapter 10, which allows leaders to develop a web of relationships with a range of people that they can later call upon for support. These interviews keep leaders in touch with the desires and beliefs of fellow participants, helping leaders define issues that will energize their base. Importantly, this approach to developing new leaders through relational meetings has provided an avenue for increasing numbers of women to take key leadership roles.

Labor Slowly Begins to Reconnect with the Community: Poor People's Unions and Worker Centers (1963–)[74]

Chavez's UFW represented the most significant, comprehensive labor-community organizing effort since the 1930s. However, other community-based labor battles were bubbling up in the 1960s, mostly among the poorest workers in America. Groups across America fought for women's rights and equal wages, and against racial discrimination in the workplace. In fact, from 1963 to 1964 "campaigns against job bias were the most common projects among the northern and western chapters" of the civil rights group CORE, and were "generally the most successful."[75]

As traditional approaches to union organizing "failed in poor communities where turnover was high and employer power was strong, . . . community support was necessary to tip the balance in the worker's favor." These efforts employed a wide range of creative tactics. In San Francisco, for example, the United Freedom Movement demanded that a supermarket chain with a racist hiring record sign a fair hiring agreement. For nine days, "protesters entered the stores, filled their grocery carts, lined up to check out, then left saying, 'I'll have more money to pay when you hire more Negroes.' " Entire job categories instead of particular workplaces also began to be organized, including domestic workers, maids, and janitors, which would have been impossible without broad community support. Approaches like these became increasingly effective in the years to come. A range of groups engaged workers in fights beyond the workplace in the political realm, including successful struggles for increases in unemployment benefits and other protections. ACORN, with its union organizing branch, was a key participant in these developments. These new approaches began in some areas to foster a broader sense of class identity that included racial, gender, and other oppressions, drawing lessons about democratic structure and recruitment from Ross' CSO and Chavez's UFW.[76]

A core strategy of these efforts was to at least initially bypass the straitjacket of standard union organizing models and begin with "direct action first"—often mass confrontations with employers. Direct action "brought workers together to act for themselves, and allowed rank-and-file leaders to gain confidence," which built "a more effective and engaging union."[77]

Despite great energy, without significant resources many early efforts had difficulty sustaining themselves as independent unions. Some survived, some failed, and some merged with larger unions. Early on, leaders of traditional unions were generally resistant and even fearful of these alien community-based strategies. They were already under siege internally from rebelling women and minorities who were increasingly unwilling to be treated as second-class citizens. The few early community-based efforts of traditional unions were top-down, with little grassroots support, accomplishing little. As they began to hemorrhage members, however, mainline unions began to recognize the potential of this new community-based approach to regaining their numbers, led by the Service Employees International Union (SEIU). SEIU sought out mergers with a number of these new efforts, and in 1986 it began its own community-based "jobs for janitors" campaigns.

Mainstream unions, however, continue to struggle to alter frequently petrified bureaucratic cultures, producing rancorous debates, leadership conflicts, and angry defections from key labor coalitions. Traditional labor's ability to refocus itself on organizing and exploit new strategies still remains an open question.

Another important community-related development in labor organizing is the emergence of "worker centers," which focus on "the most exploited and invisible workers," usually immigrants but also low-wage African Americans and others. Often in coalition with local unions, worker centers provide space for low-wage employees, especially contingent and temporary workers like day laborers and sweatshop workers, to come together. Worker centers are one of the few nonprofit organizations that have managed to maintain a focus on organizing while also providing services, ranging from ESL classes, to legal help with employment and immigration issues, to check cashing. Worker centers have successfully conducted campaigns to organize undocumented workers in different areas, showing that even apparently "unorganizable" workers can successfully fight for improved wages and against workplace discrimination. They also often conduct more traditional community organizing campaigns around issues like in-state tuition and driver cards for undocumented immigrants. And there has been work to create worker cooperatives in areas like home health care and cleaning services that allow workers to control their own employment.[78]

The Gay Rights Movement (1969–)[79]

The first real stirrings of gay rights came in the 1950s with the establishment of what came to be called "homophile" organizations. Given the fear and repression of these times, the homophile groups took a conciliatory stance, working mostly through education and trying to show that homosexuals were upstanding citizens. As the 1960s advanced, however, pressed by the example of the anti-Vietnam War movement, "the values of the homophile movement—respectability, conciliation, coats and ties at Washington pickets—[increasingly] seemed out of another era."[80]

In 1969, riots protesting a raid on the Stonewall bar in New York City changed everything. During the raid, instead of leaving as usual, a crowd collected outside the bar. When the police began arresting patrons, the crowd started "yelling, throwing bricks and bottles, and setting fire to trash cans." In one account "the police found themselves face to face with a chorus line of mocking queens, kicking their heels in the air and singing:

> We are the Stonewall girls
> We wear our hair in curls
> We wear no underwear
> We show our pubic hair . . . .

The next night crowds and the police squared off again and "the events were already beginning to take on a more political character." Signs read "THEY INVADED OUR RIGHTS; LEGALIZE GAY BARS; SUPPORT GAY POWER."

Dennis Altman called it "the Boston Tea Party of the gay movement." At the next major homophile group meeting in New York, the standard conciliatory speech of the group's president was shouted down by attendees. "We don't want acceptance, goddamn it! We want respect! Demand it! We're through hiding in dark bars."[81]

An entirely new gay liberation movement emerged. "Now, Blatant was Beautiful . . . . The key phrase is COME OUT . . . . Celebrate your sexuality." Participants sought "revolutionary change" in society and within themselves, connecting with other oppressed groups. As in the second wave, individuals shared their experiences in consciousness-raising groups, developing common themes of oppression. Groups emerged at universities and in cities around the country, and activism became more visible. The "zap" became popular, targeting politicians and other powerful figures with confrontations. And these tactics were often quite creative. At one point, the president of Fidelifacts, accused of collecting and selling information on people's sex lives, stated that "if one looks like a duck, walks like a duck, associates only with ducks, and quacks like a duck, he is probably a duck." Twelve activists dressed up in duck costumes and "were seen waddling at the entrance to Fidelifacts, quacking and carrying picket signs." On the anniversary of Stonewall, as many as twenty-thousand participated in a parade in New York, "the outrageous and the outraged splendid in their flaming colors, splendid in their . . . birthday celebration of liberation."[82]

The exhilaration of the public action was balanced by an antigay reaction. Efforts to pass rights laws competed with efforts to roll them back. Many issues emerged but did not seem likely to move quickly to resolution. Also during this time, tensions and distance grew between gays and lesbians; lesbian groups aligned themselves more closely with second-wave feminists.

And then, at the beginning of the 1980s, came AIDS. At first, no one understood what was going on. As it became clear that transmission came, in part, through unsafe sex, however, the disease seemed to threaten gay liberation's celebration of sexuality. The first response was community support for the sick as hundreds and then thousands began to die. At the same time, right-wing leaders used AIDS to paint the gay lifestyle as fundamentally diseased. Some advances continued, however, and the crisis brought lesbians and gay men closer together amid enormous fear of "a national witch-hunt, even quarantine."[83]

What began in mourning turned to anger with a Supreme Court decision in 1987 that allowed states to make gay sex—essentially *being* gay—a crime. This ruling, combined with the "Reagan and Bush administration's appalling neglect of AIDS" catalyzed a collective, militant response to oppression. Part of this response was the creation of the Aids Coalition to Unleash Power, or ACT-UP, one of the most creative and transformative groups in American history. Amid catastrophe, a "beloved community" came together, with chapters spreading across the nation and internationally. While AIDS was ACT UP's core orienting issue, it soon addressed other related issues as well. Lacking a clear central leadership—reflecting the middle-class culture of most participants and informed by women veterans of the second wave—it is perhaps inaccurate to call ACT UP an "organization." In "long and anarchic" meetings "decisions [were] made by a laborious consensus process." Groups formed within groups, each with their own related vision, coming together for direct actions, often with mini demonstrations within demonstrations. A movement with style, ACT UP actions "were known for their keen sense of political theater and an ability to attract media coverage." ACT UP forced drug companies to lower prices; increased access to experimental drugs (altering the very structure of medical trials in the process); gave people with AIDS a voice on decision-making panels; pressured government for funding; fought for needle exchange programs; and fundamentally transformed society's vision of people with AIDS.[84]

Creative direct action—political theater of different kinds—has often played a part in social struggles. The UFW, for example, used theater projects to educate migrant workers, and we noted absurdist efforts (like running a pig for president) during the anti-Vietnam War movement. More than most groups before them, ACT UP participants carefully crafted their tactics to influence specific targets even as they sought more broadly to intervene in public dialogue, to "reverse the homophobic script propelling the AIDS crisis." In ACT UP, healthy, infected, and sick activists embraced a playful attitude in the shadow of so many who had died, creating a space that allowed anger and fear and tragedy to join with a deep sense of fun, camaraderie, and empowerment. ACT UP brought partying and effective, pragmatic activism together. Participants reclaimed aspects of the gay liberation era's celebration of sexuality that AIDS had threatened. ACT UP was not just about play, however. As Benjamin Shepard notes, in effective organizing "the playful piece

[only] works well when it functions as part of a coherent, organizing strategy that includes a clear goal, direct action, and legal counsel, as well as a media and communications strategy," all of which, despite its anarchic structure, ACT UP had.[85]

The early "quack up" against Fidelifacts, described above, provides a good example of the kind of actions that later defined ACT UP. ACT UP used humor and ridicule (which Alinsky had noted is "man's most potent weapon") to "illustrate the buffoonery of those who saw AIDS as anything other than a public health issue." In the famous "Send in the Clowns demo," for example, about sixty activists put on "fuzzy clown hats" at a meeting where the right-wing-dominated Civil Rights Commission was trying to discuss AIDS. When Commission members said ridiculous things, the clowns reflected their statements in clownish actions. As one participant remembers, "the press was like, 'Oh, clown faces! Here's an image. . . . It was completely empowering because we completely wrecked it. The committee had no legitimacy. They just sort of fizzled off into nothingness, and we were really able to undercut them so severely by doing this—by being funny, by being smart, and not playing into this situation that they'd set up.'" ACT UP members were famous for their chants designed, in part, to provide sound bites for the media. For example, a group wearing lab coats and tossing around large, red-stained copies of $20 bills shouted: "We are the doctors, where is our fee? . . . What do you want? Blood money!" Perhaps better than any other group, ACT UP taught the lesson that "creative guerilla theater could reshape power structures." Its strategies also fit with the particular position of gays in America. Instead of frightening people, ACT UP wanted to "stymie people and leave them without a response," changing the focus of public dialogue in the process, so they did "the high camp thing. It was strategic."[86]

At its best, ACT UP's strategic savvy was enormously impressive. But its anarchic structure could also create potential issues. A "zap" at a Catholic Cathedral attacking a cardinal where one activist declared that he was "no man of God—he is the devil" and that "featured ACT UP members stomping on communion wafers," for example, may have antagonized people without any clear movement payoff.[87]

In the mid-1990s, internal and broader community fractures, burnout, and changes in the social context (including increased access to those in power for some) led to the fading of this branch of the gay rights movement. Like earlier "beloved communities" that were forged in fire, faith and trust slowly eroded over years of struggle; exhaustion set in, and long-standing disagreements over tactics and intergroup tensions came to the fore. The gay rights movement—which had expanded over these years to include people who were bisexual and transgender—largely shifted to less theatrical, if no less, committed efforts around gay marriage, gays in the military, and a range of other issues that continue today.[88]

Trends and Patterns

A few key trends and patterns seem evident in this historical overview. First of all, different cultural mores and patterns always influence what forms different social efforts will take. For example, men only began to participate in large numbers in the Civil Rights Movement in the South when Deacons for Defense provided a strategy that fitted better with traditions of male honor. The influence of gender on the first- and second-wave women's movements goes without saying. Social class seems especially important, reappearing as a key influence in most of the efforts discussed.

None of these influences were monolithic, however. As the Civil Rights Movement and the second-wave discussions showed, at the same moment quite different approaches could be developed in the same movement: compare the more bureaucratic structure of NOW to efforts to promote egalitarian democracy in battered women's shelters. Overall, the lesson is that organizers ignore the cultural patterns of the people they work with at their peril.

Second, social action in America has followed a roller coaster of emergence, broad activity, and then quiescence. This pattern has been driven both by exhaustion as key leaders are worn out by the demands of ongoing engagement, and, ironically, often by success, since achieving some of a movement's goals makes it increasingly difficult to maintain high participation. Winning the vote for women, for example, ended what had been an enormously vibrant movement, and it took more than forty years for another national movement around women's rights to emerge. The success of the labor movement in the 1930s led to a domesticated and largely self-satisfied union movement. The granting of standard payment schedules for welfare, among other changes, short-circuited anger at capricious bureaucracy that had earlier driven engagement, leading to the dissolution of the NWRO. Shifts back and forth between more and less progressive or conservative trends in the larger culture also clearly influence the level of success an effort achieves. In fact, success itself is part of what seems to drive conservative resurgence. We saw, for example, how the gay liberation movement catalyzed the emergence of antigay groups. In fact, those on the "losing" end can gain motivation (because they feel like they are losing) at the same time as the energy of "winning" groups declines.

Third, organizers struggle with a constant tension between fluid creativity and dependable but often restrictive structure. Sometimes catastrophe will catalyze the emergence of what Rebecca Solnit calls "paradises built in hell." A "rupture in everyday life" can bring forth a solidarity that overwhelms the normal currents of tension, disagreement, and distrust that run through every community. We saw this in the "beloved community" of the early years of SNCC, the spaces of sisterhood created by the second wave, and the reclaiming of a culture of celebration amid tragedy by ACT UP. But the historical record indicates that these somewhat utopian communities are evanescent. The deep trust and sense of shared commitment so palpable at the beginning inevitably fades as the "everyday" reasserts itself, as ongoing disagreements and tensions create fractures. As a result, organizers cannot depend upon these unpredictable, exhilarating spaces over the long term. But they can take advantage of them when they coalesce (as Alinsky and von Hoffman did in TWO), and they can build on what they accomplish as they fade—drawing from the experience gained by participants and working to spin off more coherent organizing groups as they dissolve (as when ACORN emerged out of the NWRO). Neo-Alinsky organizing has always been suspicious of "movement moments" and has generally sought a more structured, sober approach. Structure, however, can lead to sclerosis. Organizations, especially those that become dependent upon funding from more traditional sources, can easily lose their oppositional edge, feeding the growth of the nonprofit industrial complex. Neo-Alinsky organizers have also not always been as attentive as they should to the ways their vision can become dogmatic, reducing their capacity to engage effectively with the always unpredictable and shifting nature of power in modern society, and hampering the playful creativity that Alinsky himself so firmly embraced.[89]

Fourth, the achievements of social struggle are always in danger of being rolled back with the emergence of a reactionary resurgence. With the end of the NWRO, for example, came a decline of funding for welfare and increasing discomfort with the program, which led a few decades later, in 1996, to the elimination of welfare as an entitlement. By the 1990s, no organization remained with the power to effectively resist this change. The early successes of the unemployed movement in the 1930s were similarly reversed when the movement ceased to present a real threat to the powers of the time. Without power, no aspect of the social world is ever immune from attack and destruction. We have seen this most recently as those in congress become increasingly willing to discuss cutting social security, an issue that was long supposed to be the "third rail" of politics in America. If social security can be threatened—a benefit for the group in America most likely to vote—anything can be threatened.

Fifth, as with all history, there is a constant tension between the unique particulars of a specific moment and broader historical trends. One wonders whether the anti – Vietnam War movement, for example, would have been more successful had the tactically savvy Nixon not been president. For many action groups and movements, especially more hierarchical ones, the specific foibles of particular leaders can be of paramount importance. Would the UFW have maintained its strength had Chavez let go of the reigns instead of descending into autocracy at the end? Would the unemployed councils have found more traction in the later years of the Great Depression had their leaders not become co-opted by the government? Would the UNIA have survived longer had it not been so dependent on Garvey? The second-wave and environmental movements, in contrast, were much less dependent upon specific leaders, although the egalitarianism of some of their organizations brought their own challenges.

More, of course, could be said. At this point, however, we leave it to our readers to tease out further lessons. As you read though the rest of this book, other patterns and ideas will likely present themselves to you. In fact, it may benefit you to reread this chapter after you finish the rest of the book. The history will read differently once you have internalized more aspects of the neo-Alinsky model, providing a basis for better understanding and perhaps also for critiquing aspects of the strategies we discuss in the pages that follow.

The last point we would like to make is that history, by definition, is unpredictable. All of the events we discuss, above, could have turned out differently. Collective action efforts are always dependent upon their capacity to respond to and, if they are creative enough, take advantage of the unpredictable occurrences of history. It is easy, with 20/20 hindsight, to judge the actions of others. It can be difficult to remember that the participants in the Montgomery bus boycott, for example, did not know that they would win, or that success would take more than a year. Every day that they woke up to walk to work could have been the last day. Similarly, members of the unemployed councils did not know that their vibrant movement would dissipate without actually accomplishing very much on the national level. And amid the enormous rallies and marches of Garvey's UNIA, participants likely would not have believed that in only a few years it would almost completely disappear from the scene. Because of this ineradicable unpredictability—which historical writing sometimes obscures—organizing will always be a craft, not a science. Tomorrow is never entirely like today. As a result, today's organizing model may not suffice to contest tomorrow's challenges.

Notes

1. Harry Braverman, *Labor and Monopoly Capital: The Degradation of Work in the Twentieth Century* (New York: Monthly Review Press, 1975); Joseph George Rayback, *A History of American Labor* (New York: Free Press, 1966); Clayton Sinyai, *Schools of Democracy: A Political History of the American Labor Movement* (Ithaca, N.Y.: ILR Press, 2006); David Montgomery, *The Fall of the House of Labor: The Workplace, the State, and American Labor Activism, 1865–1925* (New York: Cambridge University Press, 1987); Dorothy, Sue Cobble, *The Other Women's Movement* (Princeton, NJ: Princeton University Press, 2004).

2. Braverman, *Labor and Monopoly Capital,* 66; Sinyai, *Schools of Democracy,* 43.

3. Jane Addams, *The Jane Addams Reader,* ed. Jean Bethke Elshtain (New York: Basic Books, 2002); Jean Bethke Elshtain, *Jane Addams and the Dream of American Democracy: A Life* (New York: Basic Books, 2002); Michael Reisch and Janice Andrews, *The Road Not Taken: A History of Radical Social Work in the United States* (Philadelphia, PA: Brunner-Routledge, 2001); Stanley Wenocur and Michael Reisch, *From Charity to Enterprise: The Development of American Social Work in a Market Economy* (Urbana, IL: University of Illinois Press, 1989).

4. In Aaron Schutz, *Social Class, Social Action, and Education: The Failure of Progressive Democracy* (New York: Palgrave Macmillan, 2010), Aaron actually argues that there were three different branches of progressivism, but that level of detail doesn't seem necessary here.

5. Elshtain, *Jane Addams,* 22.

6. Addams, *Jane Addams Reader,* 167.

7. See Reisch, *Road Not Taken.*

8. Colin Grant, *Negro with a Hat: The Rise and Fall of Marcus Garvey* (Oxford; New York: Oxford University Press, 2008); Michael C. Dawson, *Black Visions: The Roots of Contemporary African-American Political Ideologies* (Chicago, IL: University of Chicago Press, 2001); Roderick Bush, *We Are Not What We Seem: Black Nationalism and Class Struggle in the American Century* (New York: NYU Press, 2000) Lawrence V. Levine, "Marcus Garvey," in *Black Leaders of the Twentieth Century,* ed. John Hope Franklin (Urbana, IL: University of Illinois Press, 1982), 105–138.

9. Bush, *We Are Not What We Seem,* 98. On the establishment of black religious organizations, see Gayraud S. Wilmore, *Black Religion and Black Radicalism: An Interpretation of the Religious History of African Americans* (Maryknoll, N.Y.: Orbis Books, 1998).

10. Dawson, *Black Visions.*

11. Sara M. Evans, *Born for Liberty: A History of Women in America* (New York: Free Press, 1989); Eleanor Flexner and Ellen F. Fitzpatrick, *Century of Struggle: The Woman's Rights Movement in the United States,* Enlarged Edition (Cambridge, MA: Belknap Press of Harvard University Press, 1996); Anne Ruggles Gere, *Intimate Practices: Literacy and Cultural Work in U.S. Women's Clubs, 1880–1920* (Urbana, IL: University of Illinois Press, 1997) Eleanor Clift, *Founding Sisters and the Nineteenth Amendment* (New York: Wiley, 2003).

12. Matthews, *Rise of the New Woman*, 141; Flexner and Fitzpatrick, *Century of Struggle*, 297. The National American Women Suffrage Association actually produced a statement in response to an attack on its "open-membership policy" in 1903 noting that "each State auxiliary arranges its own affairs" and that "the most active southern women have always . . . emphasized the fact that granting suffrage to women who can read and write and pay taxes would insure white supremacy." In fact, "most white suffragists shared the not only predominant, but rarely challenged, racist views common to American society in the first half of the twentieth century." Ibid., 298–299.

13. Linda Ford, "Alice Paul and the Politics of Nonviolent Protest," in Jean H. Baker, ed., *Votes for Women: The Struggle for Suffrage Revisited* (New York: Oxford University Press, 2002), 180.

14. Tennessee was the last state needed to secure the constitutional change, and the story of the last legislative vote needed for ratification in Tennessee is a classic example of the richness of human motivation. Harry Burn, the youngest member of the legislature at twenty-four, had been elected from a district known to be anti-suffrage and was not seen as a likely supporter. But on the morning of the vote he received a letter from his mother. She wrote: "Dear Son: Hurrah, and vote for suffrage! . . . Don't forget to be a good boy and help Mrs. Catt put the 'rat' in ratification." After he voted in favor, he responded to attacks by stating, "I know that a mother's advice is always safest for a boy to follow." In an interview "many years later, he said he always believed women had a right to vote." But it was the support of his mother that gave him the strength to vote his convictions. (Interestingly, despite widespread condemnation, he was reelected to a second term.) Eleanor Clift, *Founding Sisters*, 199, 202, 204.

15. Cobble, *The Other Women's Movement*, 3.

16. Frances Fox Piven and Richard A. Cloward, *Poor People's Movements: Why They Succeed, How They Fail* (New York: Vintage, 1979); Daniel J. Leab, " 'United We Eat': The Creation and Organization of the Unemployed Councils in 1930," in *The Labor History Reader*, ed. Daniel J. Leab (Urbana, IL: University of Illinois Press, 1985), 317–332; Roy Rosenzweig, "Organizing the Unemployed: The Early Years of the Great Depression, 1929–1933," *Radical America* (September, 1976): 37–60; Roy Rosenzweig, "Radicals and the Jobless: The Musteites and the Unemployed Leagues, 1932–1936," *Labor History* 16 (1975): 52–77.

17. Piven and Cloward, *Poor People's Movements*, 49.

18. Ibid., 84. Orders handed down from the International Communist Party to US officials, however, seem not to have caused significant challenges, as local leaders often ignored these and, in any case, the party mostly supported pragmatic local efforts. Overall, Roy Rosenzweig, in "Radicals and the Jobless," argues that communist involvement didn't seem to be a key barrier to success, because other noncommunist organizers of the unemployed faced similar challenges.

19. Rosenzweig, "Organizing the Unemployed," 53.

20. Nicholas Von Hoffman, *Radical: A Portrait of Saul Alinsky* (New York: Nation Books, 2010); Sanford D. Horwitt, *Let Them Call Me Rebel: Saul Alinsky: His*

Life and Legacy (New York: Vintage, 1992); Donald C. Reitzes and Dietrich C. Reitzes, *The Alinsky Legacy: Alive and Kicking* (Greenwich, CT: Jai Press, 1987); Saul Alinsky, "Empowering People, Not Elites: An Interview with Saul Alinsky," *Playboy* (1972), http://britell.com/alinsky.html (accessed July 18, 2010); Saul Alinsky, *Rules for Radicals* (New York: Vintage, 1971); Saul Alinsky, *Reveille for Radicals* (New York: Vintage, 1946); Saul Alinsky and Marion K. Sanders, *The Professional Radical; Conversations with Saul Alinsky* (New York: Harper & Row, 1970; 1965); P. David Finks, *The Radical Vision of Saul Alinsky* (New York: Paulist Press, 1984).

21. Slayton, *Back of the Yards,* 195.
22. Finks, *Radical Vision,* 17.
23. Ibid., 18.
24. Only a few years after the victory in the packinghouses, amidst a national panic about communist infiltrators, Lewis purged the CIO of communists. With the loss of staff who had a broader vision of organizing, like March, and under the pressure of new labor laws, unions like the CIO increasingly dropped community involvement from their union campaigns. Alinsky later argued that the labor organizers in this new era were generally "poor community organizers" because of their narrow focus on workplace issues and the predictable structure of contracts (Alinsky, *Rules for Radicals,* 66). Alinsky was lucky, then, to have come into union organizing at one of the last moments when he would have seen a union organizing effort that saw community organization as an integral part of its task.
25. Miriam Pawel, *The Union of Their Dreams: Power, Hope, and Struggle in Cesar Chavez's Farm Worker Movement* (New York: Bloomsbury Press, 2009); Randy Shaw, *Beyond the Fields: Cesar Chavez, the UFW, and the Struggle for Justice in the 21st Century* (Berkeley, CA: University of California Press, 2008); Susan Ferriss, Ricardo Sandoval and Diana Hembree, *The Fight in the Fields: Cesar Chavez and the Farmworkers Movement* (New York: Harcourt Brace, 1997); Robert Fisher, *Let the People Decide: Neighborhood Organizing in America,* Updated edition (New York: Palgrave Macmillan, 1994).
26. Fisher, *Let the People Decide,* 70, 73, 80.
27. David Garrow, *Bearing the Cross: Martin Luther King, Jr., and the Southern Christian Leadership Conference* (New York: Harper Perennial Modern Classics, 2004); Michael Eric Dyson, *I May Not Get There with You: The True Martin Luther King Jr.* (New York: Free Press, 2001); Taylor Branch, *Pillar of Fire: America in the King Years 1963–65* (New York: Simon & Schuster, 1999); Taylor Branch, *Parting the Waters: America in the King Years 1954–63* (New York: Simon & Schuster, 1989); Adam Fairclough, *To Redeem the Soul of America: The Southern Christian Leadership Conference and Martin Luther King, Jr.* (Athens, GA: University of Georgia Press, 1987); Aldon D. Morris, *Origins of the Civil Rights Movement* (New York: Free Press, 1986); Doug McAdam, *Political Process and the Development of Black Insurgency, 1930–1970* (Chicago, IL: University Of Chicago Press, 1999).
28. For a more detailed discussion of SCLC, see the case study chapter in Schutz, *Social Class.*

29. Morris, *Origins of the Civil Rights Movement*; Clayborne Carson, *In Struggle: SNCC and the Black Awakening of the 1960s* (Cambridge, MA: Harvard University Press, 1995); Barbara Ransby, *Ella Baker and the Black Freedom Movement: A Radical Democratic Vision* (Durham, NC: The University of North Carolina Press, 2005); Eric Burner, *And Gently He Shall Lead Them: Robert Parris Moses and Civil Rights in Mississippi* (New York: New York University Press, 1994); McAdam, *Political Process.*

30. Ransby, *Ella Baker,* 191.

31. For a more detailed discussion of SNCC see the case study chapter of Schutz, *Social Class.*

32. See footnote #20.

33. Horwitt, *Rebel,* 330.

34. Ibid., 339.

35. Ibid., 256.

36. Ibid., 403.

37. Von Hoffman, *Radical,* 159–160. By the way, Alinsky's provocative dedication to Lucifer at the start of *Reveille* is clearly referring in large part to Milton. The dedication: "Lest we forget at least an over-the-shoulder acknowledgment to the very first radical: from all our legends, mythology, and history (and who is to know where mythology leaves off and history begins—or which is which), the first radical known to man who rebelled against the establishment and did it so effectively that he at least won his own kingdom—Lucifer." Von Hoffman's comment, in *Radical,* 180, supports this: "[Alinsky] enjoyed shaking up stuffy people who were blind to the twinkle in his eye when he carried on about how, like John Milton, he admired the Devil."

38. James Miller, *Democracy Is in the Streets: From Port Huron to the Siege of Chicago* (New York: Simon and Schuster, 1987); Fisher, *Let the People Decide.*

39. James Miller, *Democracy Is in the Streets,* 214–215.

40. See footnote #20.

41. Lance Hill, *The Deacons for Defense: Armed Resistance and the Civil Rights Movement* (Durham, NC: The University of North Carolina Press, 2006); Paul Alkebulan, *Survival Pending Revolution: The History of the Black Panther Party* (Tuscaloosa, AL: University of Alabama Press, 2007); Peniel E. Joseph, *Black Power Movement: Rethinking the Civil Rights-Black Power Era* (New York: Routledge, 2006); Jeffrey O. G. Ogbar, *Black Power: Radical Politics and African American Identity* (Baltimore, MD: The Johns Hopkins University Press, 2005); Dawson, *Black Visions*; Bush, *We Are Not What We Seem*; Francisco A. Rosales, *Chicano!: The History of the Mexican American Civil Rights Movement* (Houston, TX: Arte Público Press, 1996); Terry H. Anderson, *The Movement and the Sixties* (New York: Oxford University Press, 1996).

42. Hill, *Deacons,* 50, 264–265. Also see the case study chapter in Schutz, *Social Class.*

43. Evans, *Born for Liberty*; Sara M. Evans, *Personal Politics: The Roots of Women's Liberation in the Civil Rights Movement and the New Left* (New York: Vintage,

1980; 1979); Myra Marx Ferree and Beth B. Hess, *Controversy and Coalition: The New Feminist Movement across Three Decades of Change,* 3rd ed. (New York: Routledge, 2000); Wini Breines, "What's Love Got to Do with It? White Women, Black Women, and Feminism in the Movement Years," *Signs: Journal of Women in Culture and Society* 27, no. 4 (Summer, 2002): 1095–1133; Carmen Sirianni, "Learning Pluralism: Democracy and Diversity in Feminist Organizations," *Democratic Community* (1993): 283–312; Jo Freeman, "The Tyranny of Structurelessness," *The Second Wave* 2, no. 1 (1972–1973): 20; Van Gosse, *Rethinking the New Left: An Interpretative History* (New York: Palgrave Macmillan, 2005); Sandra Morgen, *Into Our Own Hands: The Women's Health Movement in the United States, 1969–1990* (New Brunswick, N.J.: Rutgers University Press, 2002); Susan Schechter, *Women and Male Violence: The Visions and Struggles of the Battered Women's Movement* (Boston, MA: South End Press, 1982); Maria Bevacqua, *Rape on the Public Agenda: Feminism and the Politics of Sexual Assault* (Boston, MA: Northeastern University Press, 2000); Benita Roth, *Separate Roads to Feminism: Black, Chicana, and White Feminist Movements in America's Second Wave* (New York: Cambridge University Press, 2004); Bell Hooks, *Ain't I a Woman: Black Women and Feminism* (Boston, MA: South End Press, 1981).

44. Betty Friedan, *The Feminine Mystique* (New York: Norton, 1963), 16.

45. Van Gosse, *The Movements of the New Left, 1950–1975: A Brief History with Documents* (New York: Bedford/St. Martin's, 2004), 31–32.

46. Ferree and Hess, *Controversy and Coalition.*

47. Ibid., 70.

48. Freeman, *Tyranny of Structurelessness.*

49. See Breines, "What's Love Got to Do with It?" for a discussion of the tensions between organizations for white women and those for women of color, and the complexity of this history. Also see Janet R. Jakobsen, *Working Alliances and the Politics of Difference: Diversity and Feminist Ethics* (Bloomington, IN: Indiana University Press, 1998).

50. Rik Scarce, *Eco-Warriors: Understanding the Radical Environmental Movement* (Chicago, IL: Noble Press, 1990); Thomas Raymond Wellock, *Preserving the Nation: The Conservation and Environmental Movements, 1870–2000* (Wheeling, IL: Harlan Davidson, 2007); Carolyn Merchant, *The Columbia Guide to American Environmental History* (New York: Columbia University Press, 2002).

51. Wellock, *Preserving the Nation,* 161, 163–164.

52. Horwitt, *Rebel,* 464.

53. Ibid., 498.

54. Saul Alinsky, "Empowering People, Not Elites."

55. Charles DeBenedetti and Charles Chatfield, *An American Ordeal: The Antiwar Movement of the Vietnam Era* (Syracuse, NY: Syracuse University Press, 1990); Adam M. Garfinkle, *Telltale Hearts: The Origins and Impact of the Vietnam Antiwar Movement* (New York: St. Martin's, 1995); Gosse, *Rethinking the New Left;* Anderson, *The Movement and the Sixties;* Evans, *Personal Politics.*

56. DeBenedetti, *American Ordeal,* 408.

57. Ibid., 325.
58. Fisher, *Let the People Decide*; Peter Dobkin Hall, *Inventing the Nonprofit Sector and Other Essays on Philanthropy, Voluntarism, and Nonprofit Organizations* (Baltimore, MD: The Johns Hopkins University Press, 1992); David C. Hammack, "Growth, Transformation, and Quiet Revolution in the Nonprofit Sector over Two Centuries," *Nonprofit and Voluntary Sector Quarterly* 30, no. 2 (June, 2001), 157–173; Incite! Women of Color against Violence, *The Revolution Will Not Be Funded: Beyond the Non-profit Industrial Complex* (Cambridge, MA: South End Press, 2007); John P. Kretzmann and John McKnight, *Building Communities from the Inside Out: A Path toward Finding and Mobilizing a Community's Assets* (Evanston, IL: The Asset-Based Community Development Institute, Northwestern University, 1993); Wenocur and Reisch, *From Charity to Enterprise*; Reisch and Andrews, *The Road Not Taken*.
59. Hall, *Inventing the Nonprofit*, 122.
60. Fisher, *Let the People Decide*, 121.
61. Ibid., 130.
62. Kretzmann and McKnight, *Building Communities from the Inside Out*. See Mike Miller, "A Critique of John McKnight & John Kretzmann's 'Community Organizing in the Eighties: Toward a Post-Alinsky Agenda'," *Comm-Org Papers*, 15 (2009), http://comm-org.wisc.edu/papers2009/miller.htm (accessed July 17, 2010).
63. John Atlas, *Seeds of Change: The Story of ACORN, America's Most Controversial Antipoverty Community Organizing Group* (Nashville, TN: Vanderbilt University Press, 2010).
64. Premilla Nadasen, *Welfare Warriors: The Welfare Rights Movement in the United States* (New York: Routledge, 2005); Piven and Cloward, *Poor People's Movements*.
65. Ibid., 21.
66. Ibid., 80.
67. Ibid., 134, 237.
68. Heidi J. Swarts, *Organizing Urban America: Secular and Faith-Based Progressive Movements* (Minneapolis, MN: University of Minnesota Press, 2008); Gary Delgado, *Organizing the Movement: The Roots and Growth of ACORN* (Philadelphia, PA: Temple University Press, 1986); John Atlas, *Seeds of Change*.
69. Fisher, *Let the People Decide*; Harry Chatten Boyte, *The Backyard Revolution: Understanding the New Citizen Movement* (Philadelphia: Temple University Press, 1980); David N. Pellow and Robert J. Brulle, *Power, Justice, and the Environment: A Critical Appraisal of the Environmental Justice Movement* (Cambridge, MA: MIT, 2005).
70. Boyte, *Backyard Revolution*, 3.
71. Ibid., 45.
72. Mark R. Warren, *Dry Bones Rattling: Community Building to Revitalize American Democracy* (Princeton, NJ: Princeton University Press, 2001); Edward T. D. Chambers and Michael A. Cowan, *Roots for Radicals: Organizing for Power, Action, and Justice* (New York: Continuum, 2003).

73. *Democratic Promise: Saul Alinsky and His Legacy,* directed by Bob Hercules and Bruce Ornstein (Seattle: Indieflix, 2007).

74. Vanessa Tait, *Poor Workers' Unions: Rebuilding Labor from Below* (Cambridge, MA: South End Press, 2005); Janice Fine, *Worker Centers: Organizing Communities at the Edge of the Dream* (Ithaca, NY: Cornell University Press, 2006).

75. August Meier and Elliot Rudwick cited in Tait, *Poor Worker's Unions,* 28.

76. Ibid., 32, 29.

77. Ibid., 110–111.

78. Fine, *Worker Centers,* 130.

79. The core of this section is drawn from Neil Miller, *Out of the Past: Gay and Lesbian History from 1869 to the Present* (New York: Vintage, 1995). Miller's discussion of ACT UP was supplemented by Deborah B. Gold, *Moving Politics: Emotions and ACT UP's Fight Against AIDS* (Chicago: University of Chicago Press, 2009) and Benjamin Heim Shepard, "Play as resilience: Eros Versus Thanatos in ACT UP," in Benjamin Heim Shepard, *Queer Political Performance and Protest* (New York: Routledge, 2009), 71–113.

80. Miller, *Out of the Past,* 351.

81. Ibid., 366–368.

82. Ibid., 369, 372, 379, 383.

83. Ibid., 451.

84. Ibid., 458. As Gould notes in *Moving Politics,* "ACT UP chapters were *predominantly* white, male, and middle-class" although "many women, people of color, and working-class people participated" (145). For other discussions of the majority middle-class make-up of ACT UP, see, for example, Peter F. Cohen, *Love and Anger: Essays on Aids, Activism, and Politics* (Binghamton, NY: Hayworth Press, 1998), Joshua Gamson, "Silence, Death, and the Invisible Enemy: AIDS Activism and Social Movement 'Newness,'" in Michael Burawoy et. al., ed., *Ethnography Unbound* (Berkeley, CA: University of California Press, 1991), and David Halperin, *Saint Foucault: Towards a Gay Hagiography* (New York: Oxford University Press, 1997).

85. Shepard, *Queer Political Performance,* 86, 80, 73, 130.

86. Alinsky, *Reveille,* 129; Shepard, *Queer Political Performance,* 111–112, 105–106.

87. Miller, *Queer Political Performance.*

88. Gould, in *Moving Politics,* provides an especially visceral sense of the loss that participants experienced as ACT UP disintegrated.

89. Rebecca Solnit, *A Paradise Built in Hell: The Extraordinary Communities That Arise in Disaster* (New York: Viking, 2008), 5.

CHAPTER 4

Saul Alinsky: The "Father" of Community Organizing

To hell with charity. The only thing you get is what you're strong enough to get—so you had better organize.

—Saul Alinsky, *The Alinsky Legacy*

S aul Alinsky was not the first community organizer. Far from it. Organizers have existed in myriad forms since the very beginnings of human civilization. Alinsky was, however, the first person in America to fully conceptualize organizing as an approach separate from labor organizing. In Alinsky's hands, community organizing became a coherent field of action and "community organizer" became a job description. His books, *Reveille for Radicals* in 1946 and then *Rules for Radicals* in 1971, became the central texts on collective action for the organizers that followed him. Today, nearly all community organizing groups in the United States are deeply influenced by his vision.[1]

Alinsky proved to be one of the savviest social actors of his generation. A creative strategist willing to go with his gut on a moment's notice, he was also a deep thinker who read widely (breezily quoting from Heraclites, Plato, the Bible, Montesquieu, and Jefferson) and who constantly analyzed his and others' organizing experience for new insights. Established mores, laws, and expectations in his hands became tools for struggle and action, ways to surprise, humiliate, and ridicule the opposition into taking actions that played into his hands. A pragmatist's pragmatist, he did what it took to win.

He had a legendary ability to imagine himself in the shoes of others and enormous skill for cultivating strong, often quite personal relationships with people from all walks of life. By building tight relational networks, he successfully brought people together across long-established walls of ethnic, racial,

Saul Alinsky

and religious hatred. For Alinsky and those who came after him, "relationship building" became the key tool in an organizer's toolbox.

The Education of an Organizer

Alinsky attended college at the University of Chicago and then received a graduate fellowship to study sociology, collaborating on studies of urban gangs and urban communities. As a graduate student, he worked closely with some of the luminaries of the field of urban sociology, including Robert Park, E. W. Burgess, and Clifford Shaw. In his later years, Alinsky often railed against the ignorance and stupidity of academics, presenting himself as the defender of the wisdom of the common man. He related with character- istic bluntness, for example, his astonishment with "all the horse manure" the scholars he knew "were handing out about poverty and slums . . . glossing over the misery and the despair. I mean, Christ, I'd lived in a slum. I could see through all their complacent academic jargon to the realities." "The word 'academic'," he declared, "is a synonym for irrelevant." But statements like these obscured the fact that he came to organizing equipped with the best academic preparation available at the time.[2]

From his graduate work he gained a depth of understanding about the structures and forces that led to the reproduction of poverty and oppression in urban areas. Most importantly, in his research on youth gangs, on the mobs, and in prisons, he developed skills in ethnographic fieldwork. He had an amazing capacity to immerse himself in different cultures and see the world as if from their eyes. This made it possible for him to become a great organizer in a wide range of working-class and poor communities.

He spent a few years working as an ethnographer and as staff sociologist in the juvenile justice and prison systems, giving speeches at conferences and publishing papers. This experience left him disgusted with the limitations of academia and the practice of criminology and social work. His attitude about "social workers," von Hoffman reports, "was about the same as a dog's reaction to a rodent.... He saw them as buttinskies who fostered a perpetual dependence in those they were supposed to help". (Later in life, Alinsky told a large audience at the National Association of Social Workers that "You could bomb this social worker's meeting and nobody would know the difference.")[3]

Alinsky loved to paint a romantic image of himself and his life. And to some extent this impulse was part of his success as an organizer. He used his own life, like he used everything around him, to serve the aims of his organizing. "Modesty," his biographer Sanford Horwitt noted, "was not an Alinsky virtue." He was not above exaggeration or spin if it would serve his purpose. For example, he had lived in a slum, but he didn't actually grow up there, as his quote indicates, above. Instead, most of his childhood was actually spent in a middle-class neighborhood.[4]

Most of Alinsky's fanciful stories about his life, however, were actually surprisingly accurate. Alinsky often told, for example, how he wormed into the good graces of the Chicago Mob for one of his early ethnographic studies. He had heard that a grieving mother of a murdered mobster didn't have a picture of her son. So he went to the morgue, took a photo, and had it touched up. Then he noted, "I went back to the [mobster's] wake and presented the photograph to Ms. Massina. 'Dumas gave this to me just last week', I said, 'and I'd like you to have it.' She cried and thanked me, and pretty soon word of the incident spread throughout the gang. 'That Alinsky, he's an alright motherfucker', the kids would say, and from that moment on they began to trust me." This seems to have actually happened much as Alinsky said. "Alinsky's friends over the years," Horwitt noted, "learned not to dismiss his apparently farfetched stories too quickly."[5]

In 1938, Shaw sent him into the Back of the Yards community in Chicago to conduct research and organize a community council to help delinquents.

Alinsky went much farther than Shaw had envisioned (or wanted). He combined what he had already learned with new skills drawn from union organizers working to organize the local meatpacking industry. As the previous chapter describes, he created The Back of the Yards Neighborhood Council at least partially to support this union effort. And "community organizing" as we know it today was born.

Conflict as the Lifeblood of Organizing

> Rub raw the resentments of the people of the community; fan the latent hostilities of many of the people to the point of overt expression.
> —Alinsky, *Rules for Radicals*

Alinsky stated, flatly, that "a people's organization is dedicated to an eternal war," although he always meant this in a nonviolent way. It is, he argued, "a conflict group," a fact that "must be openly and fully recognized. Its sole reason for coming into being is to wage war against all evils which cause suffering and unhappiness. . . . [I]n a world of hard reality [a People's Organization] lives in the midst of smashing forces, dashing struggles, sweeping cross-currents, ripping passions, conflict, confusion, seeming chaos, the hot and the cold, the squalor and the drama."[6]

He had little patience for those who did not understand this. Privileged liberals, he complained, preached about patience and politeness because "fights for decent housing, economic security, health programs" were, for them, "simply intellectual affinities. . . . [I]t is not *their* children who are sick; it is not *they* who are working with the specter of unemployment hanging over their heads; they are not fighting their *own* fight." Their constant search for "win-win" solutions, he believed, was usually an effort to avoid acknowledging that the "haves" would have to give up some of their privilege if the life chances of the "have nots" were ever to change significantly.[7]

Conflict was not just a reality, however. He actually sought to *fan* the flames of conflict, albeit in a nonviolent manner. "Change," he famously argued, necessarily "means movement. Movement means friction. Only in the frictionless vacuum of a nonexistent abstract world can movement or change occur without that abrasive friction of conflict." The only way the status quo can be shifted, he believed, is by generating friction and heat.[8]

Organizing a community, Alinsky argued, was really a process of "re-organization." In every community there is an established culture, a collection of organizations, and a web of relationships and antagonisms. As in the Back of the Yards, internal conflict and histories of mistrust generally keep a community from presenting a unified face to the outside world. Part of the initial job of an organizer, then, was to identify simmering problems within the community that could be used to generate anger and resentment. By focusing leaders on the predations of their collective enemies, the organizer sought to overcome divisions and allow the community to come together as an "us" vs. an outside "them."

When the time was right, the leaders of the local organizations that had been recruited would come together in a founding convention, establishing a leadership and agreeing on a constitution. The resulting community organizing group would usually start small, winning a few limited victories that proved to members that coming together did, in fact, allow them to achieve more than staying apart. These more limited efforts also provided a training ground for leaders, equipping them with the knowledge and skills necessary to take on larger campaigns.

His aim with this simple "us/them" polarization was not to insult the intelligence of participants in his organizations. In fact, he worked hard to help leaders understand the complexities of specific issues. If they didn't, victory was unlikely when confronted with an opposition that did. But he argued that while "a leader may struggle toward a decision and weigh the merits and demerits of a situation which is 52 percent positive and 48 percent negative,... once the decision is reached he must assume that his cause is 100 percent positive and the opposition 100 percent negative." Polarization, he believed, was a fundamental political necessity in the arena of conflict and struggle. Of course, this is a classic approach of other forms of working-class struggle, like union organizing.[9]

Some contemporary organizers tend not to focus so much on the "warlike" character of organizing, placing more emphasis on the need to develop relationships. Even so, however, all of the good ones understand that real recognition from the powerful is only possible if their organization represents a threat (real or imagined).

Power Is Not What You Have . . .

Alinsky sought to generate power through what he called "mass jujitsu." With ridicule and creative mass actions, his organizations sought to knock the powerful off balance, threaten their core self-interests, and force them to respond to community demands. It was crucial, Alinsky argued, that actions and threats fall *outside* the everyday experience of the opposition, while still remaining *within* the comfort zone of organization members. He told a story, for example, about a time when members of one of his organizations brought a bank to a standstill with long lines of people changing dollars into coins and asking to open new accounts. The bank didn't know how to respond to this unexpected tactic, but the action seemed reasonable enough to the organizing group's members. In this case, as in many others, Alinsky used the bank's own rules and established culture against it.

Often he didn't even carry out an action, however. Von Hoffman recalls that his frequent exhortation was to "never make a threat you are not able to carry out and even if you can carry it out, don't do it. His reasoning was that regardless of how much damage you might do to the other side by carrying out the threat, it would be less than the damage the opponents had imagined you could do." Alinsky's first rule of organizing was "power is not what you have, it is what the opposition thinks you have."[10]

A key aim of such tactics and threats was to get the opposition to make mistakes that the community organizing group could take advantage of. "The real action," Alinsky stressed, "is in the enemy's reaction," because, ultimately, "a winning tactic depends on the other side blundering into the trap you set for them." And he was "a past master at goading the other side to lose its cool." One time, for example, "in the middle of the Depression," Alinsky actually "needled the Chicago Democratic machine into canceling the free-milk program for poor kids, thus bringing a national furor down on themselves, retreating in short order and losing the skirmish."[11]

Learning Local Communities

"The foundation of a People's Organization," Alinsky argued, "is in the communal life of the local people. Therefore the first stage in the building of a People's Organization is the understanding of the life of a community, not only in terms of the individual's experiences, habits, values, and objectives, but also from the point of view of collective habits, experiences, customs, controls, and values of the whole group—the community traditions." The approach Alinsky recommended to organizers for gaining this broad understanding was the kind of extended ethnographic exploration he had learned from his work with the University of Chicago.[12]

When Alinsky first hired von Hoffman as an organizer, for example, Alinsky sent him off to a promising community and told him to send weekly reports about what he learned. That's it. It was up to von Hoffman to spend day after day going through the community talking with residents, tracking down key leaders and creating relationships with them, and digging up a range of information about the demographics and history of the community. Action usually only came after months of such work. Von Hoffman later described the process in this way:

It is a very strange thing. You go somewhere, and you know nobody . . . and you've got to organize it into something that it's never been before. . . . You don't have much going for you. You don't have prestige, you don't have muscle, you've got no money to give away. All you have are . . . your wits, charm, and whatever you can put together. So you had better form a very accurate picture of what's going on, and you had better not bring in too many a priori maps [because] if you do, you're just not going to get anywhere.[13]

The job of an organizer was to immerse himself (almost always "he" for Alinsky) into community life to the extent that he was swept "into a close" and deeply informed "identification" with it, projecting himself "into its plight."[14]

Self-Interest

Self-interest, like power, wears the black shroud of negativism and suspicion. To many the synonym for self-interest is selfishness. The word is associated with a repugnant conglomeration of vices such as narrowness, self-seeking and self-centeredness, everything that is opposite to the virtues of altruism and selflessness. . . . The myth of altruism as a motivating factor in our behavior could arise and survive only in a society bundled in the sterile gauze of New England Puritanism and Protestant morality and tied together with the ribbons of Madison Avenue public relations. It is one of the classic American fairy tales.

—Alinsky, *Rules for Radicals*

Alinsky famously believed that people were motivated by "self-interest." What he actually meant by this was more sophisticated than is commonly acknowledged, however. Many people, he noted, inaccurately think that "the synonym for self-interest is selfishness." For Alinsky, in contrast, "self-interest" represented whatever core motivation a person had for participating in an organizing effort. People needed some internal fire, whatever that might be, if they were going to sustain their commitment amidst the pressure cooker of struggle.[15]

Even churches, he found, don't really operate on the principle of selflessness. In an interview, he asked, "suppose I walked into the office of the average religious leader of any denomination and said, 'Look, I'm asking you to live up to your Christian principles, to make Jesus' words about brotherhood and social justice realities.' What do you think would happen? He'd shake my hand warmly, say 'God bless you, my son', and after I was gone he'd tell his secretary, 'If that crackpot comes around again, tell him I'm out.' " The chosen poverty of a Dorothy Day or a Gandhi is the exception and not the rule.[16]

In his first book, Alinsky told a paradigmatic story about how an authentic understanding of self-interest develops. He got David, a store owner, to join his organization by pointing out how David's participation might help advertise his business. Alinsky then walked across the street and got David's competitor, Roger, to join to make sure that "David would not take away any part of his business." At the beginning, then, David and Roger's "sole interest lay in getting as much advertising, good will, and—finally—as much business as possible. They were present to make a commercial investment." As they participated on the group's Children's Committee, however, they

> were sent into some of the West Side tenements of the neighborhood. There Roger and David personally met the children. . . . They met them face-to-face and by their first names. They saw them as living persons framed in the squalor and misery of what the children called "home." They saw the tenderness, the shyness, and the inner dignity which are in all people. They saw the children of the neighborhood for the first time in their lives. They saw them not as small gray shadows passing by the store front. They saw them not as statistical digits, not as impersonal subjects of discussion, but as real human beings. They got to know them and eventually a warm human relationship developed.

As a result, "both David and Roger came out of this experience with the anger of one who suddenly discovered that there are a lot of things in life that are wrong." "If they had been originally asked to join on grounds of pure idealism," Alinsky argued, "they would unquestionably have rejected the invitation. Similarly if the approach had been made on the basis of cooperative work they would have denounced it as radical." Yet once they began to participate, they developed a true "self-interest" in the work: no longer simply selfish. They became leaders with productive core motivations for participation over the long term.[17]

If some people remained in an organization only because of their selfishness, they might still be useful in some ways. But they would not become the kind of leaders and participants Alinsky most valued. From the beginning, therefore, Alinsky's understanding of "self-interest" was quite sophisticated.

Native Leaders

The only way that people can express themselves is through their leaders.

—Saul Alinsky, *Reveille for Radicals*

A champion of democracy, Alinsky stressed that "a program" developed by only "a few persons is a highly dictatorial action. It is not a democratic program but a monumental testament to lack of faith in the ability and intelligence of the masses of people to think their way through to the successful solution of their problems." In fact, he argued that the particular decisions made by an organization were less important than the goal of "getting people interested and participating in a democratic way." His central goal in organizing a community was to develop "a healthy, active, participating, interested, self-confident people who, through their participation and interest, become informed, educated, and above all develop faith in themselves, their fellow men, and the future." Because "the people themselves are the future, the people themselves will solve each problem that will arise."[18]

Alinsky was not simply seeking social changes by any means necessary, then. Instead, his *primary* goal was the reinvigoration of democratic participation in America. He wanted to restore the capacities of everyday people to participate in and feel they had some real power over the forces that affected their lives.

At the same time, however, he understood that it was "obviously impossible to get all of the people to talk with one another" and form a coherent plan. Thus, Alinsky argued that popular democracy needed to take the form of a *representative* democracy—a leader-based model. He noted, for example, that "*the only way that you can reach people is through their own representatives or their own leaders.* You talk to people through their leaders, and if you do not know the leaders you are in the same position as a person trying to telephone another party without knowing the telephone number."[19]

When he spoke of leaders, he was referring to people who played very specific kind of role: what he called "native leaders." A native leader needed to be recognized by some group as representing their interests in one respect or another. Native leaders' capacity for leadership grew from their rootedness in their community, from their experiential understanding of the lives and realities of those who depended on them. They commanded the respect of others because they shared the "aspirations," "hopes," and "desires" of their people. As a result, they differed radically from disconnected "leaders" of social welfare and other professionally run organizations.

Alinsky sought out the "Little Joes who are the natural leaders of their people, the biggest blades in the grass roots of American Democracy." People who looked up to the Little Joes had learned to trust them, and could use them as indicators of correct and productive action. In his efforts to convince people to join organizations, people often responded, "well what does Joe think about it?" If "Joe" hadn't joined, then they'd wave him off, but if Joe had, then they were likely to ask, "where do I sign up?"[20]

While Alinsky did try to develop new leaders, he tended to depend on long-standing leaders of community organizations in his organizations. More contemporary organizers in the Alinsky tradition, facing the dissolution of organized community in impoverished areas (especially central cities) have developed much more systematic approaches for nurturing emerging leaders, including the one-on-one process described in Chapter 10.

Organizing as Education

Alinsky believed that educating people without also providing them with the power to put that learning into concrete use, as many critical educators try to do today, was mostly a dead end. "If people feel they don't have the power to change a bad situation," he noted, "then they do not think about it. Why start figuring out how you are going to spend a million dollars if you do not have . . . a million dollars—unless you want to engage in fantasy?" Only when "people are organized so that they have the power to make changes . . . [do] they begin to think and ask questions about how to make the changes." Thus, "it is the creation of the instrument or the circumstances of power that makes knowledge essential." Only knowledge and power together, not knowledge alone, could provide a cure for collective apathy.[21]

And Alinsky did see his organizations as fundamentally educational enterprises. Thus, he noted, "the major task in popular education that confronts every People's Organization is the creation of a set of circumstances through which an educational process can function."[22]

In part, this process took place through "native leaders." What he called in his first book "The Little Joes," he said, "represent not only the most promising channels for education, but in certain respects the only channels. As the Little Joes get to know one another as human beings, prejudices are broken down and human attitudes are generated in this new relationship." But while he focused on the "Little Joes," the impact he sought was more broadly among their followers. As their leaders change their attitudes, he said, these will become "reflected among their followers so that the understanding or education begins to affect . . . thousands of people."[23]

Alinsky integrated education into the ongoing activity of his organizations. Late in his life, he did eventually create a formal training program for leaders and organizers that his followers have continued and deepened. But the most important learning, he believed (and contemporary organizers still believe), comes through *action*. "The stream of activities and programs of organizations," Alinsky explained, "provides a never-ending series of specific issues and situations that create a rich field for the learning process." At its best, "popular education becomes part of the whole participating process of a People's Organization." Leaders gain skills through the ongoing process of planning, researching, engaging directly with the opposition, and then reflecting on their actions. "The educational slogan," Alinsky stated, "has become: 'Get them to move in the right direction first. They'll explain to themselves later why they moved in that direction and that explanation will be better learning for them than anything we can do.' "[24]

Feminist and Anti-Racist Critiques of Alinsky-Style Organizing

Alinsky's work was not without controversy, of course. Feminist and anti-racist critiques of Alinsky, especially, have catalyzed ongoing changes in the field. For example, Randy Stoecker and Susan Stall as well as Rinku Sen have contrasted feminist and anti-racist approaches to organizing with the Alinsky model. They find that women and identity-based indigenous groups often focus more on the family and the immediate neighborhood, helping make these links between private and public concerns more visible. Partly as a result of differences in approach, few women and people of color participated as organizers and leaders in early Alinsky-based organizations (magnified by the fact that Alinsky resisted hiring women organizers). In fact, many women-led efforts to transform adverse conditions in their homes and neighborhoods were excluded from the public record, although these omissions are being corrected.[25]

Instead of building community around anger at common problems, as Alinsky did, feminist organizers often start by nurturing relationships, only later turning to issue development and collective action. And more recent neo-Alinsky approaches, drawing from feminist insights, have begun to refocus on intentional relationship-building efforts (see Chapter 10).

While many feminist and anti-racist-oriented organizers do employ Alinsky-based techniques and strategies, both groups frequently reject the militant language and the hierarchical structure of many neo-Alinsky groups. They also tend to blur distinctions between the roles of organizer and leader, leery about marginalizing the savvy of local people by setting organizers up as the "real experts" on social action.

Alinsky's organizations cut discrete winnable issues out of larger social problems for their campaigns. Feminist groups and anti-racist critics sometimes challenge this standard wisdom, embracing more complexity in their issues and highlighting intersecting concerns about race, gender, and class from the beginning. To neo-Alinsky organizers, this can make feminist and anti-racist-oriented efforts seem unfocused. But a more broad-based approach can also expand one's constituency. When Cindy Marano of Wider Opportunities for Women (WOW) organized local leadership teams to integrate women into nontraditional jobs (like welding, plumbing, etc.), for example, she made sure to include a wide range of representatives—employers, union representatives, job trainers, and women already employed in nontraditional jobs. She emphasized that the failure to support women in these jobs was never one person's fault. It was everyone's fault. And this meant that people from across different systems needed to help if the problem was going to be fixed.

Because of their deeply rooted distrust of established institutions, some leaders of color, as in the nationalist examples discussed in Chapter 3, have been more interested in building alternate institutions than in trying to reform existing ones. Conversely, given the severe lack of resources in poor and segregated communities, other leaders from these groups have actually been more willing to collaborate with institutions than neo-Alinsky groups. They can still "target" these institutions, when needed, however. For example, Rosa Marta Zarate of Libreria del Pueblo in San Bernardino fought tirelessly to bring needed changes to local institutions such as the public school system. At the same time, however, she was able to maintain close alliances with the local school district and the district superintendent. Leaders like Zarate can be more successful than traditional neo-Alinsky organizers at negotiating the delicate task of maintaining relationships while contesting injustice.

The Tensions of Democracy

Alinsky did not have any romantic vision of the poor, nor did he worship at the altar of majority rule. Much to the contrary. He understood the limitations of vision that come with deprivation. And he worried about the dangers of majority rule over oppressed minorities. As a result, a deep tension ran through Alinsky's conception of democratic rule—a tension that remains to a lesser extent in organizing today.

Organizers always have a great deal of influence over leaders and the direction of their campaigns. As Horwitt notes, "one ongoing dilemma was the role of the organizers vis-à-vis the citizen leadership—when was the organizer justified in stepping out front and temporarily assuming the leadership himself?" In fact, Fred Ross reported that Alinsky often complained about idealistic organizers who "go overboard about being nondirective. They get so busy trying out their little theories, they forget they've got a flesh-and-blood organization to consider. We all have to remember that while it's the organizer's function constantly to push responsibilities on the people, he must always be ready to jump in and take over himself in case the people, for some reason or another, fail to follow through. Oh, of course, many times it's okay to let them drop the ball and fumble around for a while so they'll learn. But very often you aren't allowed that luxury."[26]

Alinsky and his staff were even willing at times to stuff ballot boxes to ensure the survival of their organizations. At one point, for example, they ensured that African Americans maintained some representation in a nearly all-white organization. "Alinsky had a bluntness about such things," von Hoffman reports. "He did not try to rationalize them or deny that sometimes the majority could be so tragically and immediately wrong you could not stand aside and let the lynching process. To his way of thinking a majority trying to deprive a minority of basic rights had to be opposed." In later years he even threatened to organize against the first organization he had created, the Back of the Yards Neighborhood Council, when it supported housing discrimination against African Americans.[27]

Alinsky was a uniquely, perhaps overly flexible character when it came to such things. Organizers in established groups today are neither as morally fluid nor as beguiling as Alinsky. Something as blatant as ballot stuffing, today, is unlikely. But in more subtle ways, for many of the same reasons, it is still part of the job of the organizer to help ensure that "democracy" turns out in some useful way.

More broadly, participants in Alinsky's organizations never represented more than a small percentage of people in their communities. To some extent, then, they necessarily acted in the name of a majority who would not, or could not, act.

Given his deep and often cynical pragmatism, and his willingness to manipulate situations and people, it can be easy to miss that, at his core, Alinsky was an idealistic champion of democracy. He saw everything he did as means toward that end.

He sincerely believed, for example, that "most people are eagerly groping for some medium, some way in which they can bridge the gap between their morals and their practices." However contradictory it might seem, he saw his model of community organizing, at its core, as a way to provide people "with an opportunity for a healthy, consistent reconciliation of morals and behavior."[28]

"What does the radical want?" he asked in his first book *Reveille for Radicals*. "He wants," Alinsky answered, "a world in which the worth of the individual is recognized. He wants the creation of a kind of society where all of man's potentialities could be realized; a world where man could live in dignity, security, happiness, and peace—a world based on a morality of mankind." Alinsky did not seek chaos or to destroy government, as his enemies claimed then (and still claim today). Despite hyperbole about "rebellion," he was actually quite reformist. He respected the importance of established social institutions (something that annoyed many 1960s' revolutionaries to no end). But he wanted these institutions to respond to the people they served and affected. "He did not," von Hoffman accurately notes, "come to destroy the social order but to perfect it."[29]

"Paradoxically," Alinsky stated, in perhaps the best summation of his own character, "the roots of the radical's irreverence toward his present society lie in his reverence for the values and promises of the democratic faith, of the free and open society."[30]

Notes

1. William James, "Alinsky Discovered Organizing (Like Columbus Discovered America)," *Third Force* 4, no. 3 (July/August, 1996): 13–17.
2. Saul Alinsky, "Empowering People, Not Elites: An Interview with Saul Alinsky," *Playboy* (1972), http://britell.com/alinsky.html (accessed July 18, 2010). Saul Alinsky, *Reveille for Radicals* (New York: Vintage, 1946), ix.
3. Nicholas Von Hoffman, *Radical: A Portrait of Saul Alinsky* (New York: Nation Books, 2010), 124–126. As reported by Horowitz to Sanford D. Horwitt, *Let Them Call Me Rebel: Saul Alinsky: His Life and Legacy* (New York: Vintage, 1992), 291.
4. Horwitt, *Rebel*, 203.
5. Ibid., 4.
6. Alinsky, *Reveille*, 133, 132–133.
7. Ibid., 134.
8. Ibid., 21.
9. Ibid., 134.
10. Von Hoffman, *Radical*, 190, 85.
11. Saul Alinsky, *Rules for Radicals* (New York: Vintage, 1971), 136; Von Hoffman, *Radical*, 143, 145.
12. Alinsky, *Reveille*, 76.
13. Von Hoffman cited in Horwitt, *Rebel*, 397.
14. Alinsky, *Reveille*, 74.
15. Alinsky, *Rules*, 53.
16. Ibid., 27.
17. Alinsky, *Reveille*, 97–98.
18. Ibid., 55.
19. Ibid., 64, italics added.
20. Ibid., 158.
21. Ibid., 105–106.

22. Ibid., 158.
23. Ibid.
24. Ibid.,159, 124, 164.
25. Rinku Sen, *Stir it Up: Lessons in Community Organizing and Advocacy*, (San Francisco: Jossey-Bass, 2003); Susan Stall and Randy Stoecker, "Community Organizing Or Organizing Community? Gender and the Crafts of Empowerment," *Gender and Society 12*, no. 6 (1998), 729–756.
26. Horwitt, *Rebel*, 232.
27. Von Hoffman, *Radical*, 56–57.
28. Alinsky, *Reveille*, 94.
29. Ibid., 15. Von Hoffman, *Radical*, 210.
30. Alinsky, *Rules*, 122.

PART III

Case Studies

CHAPTER 5

Campaign versus Community Organizing: Storytelling in Obama's 2008 Presidential Campaign

A year after graduating from Columbia University, Obama was hired as a community organizer in Chicago in an organization called the "Developing Communities Project," part of the Gamaliel Foundation's national community organizing network. During his three years there, working in and around a low-income African American housing complex, he grew in his skills as an organizer. He had successes, failures, and partial successes that ended up looking like failures. He learned how to get people to meetings, how to empower leaders, and how to develop the relationships necessary to hold an organization together. He discovered the incredible capacity of elected and bureaucratic officials to obfuscate, lie, and resist. And he struggled with the immobility of a population that had experienced so much disappointment that it had largely lost belief in real change.

His grasp of the core concepts of neo-Alinsky community organizing became increasingly sophisticated. In his first book, *Dreams from My Father*, for example, he discussed his growing realization that "self-interest" is more complicated than simple selfishness: "[What the] leadership was teaching me day by day [was] that the self-interest I was supposed to be looking for extended well beyond the immediacy of issues, that beneath the small talk and sketchy biographies and received opinions people carried with them some central explanation of themselves. Stories full of terror and wonder, studded with events that still haunted and inspired them. Sacred stories." This rich understanding of human motivation is something too many involved in community organizing never really achieve.[1]

All the evidence we have available to us indicates that Obama became an especially strong organizer within the neo-Alinsky tradition.

But Obama also became increasingly dissatisfied with the limitations of this approach. The issues Obama had the power to address in Chicago were small relative to the incredible challenges facing inner-city areas. He successfully pressured the city to place an Office of Employment and Training in his neighborhood. He managed to bring the dangers of asbestos in his local housing project to public attention, although financial problems prevented complete removal. And he developed a youth mentorship program. All of these were important. None approached the transformations necessary to get at the desperate challenges facing his "people."

At only a few key moments—like the Civil Rights Movement in the 1950s and 1960s—has community organizing in America developed into broad-based struggles capable of shifting core aspects of national policy and values. Obama's experience taught him, he said, that "you can only go so far in organizing. You help people get some solutions, but it's never as big as wiping away problems."[2]

Obama also seems to have been uncomfortable with organizing's focus on confrontation. As the organizer who initially hired him, Jerry Kellman, noted, "personality-wise, Barack did not like direct confrontation. He was a very nice young man, very polite. It was a stretch for him to do Alinsky techniques. He was more comfortable in dialogue with people." Obama was willing to "challenge power." But he seemed less comfortable with the "lack of civility" that came with many organizing actions.[3]

These concerns led him away from organizing, first to law school and a position in a civil rights law firm, and then into politics.

Obama's vision of a politics of consensus produced the "politics of transcendent unity," which "appealed to so many voters" during his campaign. But this desire to avoid partisan conflict contrasts strongly with organizing's effort to "fan the flames of dissent."[4]

Differences between Community Organizing and Campaigning for Elected Office

During the campaign, the media often mentioned Obama's experience as a community organizer. But few, if any, reporters seem to have understood what community organizing in the neo-Alinsky tradition really involves. They seemed to assume that organizing was simply a more involved version of political campaigning. But organizing and political campaigns are radically different in a number of crucial ways.

As we have noted, community organizing seeks to generate collective strength for social change in oppressed communities. In the ideal, at least, community organizing groups democratically represent the interests of their members in the halls of the powerful by showing they can hold the powerful accountable. Leaders serve as representatives of this collective voice, and cannot make decisions that the "people" do not support.

Electoral politics, in contrast, focuses on electing *individuals* to public office. In the ideal, this person is supposed to represent the beliefs of her constituents. But "constituent" for an elected official has a much broader meaning than it has for a leader in an organizing group. Anyone who hopes to be reelected must respond to a broad range of interests of both voters and campaign contributors. Yes, elected officials are often willing to listen to ideas. But unless a group has the ability to pressure them in concrete ways, politicians are unlikely to do more than take its position "into account."

In fact, politicians are likely to get upset if you try to pressure them. Why do they need to be pressured? Weren't they elected by "the people?" Don't they *already* have good ideas? The case of the Community Action Program, and its demise at the hands of local elected officials upset at having to respond to empowered residents, is a good example of this kind of thinking.

In addition, once elected an official joins a new institution—a legislature, a city council, an administration—a select club with all kinds of perks and recognition. Within this institution, he or she becomes the focus of many collegial, interest groups and other pressures.

The fact is that people in or running for elected office cannot avoid constantly worrying about how they can stay in office. Your issue is just one of many that they and other constituents are worried about. If they are kicked out of office by someone who isn't even sympathetic to you, how is that going to help? So if your group doesn't have the power to make sure they can get someone reelected, then supporting you on anything controversial can be a real risk—not only to their perks of office but also to their capacity to continue to work on other issues that they may be more interested in.

Voters almost always discover that electing someone is only the first step in passing a particular agenda. Yes, it is helpful to have people in office who are sympathetic or who have made promises to you. Some people are so far on one side or another of an issue that they are nearly impossible to "move." But you also need the power to hold officials accountable after they get into office. Regardless of their sincerity, few candidates are trying to get elected to pursue a predetermined agenda. Stories about people who change their legislative priorities after an election, breaking promises by the truckload, are legion.

If a political candidate created an *independent* community organizing group to help get elected, a group focused on achieving the agendas of members and not simply her own election, this would actually be work against his or her own "interests." It would be creating a potential monster, likely to turn on the official if he or she made a decision its members didn't like. Remember a core motto of organizing: "no permanent friends, no permanent enemies."

Given these realities, should we have expected Obama to create an authentic, independent community organizing group to support his election? No.

And he didn't. While he and his supporters drew *ideas* from community organizing, what they created was a *campaign* organization focused on electing Obama.

Scott Walker Lied!

A few years ago, during the election for the new county executive, one of the candidates, Scott Walker, came to talk to the church-based organizing group that Aaron belongs to. We'll call this group CHANGE. The candidate made a promise to CHANGE. If elected, he said, he would provide three million dollars for drug treatment in the county.

After he was elected the predictable happened. "I'm so sorry," he said, "I'm afraid the budget is too tight this year. We just can't find the money I thought we could. Maybe next year we can fund drug treatment."

CHANGE leaders came together to plan a response. A few weeks later, we showed up at his office one afternoon with over 200 members carrying signs that said "Scott Walker Lied!" Although he couldn't "find the time" to meet with us (we believe he escaped out the back door), to the dismay of his staff we packed his reception area and started giving speeches and testimonials about the need for drug treatment. Then groups of participants went to the offices of their respective county board members (the legislative body that Walker was responsible to) and gave them stacks of letters about this issue.

Walker met to talk with CHANGE a week later. Somehow, he told us, he had found three million dollars to fund drug treatment in the county.

Marshall Ganz and the Importance of Stories in Organizing

The most important "community organizer" in the Obama campaign was Marshall Ganz. A lecturer at Harvard, Ganz learned his organizing skills in the hot valleys of California with Cesar Chavez, fighting for the rights of farm workers. He is one of the most accomplished organizers and organizing teachers in America.

Ganz largely designed and taught what were called "Camp Obama" workshops across the country for Obama's volunteer leaders. His curriculum focused in on an organizing strategy he had developed out of his experiences in California and elsewhere: a particular approach to "storytelling."

His vision of storytelling is best described in his Harvard course on community organizing, available online. In that course, Ganz argues that storytelling in community organizing accomplishes three main goals. An effective story

- includes a narrative of "self" that defines who a leader is and provides a model for others;
- roots a leader's story in the collective story of their community, creating a story of "us"; and
- points to a better collective future for that community if they can come together in collective action.[5]

Ganz uses the 2004 Democratic National Convention speech that first brought Obama to national prominence as a key example of an effective "story." He shows how Obama started with his story of "self," moved to a story of "us," and ended with a vision of tomorrow linked to a call to action. Through this movement from "I" to "we" to "action," Ganz argues that a powerful story reframes listeners' position in the world, providing hope and direction. Other examples include Henry V's speech in the Shakespeare play of the same name, where Henry rallied his troops at Agincourt against overwhelming odds, and Ronald Reagan's second inaugural address. "I am like you," these leaders are saying, "I can help you understand yourself, and I can provide a way for all of us together to achieve our shared goals." Through a story of this kind, a leader provides her followers with a shared understanding of the situation they are in, and a justification for coming together around her leadership.

Senate Candidate Barack Obama's Speech at the 2004 Democratic National Convention

I stand here today, grateful for the diversity of my heritage, aware that my parents' dreams live on in my precious daughters. I stand here knowing that my story is part of the larger American story, that I owe a debt to all of those who came before me, and that, in no other country on earth, is my story even possible. . . .

This year, in this election, we are called to reaffirm our values and commitments, to hold them against a hard reality and see how we are measuring up, to the legacy of our forbearers, and the promise of future generations. . . .

John Kerry believes in America. And he knows it's not enough for just some of us to prosper. For alongside our famous individualism, there's another ingredient in the American saga. A belief that we are connected as one people. If there's a child on the south side of Chicago who can't read, that matters to me, even if it's not my child. . . .

Do we participate in a politics of cynicism or a politics of hope? John Kerry calls on us to hope. John Edwards calls on us to hope. I'm not talking about blind optimism here—the almost willful ignorance that thinks unemployment will go away if we just don't talk about it, or the health care crisis will solve itself if we just ignore it. No, I'm talking about something more substantial. It's the hope of slaves sitting around a fire singing freedom songs; the hope of immigrants setting out for distant shores; the hope of a young naval lieutenant bravely patrolling the Mekong Delta. . . .

In the end . . . God's greatest gift to us [is] the bedrock of this nation; the belief in things not seen; the belief that there are better days ahead. . . .

Tonight, if you feel the same energy I do, the same urgency I do, the same passion I do, the same hopefulness I do—if we do what we must do, then I have no doubt that all across the country . . . the people will rise up in November, and John Kerry will be sworn in as president . . . and this country will reclaim its promise, and out of this long political darkness a brighter day will come.[6]

President Ronald Reagan's Second Inaugural Address, 1985

Four years ago, I spoke to you of a new beginning and we have accomplished that. But in another sense, our new beginning is a continuation of that beginning created two centuries ago when, for the first time in history, government, the people said, was not our master, it is our servant; its only power that which we the people allow it to have . . . .

By 1980, we knew it was time to renew our faith, to strive with all our strength toward the ultimate in individual freedom consistent with an orderly society . . . .

We are creating a nation once again vibrant, robust, and alive. But there are many mountains yet to climb....

My fellow citizens, our Nation is poised for greatness.... Let history say of us, "These were golden years—when the American Revolution was reborn, when freedom gained new life, when America reached for her best."....

History is a ribbon, always unfurling; history is a journey. And as we continue our journey, we think of those who traveled before us.... Now we hear again the echoes of our past: a general falls to his knees in the hard snow of Valley Forge; a lonely President paces the darkened halls, and ponders his struggle to preserve the Union; the men of the Alamo call out encouragement to each other; a settler pushes west and sings a song, and the song echoes out forever and fills the unknowing air.

It is the American sound. It is hopeful, big-hearted, idealistic, daring, decent, and fair. That's our heritage; that is our song. We sing it still. For all our problems, our differences, we are together as of old, as we raise our voices to the God who is the Author of this most tender music... called upon now to pass that dream on to a waiting and hopeful world.[7]

Henry V's St. Crispin's Day Speech from Shakespeare's _Henry V_

He which hath no stomach to this fight,
Let him depart....
We would not die in that man's company
That fears his fellowship to die with us....
From this day to the ending of the world,
But we in it shall be remember'd;
We few, we happy few, we band of brothers.
For he to-day that sheds his blood with me
Shall be my brother ...
And gentlemen in England now a-bed
Shall think themselves accursed they were not here,
And hold their manhoods cheap whiles any speaks
That fought with us upon Saint Crispin's day.[8]

More generally, Ganz argues that stories of this kind give people "the courage, love, [and] hope we need to deal with fear, loneliness and despair that inhibits our action." Unlike analytic arguments that communicate dry conceptual information, stories invite us to imaginatively participate in common *experiences*. A core function of these kinds of stories is to "mobilize" collective "hope," an idea Obama used to great effect in his 2008 campaign.[9]

Ganz defends storytelling against "a kind of suspicion of emotion that goes pretty deep—that emotion is dangerous and uncontrollable." In fact, he notes (and Alinsky certainly would have agreed) that "what moves us to action is not neck up; it's the heart. That's sort of where we can get the courage to take risks."[10]

Ganz does not promote emotion without reason, however. In organizing, he emphasizes, stories must come together with cold facts and analysis. In the St. Crispin's Day speech, for example, Henry V does not try to sugarcoat the danger he and his troops were in, or the likelihood that many of them would die. At the same time, however, he gives his army a way to see some hope and deep meaning in the coming battle. It is possible, therefore, for stories to teach both "the heart" *and* "the head." More generally, however, Ganz argues that there must be "a credible vision of how to get from here to there" for a motivating story to have any legitimacy. Thus, "the job of devising a story of hope can't be completed until the strategic work is done to articulate a vision of how to move forward." "Story" and more abstract "strategy" must come together in the effort to generate *legitimate* hope.[11]

From Organizing to Evangelism

In his Harvard community organizing course, Ganz's lecture on "storytelling" is only one component of a much broader introduction to the skills of an effective organizer and leader. In other lectures he discusses a range of approaches to getting people involved, building relationships, learning others' self-interests, and acting strategically. With a few exceptions, however, he dropped most of these other skills and concepts from his "Camp Obama" trainings. As Zack Exley, who attended a "Camp Obama," reported, participants were told that " 'stories of self' and 'stories of us' were to be the most powerful tool . . . back home [for] recruiting and motivating volunteers and building relationships."[12]

The truth is, many aspects of Ganz's wider organizing vision simply did not fit well in an electoral campaign. Campaign volunteers, for example, do not need to learn how to generate a collective policy agenda from the hopes and desires of their members. They do not have any control over their agenda—the candidate does. The job of campaign volunteers is to stick to the policy script they are given.

And while community organizing groups are trying to recruit other volunteers who will work with them over the long term, the central goal of a campaign is to get large numbers of supportive voters to the polls. The enormous numbers involved and the limited action the campaign needs from these masses of people means that there isn't time nor the need to develop rich relationships with each person. What a campaign needs, instead, is a simple way to convince people to vote for its candidate so that staff and volunteers can quickly move on to the next prospect, engaging the largest number of potential voters as possible.

What they needed was a quick strategy for "converting" voters into supporters of Obama. We use "conversion" purposefully, here, because the model Ganz developed was drawn directly from the evangelical religious tradition. The use of personal stories to encourage others to come over to a particular denominational point of view, to an acceptance of a particular religious figure (God, Jesus, Buddha, etc.), is a classic tool used by missionaries and others. In evangelical workshops members are given suggested structures for their conversion stories that look quite similar to those Ganz provided in his trainings. In fact, Ganz was quite clear that his inspiration from this approach came from these religious sources. In the training Exley attended, Ganz asked his audience several times, "Where does your hope come from?," finally getting the answer he wanted, "Faith." "Exactly," Ganz responded, "That's why faith movements and social movements have so much to do with each other."[13]

In the workshops, volunteers were taught to tell the stories of their conversion to Obama, just as evangelicals tell about how they were "born again" to those they are seeking to bring into the fold. Obama volunteers were given "materials and worksheets" that helped them give "structure and flow to the story telling process." The aim was to be able to "tell their 'story of self' in less than two minutes." Or 30 seconds if a person was phone-canvassing. Or a "couple key ideas" if someone was canvassing door to door.[14]

In fact, volunteers were instructed *not* to get into policy discussions with potential voters. One Obama trainer acknowledged, for example, that "potential voters would no doubt confront them with policy questions." But she advised them not to "go there." Instead she told volunteers to refer questioners "to Obama's web site, which includes enough material to sate any wonk." The aim was emotional, not intellectual engagement with voters. Stories, Ganz believed, would motivate voters much more powerfully than issues. "The more particular the story," he argued, "the more listeners are likely to be drawn in, identify with their own experience and want to get drawn in."[15]

Ganz did show camp attendees how to do a limited version of one-on-one interviews (which we discuss later on), which are designed to develop more in-depth relationships. These were for volunteers to use to recruit and firm up connections with other leaders who could do critical tasks and be a central part of the campaign organization. But this appears to be the only other core organizing skill, beyond storytelling, that Ganz taught.

A Canvassing Visit

Lorj[16]

Two Camp Obama trained volunteers, the foot soldiers of this "movement" were at my front door yesterday. They "loved" Obama and wanted to make sure that I would vote for the man who is transforming politics from all the bitter fighting of the past. They urged me to read his book but couldn't give me one reason why they thought his positions would be preferable to anyone else's. In fact, the best they could do is point me to his website if I was really that interested in issues.

Reinforcing Commitment

Let us emphasize that we are not arguing that the Obama strategy represented an effort to build some kind of cult or was an attempt at brainwashing. Frankly, volunteers didn't have the enormous time required to brainwash anyone even if they had wanted to. Instead, the campaign was simply trying to do what all campaigns try to do, albeit with more sophistication than most: to get people to believe in and vote for a particular person. The fact is, the very structure of electoral campaigns *necessarily* resembles evangelical efforts. As we have already noted, one must take a leap of "faith," to support someone, knowing that once they get in office there is little an individual voter can do to influence their decisions.

At the same time, the particular practice the Obama campaign used, having volunteers retell their conversion stories hundreds if not thousands of times, seems likely to have only intensified their tendency to trust Obama. In their interactions with voters, volunteers were repeatedly telling a story about themselves, who they were, how they thought, and what they cared about. Telling this story with emotion (manufactured at times or not) would seem to be a powerful tool for magnifying commitment among canvassers, something Ganz acknowledged in his organizing course. "The significance of the experience [of moving from despair to hope]," he argued, is "itself strengthened by the telling of it."[17]

Telling stories to others is also a form of public commitment making. It is probably harder to change one's mind about something when one has emphatically stressed one's commitment to others in such a public and emotional fashion than if one has simply made a private decision, or even if one has more casually mentioned one's decision to a few others. They declared their "faith" in Obama and connected this to "who" they were.

From Participants to Supporters

Obama, his key spokespersons, and the media often stated that Obama's campaign represented a "bottom-up" instead of a "top-down" approach. Interestingly enough, however, in a number of ways the Obama effort was actually more centralized than any other recent presidential campaign. For example, Obama asked donors to stop funding independent progressive organizations and to instead give the money directly to him, and a number of organizations shrunk drastically or closed their doors as a result. As a book written by one of Obama's regional field directors reported, "in Obama's campaign, nearly everything was developed centrally and scripted for organizers and local volunteers to follow." In fact, "the level of oversight from Chicago could be suffocating at times."[18]

In many ways, then, the campaign looked much like any other campaign. Volunteers were given pretty clear instructions about how to engage voters. And perhaps most importantly, again, they were stuck with Obama's policy positions (to the extent they referred to them at all). In other words, volunteers had limited power to decide *how* to campaign, and no power over *what* they would be campaigning for.

Some level of common "voice" is necessary in any collective effort. But within the campaign context, pressure to conform to a candidate's given vision (or, paradoxically at times in the Obama campaign, to not stress specific issues of policy) seems much more intense. The job of a campaign volunteer is to represent the candidate, and build trust in that person. It makes sense that this effort is necessarily largely controlled from the center.

Even the limited power of volunteers in the Obama campaign was greater than in traditional campaigning, however. Despite constant direction from Chicago, in the end, as one staff member in Texas told local volunteers, "Our job is not to run in here to tell you how it's going to be.... This is your campaign. Not our campaign." Many of the ideas that became "top-down" instructions, like urging campaigners to "Live the Campaign," and the campaign's focus on recruiting in barbershops and beauty salons, actually emerged initially as initiatives developed locally by volunteers in different areas. In fact, through the Facebook-like my.BarackObama.com site, thousands of volunteers created their own local campaign events: parties, speakers, and more. And volunteers worked largely independently, for example, "recruiting and training a crew of fellow Obama supporters to man their precincts on election day." Nonetheless, there was less flexibility than the media and the campaign generally reported in public.[19]

What about the Internet?

You will note that we haven't addressed one of the most lauded aspects of the Obama campaign in depth: its use of email and social networking technology to engage its supporters. In part this is because most communication during the campaign seems to have been top-down. By necessity the campaign seems to have largely treated supporters in the aggregate. Certainly there was no use of social networking technology to actively encourage something more like independent "organizing."

A key exception was the use of "my.BarackObama" or My BO, where people could create their own pages about their support of Obama and link, à la Facebook, to other supporters. Certainly this allowed a wide range of conversation that was not tightly controlled by the campaign. And at points supporters used these sites to put pressure on Obama around specific policy issues. For example, during the campaign over 19,000 people came together on the Web site to pressure Obama to reverse his decision as a senator to support a Bush administration spying bill. They did force Obama to respond in more detail, and led his staff to conduct an online discussion. But it did not seem to produce any significant changes in Obama's stance.[20] While other examples exist, there don't seem to have been many major instances of independent "organizing" during or after Obama's campaign on his Web site.

On the one hand, the mere fact that Obama allowed this kind of criticism is an indication of change and of an unusual openness to grassroots supporters. On the other hand, the limited number of significant examples of this kind of independence represents a continuation of the standard practice of politics. Overall, the social media used by the Obama campaign did not become a significant tool for the development of pressure groups within the campaign. In fact, it is our impression that most of the outside pressure on Obama came from outside the my.BarackObama social network—from independent blogs, etc.

Post-election

After the election, at least by the end of the first year, when we were writing this chapter, little had changed. After the election there was a discussion about what to do with the organization, but instead of letting it loose as a relatively independent organization, the administration shifted it to the Democratic National Committee, whose mission is to elect Democrats, and gave it a new name, Organizing for America (OFA).

Normally in community organizing, the activity of planning and participating in issue campaigns provides the glue that holds people in relationship. But OFA members have no control over agenda or central strategy. So, OFA staff do "listening tours" to hear what members think, run training programs to build community, and engage members in community service activities to keep people involved without doing anything controversial.

During the health-care reform debate, OFA volunteers were asked to support reform. But because the President did not get behind any specific bill, this exhortation remained fairly vague. Volunteers did make thousands of calls to their legislators, and later in the year OFA targeted Republicans from districts that went for Obama. But because it was an arm of the DNC, OFA could not ask members to target those most likely to be affected by such activity: Democratic legislators wavering in their support. Overall, OFA seems to have had little substantial impact on the health-care debate.

A recent report argued that the creation of OFA was a significant evolution of electoral politics in America. It was "the first time a political party has deployed a permanent field program with its own communications channel to contact and organize volunteers to advance a policy agenda between elections." But while OFA has maintained an unprecedented level of volunteer participation post-election, it does not resemble community organizing in any significant way.[21]

We Have the Hope. Now Where's the Audacity?

By Marshall Ganz (with Peter Drier)[22]
(Published 7 months after Barack Obama's inauguration)

The White House and its allies forgot that success . . . demands movement-building of the kind that propelled Obama's long-shot candidacy to an almost landslide victory. And it must be rooted in the moral energy that can transform people's anger, frustrations and hopes into focused public action, creating a sense of urgency equal to the crises facing the country. . . .

[I]nstead of launching a parallel strategy to mobilize supporters, most progressive organizations and Organizing for America—the group created to organize Obama's former campaign volunteers— failed to keep up. . . .

One Obama campaign volunteer from Delaware County, Pa., put it this way soon after the election: "We're all fired up now, and twiddling our thumbs!. . . Here, ALL the leader volunteers are getting bombarded by calls from volunteers essentially asking 'Nowwhatnowwhatnowwhat?' ". . .

[A traditional "insider" politics] approach replaced an "outsider" mobilizing strategy that . . . got Obama into the White House. . . .

Grass-roots mobilization raises the stakes, identifies the obstacles to reform and puts the opposition on the defensive. The right-wing fringe understood this simple organizing lesson and seized the momentum. Its leaders used tactics that energized their base, challenged specific elected officials and told a national story, enacted in locality after locality.

It is time for real reformers to take back the momentum.

Conclusion

When he was running for the State Senate in Illinois, Obama declared that politicians needed to change how they operated. He talked about the importance of using elected office to support the organization of "ordinary citizens into bottom-up democracies that create their own strategies, programs, and campaigns and that forge alliances with other disaffected Americans."[23] It is not the goal of this chapter to contest Obama's real commitment to this vision over the long term. In fact, reporting on his early years has consistently stressed his integrity and his commitment to his expressed values. Nonetheless, Obama's vision of politicians catalyzing independent "bottomup" organizing may have less relevance, or at least may be more difficult to carry out—given the pragmatic realities of the world of electoral politics,— than he had hoped, especially with his vision of politics and governance during the first year.

A few collections of local Obama supporters have begun to create their own independent groups without OFA's support, and these groups are not necessarily inclined to blind support of Obama. But the evidence indicates that not very many have gone this route.

Why not?

One answer is likely that they simply weren't taught how to operate independently, and that they were miseducated about what "organizing" is. OFA, for example, has "organizing" in its title despite having almost nothing substantive to do with organizing. In the op-ed excerpted above, Ganz and his colleague Drier complain about the failure of OFA to become a strong organizing presence. But Ganz may be partly responsible for this outcome. It was probably unreasonable to expect even a proto-populist like Obama to take the risk necessary to create an independent, aggressive organization himself. While there is nothing stopping people in OFA from creating their own organization or organizations, the training that Ganz gave them doesn't seem to have equipped them to do so.

Notes

1. Barack Obama, *Dreams from My Father* (New York: Three Rivers Press, 1995), 190.
2. David Moberg, "Obama's Community Roots," *Nation,* April 3 (2007), 2, http://www.thenation.com/doc/20070416/moberg (accessed February 2, 2010).
3. Ibid., 3.
4. Ibid.
5. Marshall Ganz, *Motivation, Story, and Celebration,* Lecture Notes from Community Organizing Course at Harvard University (2006), http://isites.harvard.edu/icb/icb.do?keyword=k2139&pageid=icb.page60814 (accessed July 18, 2010).
6. Barack Obama, "Democratic National Convention Speech," July 24 (2004), http://www.pbs.org/newshour/vote2004/demconvention/speeches/obama.html (accessed February 20, 2010).
7. Ronald Reagan, Second Inaugural Address, 1985, http://www.bartleby.com/124/pres62.html, accessed December 6, 2010.
8. Shakespeare, *Henry V,* Act IV, Scene 3, http://www.shakespeare-literature.com/Henry_V/20.html (accessed May 3, 2010).
9. Cited in Marshall Ganz, "The Power of Story in Movements," unpublished working paper (2001), 3, http://www.hks.harvard.edu/fs/mganz/publications.htm (accessed July 18, 2010).
10. Cited in Jonathan Tilove, "Barack Obama Crowd Looks Like 'Cult' or 'Craze', Pundits Say as Backlash Begins," *Newhouse News Service* (February 23, 2008), http://www.mlive.com/politics/index.ssf/2008/02/barack_obama_crowd_looks_like.html (accessed March 3, 2010).
11. Ganz, *Motivation, Story, and Celebration,* 19.
12. Zack Exley, "Stories and Numbers–A Closer Look at Camp Obama," *Huffington Post,* August 29 (2007), 2, http://www.huffingtonpost.com/zack-exley/stories-and-numbers-a-clo_b_62278.html (accessed July 18, 2010).
13. Ibid.

14. Ibid.

15. John Hill, "Obama Basic Training," Sacramento Bee (January 21, 2008), A4, http://my.barackobama.com/page/community/tag/canvassing+training+volunteers (accessed July 19, 2010), original URL http://www.sacbee.com/capitolandcalifornia/story/649427.html (accessed February 2, 2010). Kim Bardeesy, "Marshall Ganz: Lighting a Fire," *The Citizen: The Student Newspaper of the Kennedy School* (February 12, 2008), http://harvardcitizen.com/2008/02/12/marshall-ganz-lighting-a-fire/ (accessed March 3, 2009).

16. Lorj, "Bold Moves and Movement Building, Huh?" [A Comment on Paul Rosenberg's Diary, "Lakoff on Obama–If Only!"], *Open Left* (February 3, 2008), http://www.openleft.com/showDiary.do?diaryId=3607 (accessed March 3, 2009).

17. Marshall Ganz, "Notes on Storytelling," unpublished working paper (2005), 12, http://www.hks.harvard.edu/fs/mganz/publications.htm (accessed July 18, 2010).

18. Alan Kennedy-Shaffer, *The Obama Revolution* (Beverly Hills, CA: Phoenix Books, 2009), 63, 65. Also see, Tyler Rogers, "Keeping Hope Alive," New Organizing Institute (December 16, 2009), 2, http://www.neworganizing.com/jno/keeping-hope-alive-story-obama%E2%80%99s-neighborhood-teams-following-election-day (accessed July 18, 2010). Because the latter URL disappeared at the time of this book's final editing, see also http://www.openmediaboston.org/node/1140, accessed December 8, 2010, for a summary of the article.

19. Tim Dickinson, "The Machinery of Hope," *Rolling Stone March* 20 (2008), 1, http://www.rollingstone.com/news/coverstory/obamamachineryofhope (accessed February 20, 2010). Christi Parsons, "For Obama's S.C. Troops, It's a Campaign and a Lifestyle," *Chicago Tribune* (January 25, 2008), http://archives.chicagotribune.com/2008/jan/25/news/chi-obama-grassrootsjan25 (accessed February 20, 2010). Dickinson, "The Machinery of Hope," 2.

20. Ari Melber, "Online Activists Keep the Pressure on Obama," *Nation* (July 7, 2008), 1, http://www.thenation.com/doc/20080721/melber (accessed February 20, 2010).

21. Ari Melber, *Year One of Organizing for America: The Permanent Field Campaign in a Digital Age* (Washington, D.C.: techPresident, 2010), 6, http://techpresident.com/ofayear1#toc (accessed February 20, 2010).

22. Peter Drier and Marshall Ganz, "We Have the Hope. Now Where's the Audacity?" *The Washington Post* (August 30, 2009), 2–3, http://www.washingtonpost.com/wp-dyn/content/article/2009/08/28/AR2009082801817_pf.html (accessed February 24, 2010).

23. Hank De Zutter, "What Makes Obama Run?" *Chicago Reader* (December 8, 1995), 3.

CHAPTER 6

A Theology of Organizing: From Alinsky to the Modern IAF

Mark R. Warren

E rnesto Cortes, Jr., arrived back to his hometown of San Antonio in 1973, fresh from his training in Saul Alinsky's Industrial Areas Foundation (IAF).[1] His goal was to build an organization to give voice to the poor and working Mexican Americans in San Antonio's forgotten west and south sides. Within a few short years he and a group of committed Catholic clergy and lay leaders had built a powerful organization which broke the Anglo elite's monopoly on political power in San Antonio. In the process, the modern IAF came to base its organizing work almost exclusively in religious congregations and to reach deeply into religious networks to build organizations based upon religious values as much as material interests. By doing so, the IAF began to build organizations meant to last and to maintain participation over time.

* * *

On a winter's day in 1975, George Ozuna's grandmother asked him to accompany her shopping in downtown San Antonio. The high school senior got his shoes and began the long walk from the Hispanic south side of the town to Joske's Department Store, the largest retail establishment in the city. When the pair arrived, George immediately realized something was going on. Hundreds of Hispanic grandmothers, housewives, and churchgoers had gathered outside the store. They entered en masse and began trying on clothes. And they didn't stop. They continued to try on clothes all day, grinding store operations to a halt.

The protesters were all members of Catholic parishes active in Communities Organized for Public Service (COPS), a new organization fighting to improve conditions in San Antonio's impoverished and long-neglected south and west side neighborhoods. The next day COPS supporters disrupted banking operations on a busy Friday afternoon at the central branch of Frost National Bank by continuously exchanging pennies for dollars and vice versa while upstairs COPS leaders and the group's organizer, Ernesto Cortes, Jr., met with bank president Tom Frost, Jr., one of the most influential men in San Antonio.

Despite little initial success, COPS continued its protests and the tide began to turn. Prime-time television crews started covering the actions, scaring away paying customers. Pressure mounted on business leaders. The head of the Chamber of Commerce came to negotiate with Cortes. But the organizer made him wait until COPS leaders could be rounded up to participate. Through the organizing strategy discussed later in this chapter, COPS eventually won the city's commitment for $100 million worth of desperately needed improvements to its neighborhoods. For the first time, Mexican Americans had flexed their political muscle in San Antonio, and they gained new drainage projects, sidewalks, parks, and libraries for their efforts.

Militant, direct action tactics geared toward winning put COPS squarely in the tradition started by Saul Alinsky. After his encounter with Cortes, banker Tom Frost bought a case of Alinsky's books and distributed them among the power elite of San Antonio so that they could better prepare to deal with COPS.

COPS and the IAF are still known for these militant tactics. The casual observer who sees only these tactics, however, will miss the fundamental changes to Alinsky's way of organizing that Cortes began to make with his work in San Antonio. Twenty years after the tie-up at his bank, Frost, by then an influential figure in Texas state politics as well, gave this author his last remaining copy of *Rules for Radicals,* claiming it was no longer relevant. According to Frost, "I told Ernie [Cortes] he's now working out of another book. And I asked him just what is that book? Ernie said he's still writing it."

This chapter is the story of that new book. Trained under the IAF in the early 1970s, Cortes began organizing COPS using Alinsky's methods. Almost immediately, though, he began to revise Alinsky's approach. This chapter explores those changes, showing how Cortes and his colleagues in the IAF developed a new model of organizing to overcome the limitations of Alinsky's methods. The modem IAF would come to base its local organizations in the institutions and values of faith communities. Its organizers would become a permanent feature of local affiliates, using relational organizing to reach beyond pastors to foster the participation of lay leaders. Meanwhile, the IAF would come to link these leaders across racial lines, attempting to build broad-based organizations that would help ensure commitment to the common good, rather than to narrow group interests. In this way, the modern IAF developed close collaboration with people of faith, fusing religious traditions and power politics into a theology of organizing.

Communities Organized for Public Service (COPS)

While Hispanics made up a majority of San Antonio's nearly 1 million residents by the early 1970s, they were almost entirely excluded from political representation at city hall. The city politicians neglected Hispanic neighborhoods on the west and south sides of the town. Roads there were often unpaved, sidewalks nonexistent, schools poor, and floods a common and deadly occurrence. The city displayed an old-fashioned colonial atmosphere, as the growing Hispanic community remained a "sleeping giant." Cortes, however, thought the sleeping giant might be ready to wake up.

At first, Cortes followed Alinsky's methods and attempted to recruit to COPS a variety of neighborhood social organizations, including churches, PTAs, and social clubs. About 25 Catholic parishes, however, soon emerged as the bedrock of COPS, while the other institutions proved too unstable or unsuited for the ensuing political conflict. As COPS became established, the largest part of its budget came from dues paid by member parishes, the funding principle followed by all IAF affiliates.

Tapping the funds, legitimacy, and institutional leaders from the Catholic Church conformed to traditional Alinsky methods. But in organizing COPS, Cortes began to make a profound innovation. He went beyond the priests and the usually male presidents of parish councils and began to reach more deeply into the networks of lay leaders that spread out from the church. Parishes on the south and west sides served as the center for a variety of social activities through them. Cortes met with over 1,000 residents active in some way in the community.

Cortes started with the priests, got the names of potential supporters from them, and moved through the community. He recruited leaders, now mostly women, from the ranks of parish councils, fund-raising committees, and churchgoers who were active in PTAs and social clubs. Many were members of the Guadalupanas, a Catholic association of Hispanic women. Andres Sarabia, the first COPS president, and its last male president, was head of his parish council at the Holy Family Church. Beatrice Gallego, the second COPS president, was a PTA leader and active in the Council of Catholic Women in St. James parish. These new COPS leaders were also different from the Hispanic activists with whom Cortes had worked in the 1960s.

They were not individual activists committed to the cause. Instead, they were connected to parishes and rooted in the dense networks of extended families and friends that constituted San Antonio's Hispanic neighborhoods. Rather than activists committed to the cause, COPS leaders cared primarily about the needs of their families and the religion that bound them together.

Reflecting on the early years of COPS, Cortes explains that "we tried to bust the stereotypes, . . . to see leaders not necessarily as someone who could speak or persuade a crowd. We wanted to see leaders as people who have networks, relationships with other people." These leaders were often women, and many of them were excited about the opportunities the new organization offered. According to Cortes, "Many of the women leaders were real powerhouses in their private families. They had a lot to say about who does what. But that's not enough. The public side of them didn't get developed because they are invisible outside of the home. They may have gravitated to leadership in our organization because of the need to develop this aspect of their personality. We offered them the opportunity."[2]

Rather than mobilize people around an issue, Cortes engaged people's value commitments to their community. He got community leaders to talk with each other about community needs first, before identifying an issue around which to act. Specific plans for action emerged out of conversations at the bottom, rather than issues identified by activists at the top. What the IAF came to call relational organizing worked to bring community leaders together to find a common ground for action and to develop the capacity to act in the interests of the broader community.

By reaching beyond institutional leaders, the IAF unleashed the deeper capacities of the communities within these churches. Once women like Beatrice Cortez began to learn to assert themselves in public leadership, IAF organizations could become more dynamic and expansive. Compared to Alinsky's projects, which often stagnated eventually under the same small pool of institutional leaders, COPS had a method to create broader participation. By continuing to recruit from these networks, the IAF generated a continual stream of new leaders to bring fresh energy and new ideas into local organizations. Indeed, the role of the organizer was to recruit and train leaders, not run the organization themselves.

To unleash the leadership capabilities of these women, however, the IAF needed to innovate again. The organization couldn't be led by a coalition of official representatives from member social institutions as Alinsky's organizations had been run. Room had to be made for the leadership of the lay parishioners Cortes was recruiting, many of whom were women traditionally excluded from official church positions. As a result, COPS created a hybrid organizational form. Its members were institutions, that is, churches. But the organization was not a coalition, composed of institutional representatives. Its leadership was drawn more broadly from the membership of those institutions, and leaders operated together in a single organization. COPS's structure allowed member parishes and neighborhood leaders to take action for the needs of their own particular neighborhoods at the same time as the organization could also act with a single will, as something more than the sum of its parts.

COPS mobilized its strong church base to challenge the power monopoly of the Anglo elite. In these early battles for recognition, COPS acquired a reputation for pursuing militant and confrontational tactics. COPS engaged in large-scale protests at city council meetings over flooding and drainage issues. It organized disruptive actions at local symbols of economic power, like the protests at Joske's Department Store described at the beginning of the chapter. Because COPS leaders were embedded in social relationships, they could consistently provide large turnouts of hundreds of Mexican Americans to these actions, something never accomplished before in San Antonio.

While mass mobilization provided one key source of COPS' power, the organization quickly began to see the importance of voter turnout as well. In 1976 it allied with environmentalists to block the construction of a large shopping mall over the Edwards Aquifer, the city's only source of drinking water. By mobilizing their friends and neighbors, COPS leaders provided crucial votes to block the project and quickly became a force to reckon with on important public issues facing the city.

The next year COPS threw its weight behind a revision in the city charter that would serve to help institutionalize its newfound power by changing city council elections from at-large to district. With Anglos overwhelmingly voting against the charter change, many observers credit COPS with supplying the margin of victory by mobilizing Hispanic voters. Meanwhile, COPS expanded its role in determining city policy through its influence on the new councillors elected from the five districts where it was concentrated.

COPS also enhanced its power through its intervention in the Community Development Block Grant (CDBG) program in San Antonio. The federal government had established this program to help fund city-authorized projects for promoting community development. San Antonio had a particularly corrupt CDBG system at the time, in which officials went so far as to propose that federal funds be used for a golf course. COPS represented most of the neighborhoods that qualified for CDBG funds in the city and it organized its parishes to present proposals for neighborhood improvement. Through extensive research and planning, backed up by mass mobilization to the public hearings mandated by federal regulations, COPS took control of the CDBG process from city planners. The city approved 91 percent of the projects proposed by COPS.

During this period the IAF institutionalized what came to be known as "accountability sessions." Originally these public meetings would be the venues at which candidates for office would be asked to support organizational initiatives. The candidates often had a chance to meet with IAF leaders prior to these meetings for discussion. But at the sessions themselves officials would generally be limited to yes or no answers. As COPS mobilized supporters through its church base, candidates would face audiences of potential voters numbering in the hundreds, and sometimes thousands. After the meeting, COPS informed its supporters about the candidate's stand on the issues, thereby influencing the outcome of the election without a formal endorsement. If COPS gained a public commitment from a successful candidate at an accountability night, the organization would pressure the official to make good on that promise after the election.

COPS now had an organizing approach that proved powerful in gathering many kinds of resources for its neighborhoods. COPS combined careful research and planning by its leaders with large-scale mobilizations to public actions, and demonstrated its ability to turn out voters too when necessary to win its campaigns. With these methods, COPS secured funds from the county for health clinics, state funds for a community college on the south side, and federal money from the Department of Housing and Urban Development (HUD) for affordable housing programs.

To the extent local elites had expected COPS to be a "flash in the pan" organization like many other urban protest groups, they underestimated the organization's potential to grow and develop. The IAF's explicit emphasis on organization building helped COPS move from issue to issue. IAF organizers trained COPS leaders not to think primarily about the cause or the issue, but to consider whether that action would build the power of the organization. In this way, when an issue campaign was over, the organization could build upon the capacity generated in that campaign to begin to initiate another.

There was yet another way that COPS' approach marked a clear change from at least some of Alinsky's projects and helped to sustain its participatory character. COPS did not administer the programs it campaigned for itself. COPS refused to accept any government money directly. Instead, COPS would allow public agencies to handle the administration, while its leaders carefully watched to make sure the programs went as planned. COPS organizers and leaders remain focused on organizing.

Bringing Values and Interests Together

Through their long-term relationship with people of faith, IAF organizers became interested in religious traditions in a way that Alinsky never did. The IAF wanted to build institutions that would last for the long term, not rise and fall around one issue. To sustain people's participation, something more than self-interest would be necessary. The new IAF approach did not reject self-interest as one critical basis for political action. But the IAF began to see the possibilities for religion to provide a set of value commitments to combine with practical self-interest.

The new women leaders of COPS, like Beatrice Cortez, demonstrated the viability of this new approach to organizing. Mrs. Cortez and her colleagues appeared motivated to participate in COPS by something beyond self-interest. The closing of her child's school may have brought Mrs. Cortez into COPS initially. The power and status that came with her election to its presidency may have given her extra drive. But leaders like Mrs. Cortez talked about their involvement in faith terms, as part of their religious responsibility to the community. Meanwhile, if religion helped motivate leaders to action, that political experience deepened and clarified religious commitment. In discussing her participation in COPS, Mrs. Cortez recounts, "It gave more meaning to my faith. I could now relate scripture to my life. If you really care for your brother, compassion and courage become real. It's not anything you learn in school, church, or CCD [religious education]. So when we went to an action, we looked to the Bible for inspiration. That's the depth we want. We have a theology of housing!"

When Ernesto Cortes moved to East Los Angeles to organize the United Neighborhoods Organization (UNO), he continued his effort to ground IAF organizing in religious traditions, and to confront the tensions that arose in combining practical politics with faith ideals. He found many religious traditions that spoke powerfully about the obligations of people of faith to intervene in public life. Expressed in Old and New Testament stories, faith understandings proved powerful in motivating people to take action for community betterment. Father Benavides in San Antonio argued that religious symbols crystallized these traditions, but that IAF organizers could not draw from them in a utilitarian, "outsider" fashion. According to Cortes, "Albert [Benavides] brought home to me how important the symbols were to people, how deep they went. But it had to be their symbols, their stories. As an organizer, I had to be engaged and learning from them at the same time I was trying to teach." In other words, an interpenetration of religion and politics was necessary.

Over the course of the next 20 years, retelling stories from a largely Judeo-Christian tradition and identifying potent symbols of community building became central organizing tools for the IAF. The IAF drew from Paul's letters to the Corinthians to emphasize the broader public role that people of faith should play. The story of Moses became a mainstay in IAF training. IAF trainers began to call Moses the first organizer and asked participants to draw lessons about leadership from his example. As African American ministers became more involved in IAF efforts, they brought some new symbols and stories, like Ezekiel's prophecy of the valley of the dry bones, where a fractured people came together to rebuild a broken community. By the late 1970s, the IAF had identified the key theme to which every story led: the need for people of faith to take public action to build community.

In 1978 the IAF's national director, Ed Chambers, wrote "Organizing for Family and Congregation" to serve as a training guide for leaders and organizers involved in the IAF. In the pamphlet Chambers argued that religious values and self-interested political action could be combined in the IAF's theology of organizing in a way that enhanced both religion and politics. The document began with a Biblical quote, "God did not give us a spirit of timidity but a spirit of power and love and self-control" (II Timothy 1:7). It then discussed the social and economic pressures that place families under stress. The pamphlet highlighted the values of dignity, self-determination, and justice that can come from a religious tradition and be expressed through political action. Although religious institutions contribute essential values to politics, Chambers closed the document with what the IAF offers congregations in return: "In isolation, families and congregations have no chance. With the citizens' organization [the IAF affiliate] as a context and as an instrument, families and congregations can move with dignity and confidence into the arena of institutional power. Families and congregations can fight for their values. Families and congregations can win."[3]

Relational Organizing and Institution Building

IAF organizing in San Antonio built upon the strong social fabric of Hispanic Catholic communities and the viability of their parish institutions. But when he arrived in East Los Angeles, Cortes found Hispanic communities that were newer, more transient, and more fragmented. Lay leaders in UNO, the organization he founded, did not have the kind of well-established and expansive social networks available to COPS leaders. The IAF could not simply mobilize existing networks; it had to build them as well. But this task was beyond the capacity of IAF organizers alone to accomplish. The IAF staff decided to try, for the first time, to train UNO leaders in relational organizing themselves. In other words, leaders learned how to conduct the individual, relationship-building meetings IAF organizers used to recruit leaders.

In addition to individual meetings, UNO leaders also began conducting house meetings, which then became a standard part of IAF organizing as well. Cesar Chavez had used house meetings to organize farm workers in California. The IAF realized such meetings could help bring disconnected community residents together to talk about common concerns and develop plans of action. House meetings and individual meetings became ways to strengthen community and undertake political action—and to link the two together for mutual benefit.

While Cortes faced the weakness of community social fabric in Los Angeles, he had to confront the fragility of church institutions upon his return to Texas in 1978 to found a new organization in Houston called The Metropolitan Organization (TMO). In Houston the IAF faced the problem that many of the individual religious institutions within TMO were weak. They had too few members, insufficient finances, and a small leadership base. In the late 1970s and the 1980s, economic restructuring and middle-class exodus served to concentrate poverty and undermine community life in inner-city communities across the country. Although the IAF had always argued that political action would redound to the benefit of communities, it now had to pay closer attention to institution building within communities. In response to these conditions, the IAF offered the services of its organizers for "parish development." The term reveals its Catholic roots, but was meant to apply to churches in all denominations. The parish development process represented an organizing effort to articulate and unite the congregation around the institution's goals and purposes, strengthen church finances, and bring forth new lay leadership to expand church activities. To accomplish these goals, IAF organizers used the network's relational organizing technique of conversation leading to action.

Conclusion: A Synergy of Faith and Politics

By the early 1980s, Cortes and the IAF had written a good part of that "new book" to which the San Antonio banker Tom Frost referred at the beginning of this chapter. This book revised Alinsky's model of organizing in a number of significant ways. The new model served as the framework for the modern IAF's organizing efforts across the country and pushed community organizers in other networks to take faith, values, and relational organizing seriously as well.

In San Antonio, Cortes began to reach beyond institutional leaders into the social fabric of the churches on the west and south sides of the city. He chose not to start with an issue around which to mobilize. Instead, he asked lay leaders to talk among themselves to identify their concerns and find a basis for cooperative action. By doing so, he unleashed the capacity of indigenous leaders, particularly women who were immersed in and often responsible for community life. These women cared about their families, their communities, and their faith as much as about any particular issue. Where Alinsky emphasized self-interest and saw his base of religious institutions solely as repositories of hard resources like money and people, the IAF began to take faith traditions and the relational strengths of women lay leaders seriously.

While the faith/politics and values/interest combinations proved powerful in founding and sustaining IAF organizations, they were not without their inherent tensions. Too strong an emphasis on faith and values led to idealism and the failures experienced even by the COPS powerhouse in San Antonio. Too much emphasis on interests and pragmatic politics, however, led to alliances with development interests that some found unappealing.

IAF organizers began to talk about two kinds of power, unilateral and relational, a distinction it took from Bernard Loorner. Unilateral power represents "power over" others, the kind of power Alinsky generated in his projects. But the new IAF sought to create relational power as well, that is, the "power to" act collectively together. The Texas IAF organizations were not the simple interest groups Alinsky formed to mobilize resources to win an issue. Instead, they built social capital, that is, cooperative relationships, to create a more expansive form of democratic participation. The IAF has not ignored interests or power politics. Instead, it has added the "soft arts" of relational organizing in order to combine values with interests, community building with political action, creating in the process a theology of organizing.

Notes

1. For a more complete set of supporting notes, see Mark R. Warren, "Chapter Two: A Theology of Organizing," in Mark R. Warren, *Dry Bones Rattling: Community Building to Revitalize American Democracy* (Princeton, NJ: Princeton University Press, 2001), 40–71, from which much of the text of this chapter was taken.
2. Mary Beth Rogers, *Cold Anger : A Story of Faith and Power Politics* (Denton, Tex.: University of North Texas Press, 1990), 123.
3. Edward Chambers, *Organizing for Family and Congregation* (Hyde Park, NY: Industrial Areas Foundation, 1978), 1, 33.

CHAPTER 7

Organizing Through "Door Knocking" within ACORN

Heidi Swarts

BILL: We've had some powerful moments .... The best one was when [U.S. senator] Eagleton *ran over* a couple of our members!

JACKSON: He [Eagleton] was so nervous! ... Bill raised a bunch of hell! ...

BILL: I was so mad at that man. I cussed a senator. I wanted to get everyone else pissed off ... I went to block his car and he kept right on driving!

This exchange illustrates features for which ACORN was well known long before it gained notoriety during the presidential campaign of 2008: Bill, a local organizer, intentionally wanted to incite anger in grassroots members who were used to feeling passive and powerless. ACORN members felt exhilarated and empowered by direct action. The organization encouraged them not to be intimidated by powerful officials.

ACORN, the Association of Community Organizations for Reform Now, represented "low- to moderate-income" people beginning in 1970. It fell victim to unrelenting coordinated attacks from the right wing, including the John McCain presidential campaign, Fox News, and Congress. The national organization declared bankruptcy in 2010.

So why bother learning about ACORN at all? First, ACORN was uniquely structured, innovative, and successful. It made many mistakes and could be enormously inefficient in its local organizing, with high organizer turnover and an arrogance that alienated potential allies. However, nationally, its top staff was capable of strategic brilliance, and its local organizing was frequently excellent. Organizing entrepreneurs can learn volumes from both its successes and mistakes. Second, ACORN is still with us—not as a united national organization, but in the form of several surviving state-level organizations under new names. There are scores of experienced former ACORN organizers available to rebuild local, state, or even a national organization. So understanding ACORN's history and model will allow us to recognize when the model springs up again—as it will.

ACORN's particular strength was its *strategic innovation*. Among community organizations, it was structured early on to run effective national campaigns. ACORN had national ambitions as early as the 1970s, but after 2000 its rapid expansion made these more realistic—then its visibility and effectiveness made it a target, a victim of its own success. ACORN was unique partly because of the following features:

1. Unlike congregational organizing, ACORN was one centralized national organization with a unified national strategy.
2. Unlike congregational organizing, this strategy included a long-term alliance with labor.
3. Unlike congregational organizing, this strategy included direct participation in electoral politics.
4. It combined many functions and multiple legally separate organizations under its umbrella. It was a mass-based grassroots organization, a mutual benefit association, and a national public interest organization that advocated for "low- and moderate-income" Americans.
5. It experimented widely with tactics, especially in its national campaigns.

Below I discuss each of these features, but first we go back to 1970 to understand how this unique organization came to be.

Beginnings

From the start, ACORN was meant to be both a poor people's interest group and the nucleus of a broad populist movement for social change. In 1970, former organizers for the National Welfare Rights Organization (NWRO) (see discussion in Chapter 3) tried a new experiment in Arkansas. The NWRO wanted to broaden its support in the South in order to win passage of the guaranteed national income plan proposed by President Nixon's domestic advisor Daniel Patrick Moynihan. However, NWRO organizer Wade Rathke, perhaps intuiting America's imminent turn to the right, felt that winning real gains for the poor would require a broader base than welfare recipients—the working poor, the working class, and lower middle class, what ACORN called "low- to moderate-income" Americans. Rathke founded a new organization based in Arkansas, the Arkansas Community Organization for Reform Now (ACORN).[1] In Boston, the NWRO had developed a model very different from Saul Alinsky's, one that ignored existing groups and created a brand new organization after a six-week campaign. This six-week plan was the basis of the ACORN organizing model.[2]

The six-week organizing model was easily replicated by ACORN's raw, young, mostly white organizers. An organizer researched and analyzed a neighborhood, knocked on doors, made initial contacts, and established an organizing committee. This group then picked an issue, prepared for a neighborhood meeting, held the meeting, staged a collective action, and evaluated it. Ideally, the organizer made 20–40 contacts per day by knocking on doors. Following Cesar Chavez, who believed membership dues made an organization self-sufficient and helped members "own" the organization, ACORN organizers collected dues from each family. For poor families, these dues were significant. In the 1970s, dues were $1.00 per month, and $10.00 per year if paid in advance.[3] By 2008, family dues were up to $120 per year (usually paid monthly, either by bank draft or laborious monthly collection).

The goal of neighborhood organizing was that after the first issue was identified—which, Alinsky-style, should be immediate, specific, and winnable—and hopefully won, the newly hatched group would continue as an ACORN neighborhood organization. In a given city, neighborhood chapters combined to form the city organization and elect its board of directors. However, ACORN staff retained control over hiring a city's organizing director (and, indeed, shifted staff across the country at will).

Sources of Funding

Funding a poor people's organization was always an uphill battle, and family dues, endless local fundraisers, and even an extensive door-to-door canvassing operation in affluent neighborhoods (eventually abandoned) were never enough. However, as its reputation and list of accomplishments grew, the share of ACORN's income from membership dues gave it the credibility to help it win foundation grants from the U.S. Bishops' Catholic Campaign for Human Development (formed explicitly to fund poor people's empowerment) and the handful of large and small private foundations that funded community organizing.

ACORN's tactical creativity, discussed below, included its ability to find creative sources of funds, such as through settlements with corporate campaign targets. This allowed it a larger budget than other U.S. community organizing groups, although some income funded its mutual benefit services. In 2000, the total budget of all ACORN affiliates was $41.5 million. By 2008, ACORN claimed an annual budget of over $100 million, over 1,000 employees, and nearly 500,000 dues-paying families.[4]

ACORN's Development through Campaigns

ACORN's first campaign in Arkansas was designed around the needs of welfare moms in the poor neighborhoods where Rathke and his first-hired organizer Gary Delgado door-knocked. They discovered an Arkansas welfare manual's statement that poor people had a right to furniture.[5] As in the NWRO, militant (nonviolent) direct action that drew media—occupying offices and making demands at the Welfare Department, demonstrating at the governor's mansion—was the core tactic, and would remain an ACORN staple throughout its 40 years. ACORN also organized allies, including respected religious figures. Ultimately Governor Winthrop Rockefeller gave in and formed a new state agency to provide used furniture to welfare recipients.

After other victories, in 1973 ACORN took on an unusual campaign, given the group's past and future base of mostly African Americans and Latinos/Hispanics (although whites and others were always involved in ACORN). A group of white middle-class rural farmers asked ACORN to help them fight a coal-burning power plant whose pollutants might damage their crops. ACORN's winning strategy was to pressure Harvard University, the largest shareholder of the utility company whose Arkansas subsidiary would build the plant. ACORN lobbied Harvard to study the plant's environmental impacts, push for building pollution controls, and pressure the utility to create a $50 million fund for possible damages. ACORN organizers in Cambridge gathered student petitions which were given to Harvard's president and recruited student group allies. In Arkansas, the group won media coverage, the governor's support, and national university allies to research environmental impacts. Although Harvard President Derek Bok tried to bottle up the issue in committees, Harvard finally asked the utility to reconsider its plans and add emission controls. ACORN submitted research to the state utility regulator, which cut the plant's size in half; ultimately it was never built.

This campaign bore the hallmarks of ACORN's successful future campaigns. Research—here on the utility's shareholders (which identified Harvard), and later on environmental impacts—by bright, often highly educated staffers was essential. ACORN creatively used multiple tactics to win the campaign.

ACORN always understood that victories build the organization. After the power plant victory, ACORN not only spread throughout Arkansas, but by 1975 had expanded to Texas and South Dakota, with a string of impressive achievements. The group's name was changed to *Association of Community Organizations for Reform Now.* As early as the 1970s, Rathke challenged a shibboleth of Saul Alinsky's organizing—remain neutral in electoral politics—and experimented with running local ACORN candidates for office in Little Rock, Arkansas.[6]

It was a characteristic combination of hubris, naïveté, and creativity that led ACORN to aim a campaign at the 1980 presidential election when it was only 6 years old. In 1976 Rathke proposed the 20/80 campaign—an audacious plan to expand ACORN from 3 to 20 states by 1980 and run delegates in caucus states. The goal was to win policies benefiting poor people on the national Democratic platform—and, as always, to build ACORN. By 1978, ACORN had chapters in 12 states. ACORN failed to win its demands, but the campaign expanded ACORN and won it national visibility. By not endorsing a candidate, however, it lost such potential allies as labor, which embraced the Democratic Party after Reagan's 1980 victory. ACORN did not realize that presidential campaigns are candidate driven; later, its political action committee not only endorsed presidential and other candidates but also ran local candidates for office. ACORN failed with the Democrats, but expanded to 20 states.[7]

Affordable Housing, Community Reinvestment, and Predatory Lending

Ronald Reagan's election in 1980 ushered in a period of budget cuts to cities and social programs. ACORN members always struggled for affordable housing, and rust belt cities with middle-class flight and plummeting home values in concentrated-poverty neighborhoods were rife with houses abandoned by absentee owners. In 1979 ACORN launched a squatting campaign aiming to publicize the lack of good housing and, through sweat equity, encouraged members to renovate abandoned homes. Perhaps its most important result was the radical claim that the right to good housing trumped the rights of private property owners who abandoned their buildings.

ACORN's use of the Community Reinvestment Act (CRA) produced more concrete wins. During the 1970s, ACORN played a role in the campaign for community reinvestment led by National People's Action (NPA). This national campaign, rare in community organizing, produced the Home Mortgage Disclosure Act (HMDA) in 1975, which required banks to disclose the location of mortgage applications they accepted and rejected. This enabled organizations to challenge banks with racial bias for refusing to lend in inner-city neighborhoods. This led to the successful campaign for the CRA, passed by the Congress in 1977. The CRA made federal bank regulators' approval of mergers and acquisitions conditional on investment in their local communities. It relied on citizen groups to file challenges to banks applying for merger and acquisition approval. Groups like ACORN could force them to the bargaining table, as banks typically preferred a settlement with a community group to full-scale review by a federal supervisory agency. Throughout its history, ACORN fought numerous attempts to weaken the CRA. In 1991 it staged a two-day takeover of a House Banking Committee hearing.

ACORN filed its first CRA challenge in St. Louis in 1985. The group became adept at researching discriminatory lending practices, challenging bank mergers, and winning new mortgage products for its low-income members. ACORN's creativity and openness to new vehicles for action led it to found the ACORN Housing Corporation, which handled CRA bank challenges and subsequent negotiations for new, lower-interest mortgages for first-time home buyers in urban neighborhoods. Settlements even included funding for the housing corporation to recruit qualifying home buyers, handle their applications, and train them in responsible homeownership.

The 1990s saw a massive wave of bank mergers and acquisitions. This created the opportunity for ACORN Housing Corporation to use the CRA to demand more local investment as a condition of the mergers. ACORN Housing made over 45 agreements with banks; the mortgages from 1995 to 2004 alone were worth $4.6 billion. These campaigns fulfilled multiple goals. They extracted resources for poor and working-class people. This allowed thousands of families to realize the American dream of homeownership. These campaigns also increased ACORN's visibility and value to members, recruited new potential members, and funded the ACORN Housing Corporation, some of whose budget supported organizing.[8]

Contrary to right-wing propaganda after the recession of 2008, the crisis caused by bundling bad home mortgages as investment vehicles was not caused by ACORN. In fact, ACORN was in the forefront of the fight against predatory lending. Beginning in the late 1990s, ACORN heard increasing complaints of mortgage scams with outrageous interest rates and provisions that often were not disclosed to borrowers. One of ACORN's biggest victories was its 3-year campaign against Household Finance (as of 2010, owned by HSBC Finance Corporation). Household extended extremely high rate second mortgages to borrowers, often designed so that borrowers could make virtually no progress in paying them off, despite making required monthly payments. Ironically, many ACORN homeowners could have qualified for "A"-level mortgages (those with the best interest rates and provisions), but because of racial profiling or borrowers' lack of knowledge, they were trapped in subprime loans.

This campaign illustrates ACORN's strategic creativity, and how its structure as one centralized, national organization with national, state, city, and neighborhood chapters could be coordinated. In 2003 the Household Finance campaign, which included a class-action lawsuit, produced a proposed settlement including a $72 million foreclosure avoidance program for Household borrowers at risk of losing their homes, as well as an earlier $484 million settlement between Household, all 50 state attorneys general, and state bank regulators, which provided restitution to exploited borrowers. Household also reformed its lending practices.[9]

This campaign exemplifies the power of ACORN's strategic capacity after 30 years of experience and organizational growth. Significantly, its expansion into 80 cities by 2000, the multiplication of national staffers with specific expertise, and the strategic capacity to recruit powerful state allies made this victory against a multinational corporation possible. However, such achievements no doubt put ACORN on the radar screen of powerful opponents in business and Republican politics, as we will see below.

Insurance Redlining

ACORN learned that homeowners' insurance redlining—the practice of denying insurance to specific geographic areas, based on risk but often simply just racial discrimination—was a problem for many of its new homeowners and others. In 1993, ACORN began to fight it, and won agreements with Allstate Insurance (a $10 million partnership with ACORN and Nations-Bank) and Travelers Insurance, which widened access to insurance in return for public safety programs.

Organizing for Better Schools

ACORN long worked on improving schools in its members' neighborhoods. It organized parent groups, allied with teachers' unions, advocated for adequate textbooks and school repairs, and even founded ACORN-sponsored charter schools.

Responding to Hurricane Katrina

Wade Rathke's home and one of the national ACORN offices were located in New Orleans, as well as a large ACORN local organization, so ACORN members were extremely active in helping their Gulf Coast members advocate for assistance, relocation, and return to their homes. The organization gutted and rebuilt over 1,850 homes, and bused displaced New Orleans residents back to the city for several elections.

What Made ACORN Unique?

At this chapter's beginning, several features of ACORN were identified that help explain its uniqueness as an organization. The brief preceding history sets the context for the fuller explanation that follows.

1. *ACORN was one centralized national organization with a unified national strategy.*

Unlike congregation-based organizing, ACORN was not a "network" or federation of affiliated but legally distinct organizations. It was one national organization with local and state chapters. This structure allowed it to mobilize coordinated national campaigns. While the boards of directors of ACORN locals set local policy, crucially, the national Chief Organizer (since 1970, Wade Rathke), not the elected local ACORN boards, had the ultimate authority to hire and fire *all* staff. Therefore, organizers reported to the ACORN national office and only secondarily to the local board.[10]

ACORN senior national staff wielded enormous influence in choosing campaigns and strategies. Many would agree that this compromised ACORN's degree of internal democracy, in direct contradiction to its public ideology. On the other hand, centralized direction is streamlined and efficient, and most ACORN issues were pursued because local members identified them as problems. Furthermore, senior staffers' exceptional strategic expertise often made ACORN's most groundbreaking campaigns possible.

2. *Unlike congregational organizing, this strategy included a long-term alliance with labor.*

A classic maxim of congregational organizing is "no permanent friends, no permanent enemies." However, while congregation-based groups may often collaborate with labor, ACORN saw labor as a "permanent friend." ACORN saw a long-term shared class interest with the labor movement. Former ACORN Executive Director Steve Kest argued that ACORN and labor are natural allies because they share the same constituency; they are not just advocacy or policy organizations, but membership organizations who could offer each other the ability to mobilize a mass base, and both sought long-term power for political and social change.[11]

Always experimenting, in 1978 Wade Rathke convinced the ACORN national board to fill a gap in union organizing: low-wage workers in fast-food, home health-care, and hotel work. It began organizing Burger King and

McDonald's workers in Detroit. While ultimately ACORN's United Labor Unions (ULU) failed to take off, it trained a host of future labor organizers, and its locals eventually affiliated with the Service Employees International Union.

The living wage movement, in which ACORN played a key role, tackled a labor issue and enlisted a broad range of religious, civic, and labor groups. Living wage ordinances require private companies that have contracts with cities and other municipalities, or that receive public subsidies, to pay their workers an above-minimum wage that enables them to support their families decently, above the poverty level. These policies only affect a fraction of a city's workers—but more importantly, they reframe the issue of wages as a moral issue, and build constituencies for larger efforts.

The living wage campaign that sparked the movement was originated in 1994 not by ACORN, but by the Baltimore affiliate of the Industrial Areas Foundation (IAF). The IAF's balkanized structure prevented the tactic's diffusion within that network—five or six decentralized regional organizations, each with its own powerful organizer-director. However, ACORN's centralized and unified national organization enabled it to make the issue a priority round the country. ACORN sought to build this movement because when it began in the mid-1990s, the Clinton administration had already passed a federal minimum wage increase to $5.15—still a poverty wage—and a further federal increase was politically impossible. ACORN then tried a state-level campaign in Missouri in 1996, but failed. Working at the city level was a strategic decision that, once successful, allowed ACORN to return to state-level campaigns.

ACORN has led or helped lead only 15 of the more than 140 successful local campaigns, in major cities such as Chicago, Boston, New York, Oakland, St. Louis, and Denver. Helping lead the national living wage movement was nonetheless a national ACORN strategy. ACORN staffed a national Living Wage Resource Center that provided technical assistance to living wage campaigns, organized conferences open to all for sharing strategies, and monitored the growing number of ordinances, besides leading and participating in local campaigns.

Once scores of living wage ordinances were passed by cities, ACORN quickly set its sights higher. Illustrating many national staffers' strategic acumen, Florida ACORN director Brian Kettenring took advantage of the 2004 presidential election and proposed a Florida-wide minimum wage increase ballot initiative. However, Florida ACORN lacked the funds. By enrolling labor unions and the Democratic Party, the Floridians for All Campaign received the funds and volunteers it needed. Florida ACORN collected close to a million signatures to place its wage increase on the

November ballot, partly as a strategy to boost low-income (likely Democratic) voter turnout for the presidential vote. The measure passed by 72 to 28 percent and raised the minimum wage to $6.15, indexed annually to inflation. About 850,000 workers each gained $2,000 of additional annual full-time income in May 2005. The campaign set a precedent: It was the first time a minimum wage increase was passed in a Southern state.[12]

Like the labor movement, ACORN saw direct engagement in electoral politics as an essential route to achieve its goals.

3. ACORN's strategy included direct participation in electoral politics.

All community organizations that challenge authorities for policy changes address the political system, at least as pressure groups. However, groups (including churches) that are classified as 501(c)(3) nonprofits may legally accept tax-deductible donations only if they limit their "lobbying" activity. They cannot make partisan endorsements or run candidates, but can educate and organize on the basis of issues.

In contrast, ACORN had no Internal Revenue Service (IRS) status that limited its involvement in politics (although its *affiliated* "educational"/training organization was a 501(c)(3)). It ran candidates for office in its earliest days. Later, it was a key founder of the New Party, and the most successful recent third party, the Working Families Party. ACORN has brought lawsuits to remove obstacles to voter registration, such as violations of the National Voter Registration Act of 1993 ("Motor Voter Act").

In 2003, ACORN assumed the management of Project Vote, a leading voter mobilization organization since 1982.[13] In 2004, using ACORN's network of neighborhood chapters, Project Vote mounted a massive voter mobilization. In the 2008 election, it aimed to register and mobilize 1.3 million new voters from among its constituency, the low-income, African American, and Latino populations. In an unprecedented effort by thousands of workers, ACORN gathered over 1.3 million voter registration forms in 21 states. However, after screening out incomplete, incorrect, or phony forms, according to former ACORN Executive Director Steve Kest, the campaign yielded about 866,000 successful registrations. Of these, approximately,

- 70 percent were people of color (predominantly African American).
- 68 percent were low income ($40,000 or less, most under $25,000).
- The states with the highest number of successful applications were Ohio, Michigan, Florida, and Pennsylvania.

- 432,440 of these successful registrants actually voted in the 2008 general election. All told, 746,000 people who cast ballots had been successfully registered by ACORN and Project Vote since 2004 and remained on the rolls in 2008.[14]

This unprecedented enfranchisement of probable Democratic Party supporters in a presidential election got attention, including unwanted attention, from ACORN's opponents. As we will see, inaccurate accusations of "voter fraud" began the cycle of events that led to ACORN's downfall.

4. *ACORN combined the mass base of a grassroots organization, the services of a mutual benefit association, and the advocacy of a national public interest organization.*[15]

ACORN continuously experimented with new organizational forms. It has been a pressure group, a labor union, a voter registration organization, a political action committee, a housing developer, a low-income financial services broker, a charter school founder, and a leadership training institute. Its related organizations included ACORN Housing Corporation, the American Institute for Social Justice, (its separate tax-deductible 501(c)(3) education and training arm), ACORN political action committees, and Project Vote. In New York City alone, ACORN Housing helped develop about 500 housing units; a local ACORN Schools Office helped plan community-controlled charter schools and directed education campaigns; a community hiring hall channeled low-income local residents to jobs; and a workers organizing committee organized workfare participants.

New ACORN-affiliated organizations often emerged from issue campaigns. For example, in 1979 ACORN began dramatic, well-publicized squatting campaigns in the 30,000 vacant houses in Philadelphia. In 1982 it set up a squatters' tent city behind the White House. This campaign led to the ACORN Housing Corporation, which at its peak operated in about 40 cities.

Part of ACORN's motivation for experimenting with new functions and tactics was the imperative for identifying new sources of funds. In the best campaigns, creative sources of funding, tactical innovation, and winning gains for poor and working people went hand in hand. One example is ACORN's Earned Income Tax Credit Campaign. Instead of targeting a bank or corporation for concessions, it won a private foundation grant to help eligible low-wage workers apply for the tax credit. The Earned Income Tax Credit is now the largest remaining federal entitlement for income support, and lifts more children out of poverty than any other government program.[16] In 2003, the Marguerite Casey Foundation awarded ACORN a 2-year $1.5 million grant to recruit low-income families to apply for credit in three pilot cities. ACORN's unlikely partner was the IRS. Because ACORN could mobilize its grassroots network of neighborhood chapters door to door, in 2003 ACORN exceeded its goal and directed $3.8 million in tax credits to new applicants—reaching far more people compared to the hundreds of other community groups participating. Organizers conducted door-to-door education in multiple languages. Staffers and member volunteers with hand-held electronic devices could determine a person's eligibility at their doorstep. They staffed free tax preparation centers, which saved applicants tax preparation fees as well as the high-interest "refund anticipation loans" (RALs), which commercial tax preparers offer. The IRS found ACORN so effective that it expanded ACORN's participation from 3 cities in 2003, to 45 in 2004, and 80 in 2005.[17]

This campaign exemplified synergy—it mobilized resources for ACORN, won gains for constituents ripe for membership recruitment, and was consistent with ACORN's ultimate mission: political and economic gains for lower-income Americans.

5. *ACORN's tactical experimentation combined many simultaneous tactics and targets in the same national campaign.*

While entire movements typically include diverse organizations using varied tactics, it is less common for one organization to do so. Using numerous tactics builds a synergistic effect, allowing tactics to reinforce each other. For example, ACORN used a dizzying array of simultaneous local, state, and national tactics to build pressure on Household Finance. The box below shows the major tactics used in this campaign against predatory lending.

Just to follow one "pathway" of effects, publicizing Household's abuses helped ACORN identify more borrowers who were victim to predatory loans. This helped document abuses, which helped make the legal and political case for reform—and it provided another vehicle to recruit new ACORN members, which built the campaign's mass base, built pressure on government officials and corporations for reform, and provided more data and individuals for reporters to interview for news stories. Positive media coverage not only gives a campaign credibility but it also helps reframe borrowers' experiences, from shameful *personal failure* to *collective political injustice*. This builds solidarity and participation and recruits activists for other battles.

Multilevel Tactics Used in Campaign against Predatory Lending by Household Finance

Local chapter tactics:

- Identified loan victims
- Documented predatory business practices
- Protested at local Household offices
- Launched local media campaigns
- Sought local legislation to curb loan practices

State-level tactics:

- Legal: pushed state attorneys general to sue Household
- Legislative: sought local legislation to curb loan practices
- Regulatory: pushed banking regulators to act

National-level tactics:

- Legal: two class-action lawsuits
- Pressure through allies: American Federation of Labor and Congress of Industrial Organizations (AFL-CIO), which had contracts with Household to provide discounted loans to union members, lobbied Household
- Shareholders: resolution introduced at Household shareholders meeting, which in 2001 received 30 percent support
- Media campaign about loan practices directed at Wall Street analysts

ACORN's Many Warts

As impressive as ACORN's achievements are, so are the criticisms, which emerged long before 2008—from both insiders and outsiders. ACORN founder Wade Rathke was its Chief Organizer for its entire 40 years, and exerted enormous control—counterbalanced, however, by other staffers with tenures almost as long. However, to function, organizers and leaders had to share a mind-set that resisted criticism from the outside—for disregarding other groups' "turf," reneging on agreements with outsiders, refusing any coalitions that it could not dominate, chewing up organizers like fodder, using shoddy or no financial management—and so on. ACORN came under fire for fighting the unionizing efforts of some of its own staff. It paid poverty wages and demanded endless hours. Its model was one of staff sacrifice to a calling. No wonder it needed a powerful ideology of its value and superiority to sustain commitment; some likened it to a cult. Black and Latino organizers were bitter about the fact that the long-time senior staff were white and mostly male.[18] ACORN's informal culture of machismo was not particularly friendly to women, although a number of women were among its top national leaders.

To be fair, ACORN made efforts to change. In the 1970s and 1980s, only 10 percent of ACORN's organizers were of color; by 2003, this had increased to 64 percent[19] Furthermore, in its last decade, ACORN made unprecedented efforts to forge cooperative efforts. Often success in city-level efforts depended on the quality of local relationships. Nationally, top ACORN staffers built relationships with their counterparts at both the faith-based PICO National Network and the Gamaliel Foundation, and many other groups. In July 2008, shortly before its demise, ACORN and PICO held their first joint action, a press conference in Washington, D.C., with member testimonies from both groups about home loan disasters, to launch the new coalition Americans for Financial Reform. Tragically, it was to be their last.

ACORN's Demise

ACORN had a long history of challenging government and corporations alike, and as it gained capacity—80–100 city chapters by 2008—and registered half a million new likely Democratic voters for the 2008 election, it was large enough for the right wing to take note—and target it for an overwhelming attack. The McCain campaign, Fox Network, conservative blogs, Republican state officials, and others converged to attack ACORN for "voter fraud"—patently false charges, as voter fraud occurs during the election itself, not during voter *registration*. Some ACORN workers submitted fraudulent registration forms, but any incomplete forms or forms whose accuracy could not be confirmed by multiple telephone calls, *by law,* had to be turned in to each state's board of elections, flagged as possibly invalid. Only boards of elections are permitted to discard voter registration forms, in case they are legitimate. Therefore, conservatives accused ACORN of intentional fraud even though they were simply complying with the law.[20]

But there was more. On July 9, 2008, *The New York Times* reported that Wade Rathke's brother Dale had embezzled $948,607.50 from ACORN in 1999–2000.[21] The Rathkes made arrangements for full repayment, but did not inform most national board members. ACORN's culture of secrecy and control had come home to roost. The board of directors was furious and demanded that Rathke step down as ACORN's chief organizer. Longtime New York ACORN senior organizer Bertha Lewis took over and the group hired outside consultants to reform their management practices. However, it was too late—the negative publicity fed ACORN's image as a crooked organization.

The final straw came in 2009, when two conservative activists released misleading, highly edited videos filmed with a hidden camera, which showed low-level ACORN employees appearing to advise them how to illegally fund a prostitution ring. (The activists visited eight ACORN offices and didn't report the ACORN staffers who covertly took cell phone pictures of them as evidence against them, sought other incriminating evidence for the police, or threw them out of the office.) This broke the camel's back. Congress, including Democrats eager to disassociate themselves from ACORN, rushed to eliminate its federal funding (only 10 percent of its budget). The real damage was done by private foundations, which, following Congress, cut their grants to ACORN. By March 2010, half of ACORN's 30 state chapters had closed. Later that month, ACORN disbanded because of lack of funds. Multiple investigations determined that, while ACORN needed to reform its management practices, it was innocent of all charges. But the damage had been done.[22]

By March 2010, 15 of ACORN's 30 state chapters had closed and at least 2 others had severed ties with ACORN.

ACORN Is Dead; Long Live ACORN

Several of ACORN's largest state organizations regrouped under new names and continue to organize. California ACORN became the Alliance of Californians for Community Empowerment, while New York ACORN became New York Communities for Change. Even before the scandals, longtime Chicago organizer Madeline Talbott, disgusted with ACORN's internal culture and management problems, had pulled ACORN's Chicago organization away and reorganized it as Action Now.[23]

Some critics have asked, "Did ACORN get too large?" The answer is no. No mass-based social justice organization can get too large. ACORN may have expanded too quickly after 2000; it certainly suffered from cultural and management flaws that made it vulnerable to attack. The real answer to that question is that it got too large for the comfort of right-wing corporate interests and their political and media allies. With corporate mass media like Fox News and a cowardly and passive liberal media and foundation sector, the deck was stacked against ACORN. Can a revitalized and reformed national version of ACORN rise again? For those who seek social justice, we must hope it will.[24]

Notes

1. This brief history of ACORN is drawn from Gary Delgado, *Organizing the Movement: The Roots and Growth of ACORN* (Philadelphia, PA: Temple University Press, 1986); John Atlas, *Seeds of Change: The Story of ACORN, America's Most Controversial Antipoverty Community Organizing Group* (Nashville, TN: Vanderbilt University Press, 2010).
2. See the discussion of the NWRO in Chapter 3.
3. On the original dues, see Atlas, *Seeds of Change*, x; on 2008 dues, see Nathan Newman, "ACORN Praised by Prosecutors for Fighting Voter Registration Fraud," TPM Café (September 9, 2009), http://tpmcafe.talkingpointsmemo.com/2009/09/09/ACORN_praised_by_prosecutors_for_fighting_voter_re/ (accessed July 5, 2010).
4. See Peter Drier and John Atlas, "ACORN under the Microscope," *Huffington Post* (July 14, 2008), http://www.huffingtonpost.com/john-atlas/ACORN-under-the-microscop_b_112503.html (accessed July 5, 2010). Note: Like almost all grassroots organizations, ACORN's membership claims were typically inflated; however, the budget figures are probably accurate.
5. Information on major early campaigns is drawn from John Atlas' important history of ACORN, *Seeds of Change*.
6. Nicholas von Hoffman reports that Alinsky was actually quite interested in electoral politics, although he never found a moment when he thought it was the right strategy for one of his organizations. Nicholas von Hoffman, *Radical: A Portrait of Saul Alinsky* (New York: Nation Books, 2010).
7. At the 1980 convention, Democratic Party leaders agreed to establish a poor people's commission, but it never happened. Delgado, *Organizing the Movement*.
8. Lisa Ranghelli, "The Monetary Impact of ACORN Campaigns: A Ten Year Retrospective," unpublished draft paper (February 16, 2005), in author's possession. Ranghelli was an external consultant. The figure was arrived at using ACORN Housing records, indicating that its offices "in 38 cities educated 175,057 potential buyers, counseled 115,660 clients, and assisted families in securing 48,566 mortgages" whose estimated average value was $95,500: "Multiplying the average house price by the number of mortgages produces an aggregate of $4,638,053,000 in housing values." ACORN negotiated aggressively for the banks to cover some loan costs that would normally be passed on to borrowers, based on observation by this author of negotiations in 1998.
9. News release, "States Settle with Household Finance," *Washington State Office of the Attorney General* (nd), http://web.archive.org/web/20060922203225/www.atg.wa.gov/releases/rel_house_101102.html (accessed July 4, 2010).
10. ACORN Bylaws, author's collection.

11. Steve Kest, "ACORN's Experience Working with Labor," working paper (nd), in author's possession.

12. Interview, anonymous ACORN organizer.

13. Project Vote, "Our Mission," http://projectvote.org/index.php?id=119 (accessed July 18, 2010). It was independent until 2003, when it approached the Industrial Areas Foundation and ACORN to pursue affiliation. ACORN accepted the offer.

14. This was based on an independent report by the New Organizing Institute on the 2008 election cycle. Steve Kest, Memo (December 18, 2009), in author's possession.

15. Sections numbered 4 and 5 are adapted from Heidi Swarts, *Organizing Urban America: Secular and Faith-Based Progressive Movements* (Minneapolis, MN: University of Minnesota Press, 2009), chapter 4.

16. According to the Center on Budget and Policy Priorities, in 2002 this included 4.9 million people, including 2.7 million children. Joseph Llobrera and Bob Zahradnik, *A Hand Up: How State Earned Income Tax Credits Help Working Families Escape Poverty in 2004,* Summary (Washington, D.C.: Center on Budget and Policy Priorities, 2004), http://www.cbpp.org/5-14-04sfp.pdf (accessed June 20, 2005).

17. Ron Smith, IRS Chief of Corporate Partnerships, telephone interview, June 24, 2005.

18. See Delgado, *Organizing the Movement.* For an immediate sense of the complaints by lower-level ACORN organizers and organizers of color, see the comments of "JohnBrownz" to Peter Dreier and John Atlas, "ACORN under the Microscope."

19. F. Brooks, "Racial Diversity on ACORN's Organizing Staff, 1970–2003," *Administration in Social Work,* 31, no. 1 (2007): 27–48.

20. Note: ACORN claimed various numbers of active city affiliates, but, like all community organizations, some affiliates were barely active and needed to be organized or reorganized.

21. Strom, Stephanie, "Funds Misappropriated at 2 Nonprofit Groups," *The New York Times* (July 9, 2008), http://www.nytimes.com/2008/07/09/us/09embezzle.html (accessed July 6, 2010).

22. An internal investigation (which ACORN commissioned) by former Massachusetts attorney general Scott Harshbarger found "there was no criminal conduct by employees who offered advice on how to hide assets and falsify lending documents." Frank James, "ACORN Workers Cleared of Illegality by Outside Probe," National Public Radio (December 7, 2009), http://www.npr.org/blogs/thetwo-way/2009/12/ACORN_workers_cleared_of_illeg.htm (accessed July 6, 2010); also see Editors, "NPQ on ACORN Investigation Results," *Nonprofit Quarterly* (January 26, 2010), http://www.nonprofitquarterly.org/index.php?option=com_content&view=article&id=1654:npq-on-ACORN-investigation-results&catid=58:npq-in-the-news&Itemid=54 (accessed July 6, 2010).

    On March 1, 2010, the Brooklyn district attorney cleared ACORN of any criminal wrongdoing; see Andrew Newman, "Advice to Fake Pimp Was No

Crime, Prosecutor Says," *The New York Times* (March 1, 2010), http://www.nytimes.com/2010/03/02/nyregion/02ACORN.html (accessed July 6, 2010).

An investigation by California Attorney General Jerry Brown released on April 1, 2010, found videos from California ACORN offices to be "severely edited" and found no evidence of criminal conduct by ACORN employees. "Brown Releases Report Detailing a Litany of Problems with ACORN, But No Criminality," *California Office of Attorney General* (April 1, 2010), http://ag.ca.gov/newsalerts/release.php?id=1888& (accessed July 6, 2010).

23. For the California organization, see http://www.calorganize.org; for New York, see http://www.nycommunities.org/; and for Chicago, see http://actionnow.org. Other former ACORN affiliates have reorganized as well.

24. Sharon Theimer and Pete Yost, "Did ACORN Get Too Big for Its Own Good?" Associated Press (September 9, 2009), http://www.msnbc.msn.com/id/32925682/ns/politics-more_politics/ (accessed July 18, 2010).

CHAPTER 8

Mixing Metaphors and Integrating Organizing Models

Marie Sandy

This book primarily concerns itself with the Alinsky tradition of community organizing, but there are many other important figures and movements as well, as described Chapter 3. As organizer Rinku Sen reminds us, "there are no pure models" for community organizing. I think of organizing histories and examples as a kind of "banyan tree;" it is difficult (and sometimes pointless) to see where one root begins and another ends. While they may have historic moments where they began or became prevalent, they all inform one another, like intertwined branches and roots. New roots shoot up, and new branches become rooted. People trained from one branch may join another one or even start a new organizing initiative. People may even argue about what is a legitimate part of one branch, and what constitutes something distinct. Importantly, the critique of organizing efforts, particularly the antiracist and feminist critiques of Alinsky, also bear fruit and help form new branches and roots. Even if a branch or trunk "dies," the group may have trained generations of organizers that go on to develop new organizing practices and theories. In this way, organizing is an authentic living tradition that continues to evolve.

While keeping in mind how entangled all of these organizing branches are, it is usually helpful to know some of the basic organizing "types" or traditions. Here is my attempt at sketching a "tree of organizing history" based on Rinku Sen's excellent description of the field. The soil beneath the banyan tree is comprised of the historical context and current conditions that allow community organizing to flourish in the United States, including the established tradition of labor organizing, the settlement movement, and racial justice

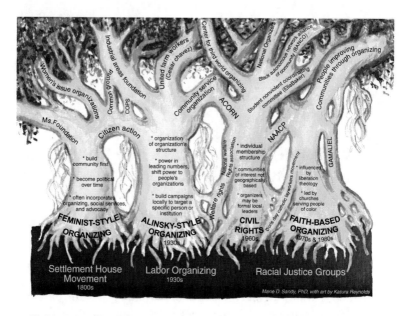

All of the roots and branches are intertwined in a banyan tree, and so too with the organizing tradition in the United States. Most organizers have been influenced by Alinsky-style organizing, so while the PICO and Gamaliel groups are listed as part of Faith-Based Organizing because theological interpretations and congregation based practices created a distinct form of organizing, their founders also trained with Alinsky.

The soil beneath the banyan tree is comprised of the historical context and current conditions that allow community organizing to flourish in the United States, including labor organizing, the settlement movement, and racial justice groups.

The smaller dangling vines in the illustration represent new growth provided by the various organizing training programs, such as the Midwest Academy, leadership school, training institutes led by the Center for Third World Organizing, the Industrial Areas Foundation, DART, the National Organizers Alliance, and some university-based programs.

groups. The main "trunks" described here include feminist-style organizing, Alinsky-style organizing, civil rights movement organizing, and faith-based organizing. Organizations associated with the Alinsky model include "organization of organizations" groups such as the Industrial Area Foundation's (IAF's) Communities Organized for Public Service (COPS) in San Antonio. Modified iterations of this model include Community Service Organization (CSO) and the United Farm Workers. Organizations associated with the feminist branch include the Ms. Foundation and the National Organization for Women. The antiracism, welfare rights branch of organizing includes the National Welfare Rights Association (NWRO), the Association of Community Organizations for Reform Now (ACORN), the Center for Third World Organizing, and the National Organizers Alliance. Organizations associated with the faith-based tradition of organizing include the People Improving Communities through Organizing (PICO).

The smaller dangling vines on the illustration represent new growth provided by the various organizing training programs, such as the Midwest Academy, ACORN's leadership school, training institutes led by the Center for Third World Organizing, the Industrial Areas Foundation, DART, the National Organizers Alliance, and some university-based programs. Most organizers are influenced by one or more "branches of this tree. For example, I apprenticed with Cindy Marano of Wider Opportunities for Women (WOW), where Alinsky-style organizing strategies were informed by the experiences of woman-centered organizing work as well as the feminist critique of Alinsky's organizing practices. While not listed here, organizers in the gay rights movement, the antiwar movement, and the environmental movement have been greatly influenced by the Civil Rights organizing, particularly with its emphasis on communities of identity, and feminist organizing. Global organizing might be seen as the canopy of networked branches and leaves above these (and other) trunks and roots.

Because this chapter concerns a case study in which I (Marie) participated, I thought it would be helpful to provide some background about my own roots and influences. I am grateful to those who have nurtured my own leadership capacity to engage in this work and two people stand out in particular, Cindy Marano and Lourdes Arguelles. Under the mentorship of Cindy Marano, the former executive director of WOW in Washington, D.C., I learned a great deal on how to "do" community organizing while working as a project director for a program on integrating women in nontraditional jobs, and then as director of our statewide organizing project, the Family Economic Self-Sufficiency Project, which was implemented in six different states. I later became the deputy director of WOW. WOW's model of organizing included the creation of community-wide leadership teams in different cities. In the case of the Nontraditional Employment Training project, these consisted of women currently working in nontraditional jobs and women-led support groups for women in these jobs, employers, unions, community colleges, private industry councils, and job trainers. In the Self-Sufficiency Project, teams were comprised of women currently receiving public assistance as well as a coalition of a wide variety of women's organizations throughout the state. In particular, the New Voices Project in Pennsylvania helped provide intensive leadership training for women recipients of Temporary Assistance to Needy Families (TANF) to testify in front of state legislative bodies and to become leaders in the statewide coalition advocating for the adoption of effective statewide TANF laws. Cindy taught me the art of engaging our constituency, motivating targets, planning effective actions to change public policy, and developing follow-up actions to make sure legal changes made a real difference on the ground. Cindy never wanted to move to Canada or plan to "count the homeless bodies" after welfare reform went into effect in the 1990s. Instead, she encouraged us all to work harder and fight longer. It was an enormous loss to the world of community organizing and to progressive public policy change agents when she died in 2005.

As a doctoral student at Claremont Graduate University in California in the late 1990s and early 2000s, I worked closely with Dr. Lourdes Arguelles. She helped support a number of efforts led by indigenous people, and has been deeply engaged with local communities and in communities in many different parts of the world. With her, I learned much about being a community-based scholar and how to participate in communities that are always in flux. Dr. Arguelles' work often focuses on building alternative institutions when current systems are too broken to fix. She also leads dialogue projects for groups that are deeply opposed to one another, such as migrating immigrants and the patriot fighters engaged in (illegally) capturing migrating workers along the border. I have no words to express my gratitude and love for my advisor, Dr. Lourdes Arguelles. My conversations with her, and the questions she raised with me during the years I have known her, are woven throughout my practice.

The Grassroots Think Tank of Ontario, California

And everything that has to do with growth has to have "power tools." And the power tools, fortunately are the people that are a part of the group.

—Sue Gomez, grassroots think tank member

While in graduate school, I helped to cultivate an intermediary "semi-public" civic space in southern California that integrated community organizing, community building, and community-based participatory research into its practices. Although it wasn't explicitly based on a feminist or antiracist model, the participants sought to incorporate these sentiments into their work together. Like the work of many feminist-style organizing efforts, this group engaged in political organizing activities at the same time as it piloted more typical "service" programs that they worked to institutionalize in local nonprofit organizations. Residents voluntarily came together to identify strengths and challenges in their community. They implemented research, outreach, and direct action efforts on issues they defined. They drew on university partners for support of their work with research and technical assistance. And they engaged in many of the same activities as Alinsky-style organizing groups, including defining the organization's mission and goals, building their leadership capacity, recruiting new leaders in the community, and implementing and debriefing direct action campaigns and events.

The grassroots think tank was located in the most densely populated part of Ontario in southern California, a small city of about 100,000 people. About 60 percent of residents are Latino, 30 percent are white, and the remaining 10 percent are African American, Asian, or "other." The western end of the city, where the grassroots think tank was based, was predominantly Latino, comprised of new and recent immigrants as well as some second- and third-generation residents. We focused largely on the zip codes consisting of the lowest-income residents. The group's operations were based for many years at the Pitzer in Ontario House, and its existence was in part a result of the previous work of Pitzer College in the city of Ontario, which had been ongoing for several years. It was eventually sponsored by Claremont Graduate University through a U.S. Department of Housing and Urban Development (HUD) grant. The grassroots think tank functioned largely as an association, although there was eventually a paid staff in place through the support of the HUD Community Outreach Partnership Center grant. Place-based associations like this one are typically local, ad hoc, and voluntary, dependent on the number of people participants are likely to get to know well and to work with at any given time. While less "permanent" than more formal institutions, they represent an essential building block for healthy communities. The grassroots think tank was in existence between 2001 and 2005.

Also known as the Ontario Community University Partnership (OCUP), the grassroots think tank was comprised of nearly 40 Ontario residents, with some representatives from community-based organizations, schools, and city employees, as well as Claremont Graduate University and Pitzer College faculty and students. Perhaps because I helped lead this group in the beginning, more women than men participated—about 70 percent of the participants were women, and nearly all were people of color, primarily Latino/a. Most of the men who participated were already recognized as leaders in the community, and were usually ministers or administrators of organizations.

In the beginning, Professor Arguelles invited me to be a part of some conversations in Ontario with her to see if we might identify positive ways for the university to collaborate with residents, churches, and community groups there, and to see what might emerge through our association together. Based on the enthusiasm and the direction of those who participated in these informal events, and shaped by my previous experiences working with WOW, we then began to regularly hold a series of conversations together at the Pitzer in Ontario house, which helped organize our work together. "At-large" meetings comprised of everyone involved, and they were held every 3–4 months. After conducting bilingual community surveys designed by group members, our association organized itself into three subcommittees focusing on health, education, and housing. Members of the partnership self-selected which subcommittee or subcommittees they wished to join, and these smaller groups met monthly or even biweekly at times. Most members said that they joined a particular subcommittee because the issue directly impacted them or their families. People without health insurance or who were experiencing health problems joined the health-care subcommittee. People who were currently homeless or who had experienced bouts of homelessness in the past joined the housing subcommittee. Immigration issues, of course, cut across all of the subcommittee issues and this was never an issue we were able to adequately address. We lost some grassroots think tank members because they were deported.

A member of the group, Susan Gomez, described the structure that we eventually came up with through her creative use of the metaphor of a house.

The House Metaphor

Sue Gomez

When you build something, you feed from everyone else in your community. That's how things get done. So what we did is, I had the idea of building a house of OCUP. So, from the house, we figured that we'd build in the rooms, putting in the three pieces that were our goals. And each piece of the house is one of the rooms, and in that we also left room for home improvements, maybe the construction of add-on pieces of the house or remodeling of the rooms. But our basis of the house is the foundation. And the foundation of the house is located in Ontario, and that's where everything with OCUP takes place, so that's the ground here. And the foundation is the partners of our group.

And without our partners, there's no foundation. And then comes the steps here, they are the partners coming together. And each of the rooms included the members itself, the outreach that we were doing, the research that it took to complete the projects, the things where we needed to fight to get things like a health clinic for our community. Because we couldn't do that on our own and they weren't going to just give it to us.

My room was the health room. Our promotoras project in the health room kind of was built off of [the education work of a local non-profit], because we knew that people were there wanting to learn so we decided to have the promotoras program there. Our health sub-committee got this idea for a promotoras de salud program from the Por la Vida program which is in Montclair. We also wanted to get a clinic for adults here instead of having to go all the way to the Pomona Valley emergency room.... We have to trust each other to start this organization, and we have to trust that we can complete it. You know, a lot of people in our group had the same problems that we were try-ing to fix. We needed to take into consideration [the group members'] personal life problems without divulging and going out and spread-ing the word to everybody else. The confidence and the trust was very important for building our house.

Building Trust, Cultivating Community and Building Skills

We were aware of the difficulties involved in holding conversations in such a diverse group due to differences in access to and possession of "power," race, gender, class, and education levels. But the grassroots think tank began with the assumption that it would be possible for people with traditional access to power to hold conversations with and act in concert with people in Ontario, many of whom would likely be described by some as "subaltern." We were hopeful that we could work through some of these prejudices and

Denise Teaching

pre-understandings to begin to hear one another. We knew our conversations would not be perfect—indeed they were not—but the work that we did together over a 4-year period of time seems to have borne out some measure of success.[1]

Most of the core adult participants in the grassroots think tank had a high school diploma or equivalent, although some did not. At least one resident member had taken a few college-level classes before dropping out, and more people working at community service agencies in professional-level capacities had college-level degrees. A college education was valued, and perhaps also resented by some of the members.

Just a Piece of Paper

COMMUNITY PARTNER: There are too many people "UP THERE," who don't know what they're doing and never experienced things although they have this piece of paper. And, I know I have, I know Rosa has, and I know a whole lot of other people who have worked in a place or who have worked in some organization where someone very, very young, 24-years old, and just got his or her bachelor's degree, and they have just been hired as your boss. And they don't have a clue as to how to do things.

When I worked for the school district, the girl who was my boss, she was the sweetest thing and the thing that I liked about her is that she knew she didn't know what she was doing, so she was very, very open to getting help. She made, maybe four or five times more than any of us did. And we had to teach her. All she had was a piece of paper that said she went to college. That's it! And she got that big amount of money. And because we didn't have that piece of paper, we had to teach her how to do the job that she was paid so much money to do.

Our group actually "inverted" who we usually think of as powerful in our meetings. As the local residents were the ones closest to the problems we were discussing, they usually had the best ideas about what to do about them, and they usually had the most flexibility in their schedule and willingness to carry out and participate in activities. Subsequently, the residents usually had the most power in the grassroots think tank. They were always the majority of participants at meetings, and there was additional strength in numbers. This sometimes rankled people with traditional access to power.

Talking

Thought alone moves nothing. Only thought that is tied to action can do so.

—Aristotle

In organizing, one might also say, "Talk alone moves nothing. Only talk that is tied to action can do so." The relationships that the grassroots think tank members cultivated with one another were more formal and "public" in the beginning as the at-large meetings grew to a critical mass. As people began to form public relationships with one another, many personal friendships emerged, and people often learned from members about other local resources that were beyond the scope of the think tank's objectives. New collaborations formed among local nonprofits and some members found jobs through its network. Many people reported that the sense of community that they felt with one another was an important reason that they continued to be involved, and the personal and public connections became increasingly entwined over the years. "Gossip gets things done," is how one community partner member put it, and we always left some informal time—with refreshments—at the start of meetings so people would have some time to make these connections and think together. We tried to stay as much on task during the meetings, and always ended on time or a little early. Different people took turns leading meetings after the group was in existence for a while.[2]

Working and Learning

COMMUNITY PARTNER 1: At our meetings, there was a feeling of we're going to accomplish something. We're not here to just say hello, network, and then say goodbye. We're here because we want to make something happen. And what is that something going to be, and what do you guys want to do? Now you've opened the door to say, "What can we do?" And we listened to everybody, and gave them enough time to say their spiel, but at the same time to stay focused. You know in a meeting where everybody talks and that's it and you get up and you wonder what anybody said? But see in our meetings we wrote it [on poster paper], it meant that they heard it, they can see it, and in some cases they could feel it because they could see it in the person's emphasis with it. So those things were important. And they participated. They owned it. And because they owned it, they wanted to be a part of it even more. It is like I think that process of owning something that is being created really was important and that is what we provided.

COMMUNITY PARTNER 2: I think I learned how to conduct those meetings from those experiences with the Partnership. Because a lot of times, you know, things would go off to other subjects, and I had to pull it back in. And I just thought about the [at-large] think tank meetings, how you would pull us all back in to focus on this particular thing, you know, but in a really nice way. You didn't say, OK everybody, let's stop talking. You validate the conversation, which is very important, to validate what people are saying, that what they're saying is important and that you're listening. But at the same time, we do want to focus on this next thing because we only have so much time, and that, so. They were fun. There was laughter. You know, you could relax.

COMMUNITY PARTNER 3: And that we've had the encouragement of others, you know, where some people say, "I'm tired, I don't want to do this anymore." And there were other people there doing it with you and it was fun, and refreshing.

Gossip got things done, and it also meant that my own life was an open book. I actually lived at the Pitzer in Ontario House during the time I was doing the grassroots think tank, so this compounded things even more. But the informal connections, usually before or after meetings, is where a lot of sharing of information happened.

Sharing

COMMUNITY PARTNER 3: So, I'm planning her [Marie's] wedding.

COMMUNITY PARTNER 2: Yes, it's a done deal. [laughter]

MARIE: I really have very little to say about the matter. [laughter]

COMMUNITY PARTNER 1: All we need is the dress and the date. . . . [T]he menu has been set.

COMMUNITY PARTNER 2: And we've even got a guy picked out! [laughter]

COMMUNITY PARTNER 1: And I told those girls [Sandy and Marie] to go for the guys with the good legs and the cute butt, and they did! [everybody laughs]

COMMUNITY PARTNER 2: But he's so sweet too!

COMMUNITY PARTNER 3: We were going to make sure she got a good one.

COMMUNITY PARTNER 2: Yeah, he had to pass the test first!

MARIE: Do you need help with this? [carrying food; bottles clink]

COMMUNITY PARTNER 2: Do you want the salsa?

MARIE: Do you want to take the soda too?

COMMUNITY PARTNER 1: I think we better go.

COMMUNITY PARTNER 4: I gotta go, . . . and see what my little granddaughter is going to be doing. [This partner had come back to the group after a long absence—she had lost her job and, subsequently, her apartment.]

MARIE: It was great to see you, Terry.

COMMUNITY PARTNER 3: You look fabulous.

MARIE: You do, you look great.

COMMUNITY PARTNER 1: Do I have your number?

COMMUNITY PARTNER 4: I think Marie has it.

MARIE: I'm not sure I have your new one. Do you have my number?

COMMUNITY PARTNER 4: Well you're at Gilbert's.

MARIE: The program number is exactly the same.

COMMUNITY PARTNER 1: But I'll ask Ray if she has a good connection at the David and Margaret home [residential facility for troubled youth] for you.

COMMUNITY PARTNER 4: OK.

COMMUNITY PARTNER 1: So call the program number. So we'll find out what it takes to get her [granddaughter] in. When my kids were growing up, I'm not kidding, I was ready to put Tim into a home.

COMMUNITY PARTNER 4: One of my daughters is in the hospital. And that's Christine and that's her mother. So you know . . .

COMMUNITY PARTNER 1: But you know, when we went. . . . [A]nd right away Leo said, no, we can't do that, he's gonna turn out worse, he'll be with worse kids, and blah blah blah, I should have. . . . But you know, he turned out to be a pretty good kid. He really did, and maybe it was because of all the love that Leo gave him and that he wouldn't quit on him. I was ready to stick him in a home. [people laugh]

COMMUNITY PARTNER 1: I'm not kidding! I'd throw him out and he'd sleep in the park for two or three days and my neighbor would come over—Ray, the one I was telling you about. All gentle, "Susan, Tim's out in the park." I KNOW! I threw the kid away. [people laugh] But I couldn't stand him.

COMMUNITY PARTNER 4: I understand.

COMMUNITY PARTNER 1: I couldn't stand him. I was to a point where I was ready to hit the walls.

COMMUNITY PARTNER 4: I understand, I understand perfectly.

COMMUNITY PARTNER 1: But with his dad it was a different story. [laughing more]

COMMUNITY PARTNER 3: He's just a, you know.

MARIE: He's a really good guy.

COMMUNITY PARTNER 3: Yeah, he's a really nice guy, but to piss HER off.

COMMUNITY PARTNER 4: It takes a lot to piss her off.

Practicing Organizing in Politically Conservative Territory: Combining Service and Organizing Work

In the early and mid-2000s, Ontario was fairly conservative politically and most of the grassroots social change work was led by right-wing grassroots populists, primarily ministers, and sponsored by local churches. Appealing directly to progressive or liberal values was likely to be met with suspicion, and the tradition of Alinsky-style organizing was not practiced. Because of religious or personal reasons, some of the members were not willing to engage in direct actions of a political nature or to vote in public elections. Others chose not to participate in overtly political work because of their legal status. But these same members were still able to participate in conversations to help define the issues, create supportive service projects, identify targets, and provide support for residents who were interested in engaging in this work. Some members who had never considered being involved in direct action efforts before became more political through their participation in the grassroots think tank campaigns, and they continue to be political forces in their communities.

"I Am NOT an Activist"

LILY: Remember when we went to Claudia's [a professor on campus] and we had like a breakfast or something. They [academics] wigged me out. And they asked me, "what do you do," and I was, 'oh I'm in Pitzer's Ontario Partnership and it's the Grassroots Think tank.

So what did they call us? I forgot, what was it they called me? Oh, you're like those people who go into the communities and like stir things up. What's the word?

MARIE: An agitator?

LILY: No not the agitator, what's the word . . . An ACTIVIST. They called me an activist. Oh my God. I am NOT an activist. [laughs] I always think of the activist is like a troublemaker, the one who's always getting chased out, and I'm like NOOO, I'm not an activist.

[everyone laughs]

LILY: I haven't been chased out yet.

TERRY: But everything we do. It was like you know what? This is not a cause, this is what we deal with every day. This is what we do. This is everyday.

ROSA: Like, "Hello?" These are the issues any of us may be dealing with too, you know.

TERRY: It wasn't something that I didn't have in common with, because it's like you know what? At some stage in my life I may deal with this or have dealt with this. And you have to do something. It's like, get out of the cocoon, bro, you know, do something.

[everybody laughs]

Combining Service and Direct Action

Like the experiences of many other small groups, the service work was initiated first. One of the first projects that we did was to collaborate on authoring a bilingual resource directory for other residents that outlined local services such as battered women's shelters, food pantries, and low-cost clinics. We quickly became known as "that green book" group, and more people wanted to join us and see what we were about. While a useful calling card, it also served an important research function for us and helped document inequalities of access. The directory quickly led to discussions about *why* there were no low-cost clinics or hospitals serving adults in the City of Ontario, the most population-dense portion of San Bernardino County. Questions about basic health infrastructure quickly formed the basis of organizing work of the health care access committee, and the group began to frame an issue on obtaining a low-cost clinic for adults in Ontario, with the county superintendent as our target. Several members of the group prepared testimony to present at meetings of the county superintendent and held public meetings for local hospitals to explain the placement of local clinics and to make public the results of their state-mandated community health care needs assessments. (While it is required that all hospitals undertake these assessments, there is no similar requirement for them to publicize this information, and our group found this information fairly difficult to obtain). Fortunately, the sub-committee was able to rely on the support of a hospital in a neighboring county as a secondary target who was interested in reducing the cost of their emergency room visits, as a large number of their low-income and indigent visitors were from Ontario. They were able to put pressure on our primary target. It took years to obtain the desired clinic, but it did happen. Interestingly, a number of for-profit health care operations took a greater interest in locating in this region because of the work the group did to point to the gap, and there was actually competition about which entity would fill this need.

A few members of the health care subcommittee possessed religious convictions that prevented them from participating in explicitly political activities, and they opted out of this component of the subcommittee's work. Others who did participate in it described it as the most important work they ever did. Some of them went on to participate in the housing subcommittee's work that linked to statewide efforts sponsored by the California Coalition to End Hunger and Homelessness and worked to obtain affordable housing in Ontario and the Inland Empire.

While an imperfect arrangement, this blending of service and organizing worked reasonably well, and enabled us to obtain federal financial support that would have otherwise been unavailable to us. By integrating services, research design, as well as explicit attention on organizing, the grassroots think tank benefited from a broader participation of residents than we could have had if we were "only" an organizing group. It also meant that there was always work for everyone to do in between the direct action activities of our organizing campaigns. A downside of this arrangement was that the group probably took on fewer direct action activities related to our overall organizing strategy because we were also involved with implementing other activities such as education activities for homeless families and children and designing resource publications. A common thread for all of the activities we undertook, however, is that they were designed and implemented by the people closest to the problem. Here is an example of a conversation where a pilot social services project led to more political actions:

From Service to Action

COMMUNITY PARTNER 1: Now the neat thing about it is that the promotoras [health education outreach] program, it's been great. But yet, the city doesn't want to pay for it. You know, it's all...which is fine.

COMMUNITY PARTNER 2: But still...

COMMUNITY PARTNER 3: What's her name? The one that's in charge of the community centers...what's her first name? What about a meeting with OCUP and her? They said that they liked it. We know it works. Pay up or shut up. What about getting block grant funds. That's what I'm saying.

COMMUNITY PARTNER 2: We need to meet with the department of rec...

COMMUNITY PARTNER 3: That's what I'm saying, with the City. We have to have a meeting with 'em.

COMMUNITY PARTNER 2: The center's community director, and if you get in good with that community director, you can do whatever you want. Everything that they have is, naturally, free, gratis from us to them.

COMMUNITY PARTNER 4: We've got to change that.

COMMUNITY PARTNER 1: That's the problem, because, I mean, unless we have grant money to sustain...

COMMUNITY PARTNER 2: Okay, because this is what we're doing.... [laughter] [L]et's say we all go to "Bob" and asked him to get involved in this. See, this is my concern right now, that our promotoras—they don't get paid, okay, but yet I have to have them 10 weeks in a certain location and they need maybe refreshments or something.

COMMUNITY PARTNER 1: And child care.

COMMUNITY PARTNER 2: Yeah child care services.

COMMUNITY PARTNER 1: And a stipend of some sort.

COMMUNITY PARTNER 2: So this fits into the health stuff that the city is already supposed to be doing. They should provide most of those things already to you. You've set it up over there [another part of San Bernardino County]. That was the arrangement that we did directly through County Parks and Rec—And then the Parks and Rec, what they did is that, number one, we didn't have to pay for the park, because they were a co-sponsor. What I'm saying is that

> there are things they could be brought to do . . . refreshments, and
> then they have to pay for babysitting. Montclair does this. I can
> definitely see them doing the babysitting, and . . . statewide. . . .
> COMMUNITY PARTNER 3: Mandated.
> COMMUNITY PARTNER 2: There's the word . . . it's mandated, so
> they have to prove to the State of California, to Arnold, that they
> are complying with that component, so it could be under the health
> and parks.
> MARIE: Okay, so we have a job to do . . . who wants to work on
> pushing to make the promotoras a part of the parks and rec budget?
> COMMUNITY PARTNER 1: So I just got homework.

University Sponsorship

The university sponsorship involved benefits and limitations for this group.
The university connection provided a physical space, communication infrastructure, and some financial support, but, to be effective, the think tank had
to carve out its own identity when working on issues. The group's issues were
not necessarily topics with which the university wished to be entangled, but,
for the most part, this group had a great deal of autonomy to define its agenda
and to design research and action campaigns on these issues. The accounting staff at the sponsoring university sometimes raised their eyebrows when
requests for reimbursement for babysitting or refreshments crossed their desk,
but all in all it worked reasonably well. Some resources were relatively easy for
the higher education institution to provide, such as physical meeting space,
phone lines, use of photocopying machines, hosting the Web site, etc. The
people power involved, particularly if they were students, was more difficult
to sustain over time. As organizing efforts become more difficult to support,
however, I encourage other higher education institutions to bring their assets
to bear to support other related initiatives.[3]

Values and Ideology in the Grassroots Think Tank

Hans-Georg Gadamer reminds us that "what ties us to each other and holds
us together stretches far beyond what we can give an objective account of."
We can certainly say that there was not a consistent ideological perspective
among all of the members of the grassroots think tank, however. The political
persuasion of the university partners was generally quite a bit different, that
is, liberal, from the community partners, and Alinksy's recommendation to
remain ideologically neutral while focusing on concrete projects rang largely

true here. This may be because, as in Alinksy's organizing experiences, this work was place based, not based on particular communities of interest that transcend place.[4]

Lourdes Arguelles and Marie once had a conversation where the two of us remarked how unusual it was that one of our community partners, a grassroots right-wing populist fundamentalist Christian director of a nonprofit, regularly entered into collaborative work – based and financial arrangements with a liberation theology/indigenous spirituality nonprofit whose prominent leaders had once been accused of being communists. Lourdes remarked that perhaps outsiders were the ones that perceived and even created some these ideological divisions that did not matter on the ground. "Very interesting," I thought. Months later, I thought nothing of the fact that I had agreed to become a board member for a small nonprofit whose religious and political ideology had nothing to do with my own. I had altogether forgotten about my earlier "curious" observation, as I was just trying to help this group—my friends—file their paperwork.

Howard Becker wrote an interesting article about the Chicago School and drew on the work of Samuel Gilmore in his critique of contemporary musical composers. Gilmore wrote that, oftentimes, composers that are considered to be part of the same "school," because of style, etc., have often never met one another, and people who are often considered to be from different "schools" collaborate all the time on musical endeavors. Becker calls this first type a "school of thought" and the second type a "school of activity." People belonging to the same "school of activity" may disagree violently on matters of ideology, but work together all the time. People belonging to the same "school of thought," which is largely defined by outsiders, may never act together at all.[5]

Prior to working in Ontario, California, I had always worked on interest-based organizing campaigns with people from the same school of thought, those who were concerned with issues related to women and poverty. In Ontario, I became a part of a "school of activity" and had to reconcile myself to the fact that I worked wholeheartedly with people whose ideas about virtually every public issue in national politics, gay rights, the Middle East, the environment, etc., were vastly different from my own. And I liked them, had enormous respect for them. And, I could hang on to the fact that we remained committed to being a community of practice here.

If I had to do it all over again, I would be more vocal about my personal ideological perspectives and not less, so this could enter into public conversation. While interest organizing remains an absolutely critical aspect of community organizing today, I believe we lose something terribly vital if we move away from place-based organizing altogether.

Managing Internal Power Dynamics

You bump into the walls until you find which one is the door!

—Community partner

All groups, informal or not, should think clearly about the type of structure they are building and what the implications of that will be. The inclusion of residents, as well as prominent leaders from community-based organizations and city agencies, ensured the grassroots think tank's work was noticed, which encouraged others to join us, but it was challenging in terms of managing the power dynamics of the group. We originally had an "open door" approach to who could participate in the grassroots think tank meetings. While residents were the core members, we had always had a few representatives from local community-based organizations, churches, schools, and other institutions.

The most critical disagreements about race began to occur about 3 months after we received the HUD/COPC grant. Suddenly, more "institutional representatives" and other people with greater access to power began to regularly attend the subcommittee meetings. The knowledge that the association now involved "real" money may have been the tipping point. This inclusion of a greater number of high-ranking hospital officials, city personnel, and school district officials meant that there were more people in formal business attire at our meetings, and most of these people were white, whereas the majority of our group had always been—and continued to be—people of color. Some of these new members were also current or former supervisors of the "original" members of our group. Decision-making power was always made by who attended the meetings, and not by institutional authority, but I knew that the influx of new people would likely change our discourse together. What I did not know was how, or the extent to which, these changes would affect us, and I made the serious mistake of not holding conversations with the group about these changes.

During the subcommittee meetings following the university's receipt of the grant, I did what I had been doing before, which included listening to everyone's suggestions and writing them on poster paper. Additionally, the newest members, who were usually white, were quite talkative, and often dominant. For a lot of people in the partnership, this was an insult. A couple of the members revealed to me privately that a good number of them felt that I was going to "side" with the suggestions of the white people because I am white. Also, they felt that their suggestions should carry more clout since they had been there from the beginning. They also expressed their dissatisfaction with our choice in the project director and wondered why they had not been a part of the selection process when they had been involved with everything else, up to that point. Although I was grateful that they trusted me enough to tell me this, I was deeply, deeply hurt by this information, and wondered if I was going to help build another organization that would serve to oppress people.

After an at-large meeting where we discussed these problems in an open forum, we agreed to restructure our grant budget to hire a bilingual coordinator, who would be interviewed by a team of think tank members. We also developed specific processes for how people could enter the group. Holding explicit conversations and attending workshops about race, power, and wielding power in public settings became a greater part of our work in the subsequent years of the partnership. People now had to be vetted in by attending an orientation on the project run by experienced leaders in the group, where they learned about the meeting participation ground rules, etc. Our meetings also used more of a "majority rule" format and the residents were always in the majority. During one health-care subcommittee, I also decided to openly back the "original" members of the group on a key decision regarding the health-care directory. This had important consequences for everyone involved. I cannot say definitively whether or not my decisions were correct, of course. People with more experience than I had at the time may have come to other conclusions. I am happy that virtually all of the original members of the group have remained a part of it for the past three years, although several of the key power brokers in the city began attending the subcommittee meetings much less frequently.

Mixed or Muddled?

Combining different social change strategies together can be powerful . . . or just a big mess. Part of the art of fusion requires experience "in the kitchen"— and maybe getting burned—but having a general understanding of the key elements of each strategy is very helpful. Want to engage in a decent community organizing effort? You're probably going to look for a local, relatively permanent entity with a concerted effort to alter the existing power relations over the long term, where the people closest to the problem participate in the design and implementation of campaigns to win real improvements in their lives, and through which they build their own power in the process. In the Alinsky tradition, one might expect an organizing effort to include honing in on particular targets and the creative use of confrontational tactics. There are probably paid organizers involved that may or may not come originally from the local area. In an organizing effort with more assertive feminist influences, one might see a more direct focus on community building, leadership development, and collaborative as well as confrontational tactics.

We are more likely to be able to be adept at fusing social change strategies rather than participating in ineffective social experiments if we understand the foundations of these different models, and this may also give us a better understanding of why certain organizing efforts fail. Here are some examples when attempts at organizing became confused with other social change strategies:

- A nonprofit organization, which operates on both a community *service* model and a community *organizing* model, finds that when it organizes people to fight city hall, city hall retaliates by cutting off the funding for the service program. This is why a lot of organizers do not want to integrate service with organizing work—it is usually not possible to bite the hand that feeds you.

- The Midwest Academy reports that a nonprofit community development corporation (CDC) set up and staffed a tenant organization designed to fight for tenant rights in buildings that it owned and managed. The tenants then start to fight "the landlord," and the organizing staff is told by the executive director and board to make the tenants stop complaining.

- A blue-ribbon leadership team to help homeless people advocate for their rights includes a few homeless people, local homeowners who want the homeless moved out of their neighborhood, and the directors of local nonprofit service providers for the homeless. The people currently experiencing homelessness feel that their voices are drowned out on the board and that they are being asked to rubber-stamp decisions that are not their own and not in their interests.

Combining organizing models is often a matter of taste, experience, and local organizing conditions. The grassroots think tank combined some feminist organizing strategies relatively well, such as an explicit focus on building community and integrating service work with organizing campaigns. We also incorporated key Alinsky-style elements into our work, and drew on the support of a community-university partnership to support our work, something that is uncommon in most community organizing practices that stress the importance of the autonomy of a durable organization. Part of our legacy is not readily apparent, but no less real. While not in existence today, many of the former members of the grassroots think tank are involved in various social change efforts throughout southern California. For me, participating in the grassroots think tank was one of the most gratifying experiences of my life, and while I see our members much less frequently than I used to, our friendships endure.

Notes

1. On subaltern studies, see Ranajit Guha and Gayatri Chakravorty Spivak, *Selected Subaltern Studies* (New York: Oxford University Press, 1988).
2. Marie Sandy, "Hermeneutic Passages in Academia and Community" (Ph.D., Claremont Graduate School).
3. For a more in-depth discussion of how education institutions can support local organizing work, see Sandy, *Hermeneutic Passages.*
4. Jean Grondin, *Introduction to Philosophical Hermeneutics* (New Haven, CT: Yale University Press, 1994), 318.
5. Howard S. Becker, "The Chicago School, So-Called," *Qualitative Sociology* 22, no. 1 (March, 1999), 3–12.

PART IV

Key Concepts

CHAPTER 9

Private—Civic—Public

It's not business, it's personal!

—Billboard advertising a local bank

The billboard quoted above is a classic example of a common strategy used by those in power to confuse and control ordinary people. In actual fact, the bank doesn't *care* about individual clients. If you don't live up to your responsibilities to a bank you will find this out quite quickly, regardless of how nice the tellers and mortgage brokers have been in the past.

Organizers have generalized from examples like this, developing a critical distinction between "public" and "private" relationships. In the simplest sense, organizers argue, private relationships should be based on loyalty and love, while public ones should be grounded in respect, accountability, and self-interest.[1]

Your family and your close friends are supposed to love you no matter what (whether they do or not is a different issue). They are supposed to support and care about you despite your imperfections and mistakes. But beyond a limited collection of relationships, we increasingly encounter a world where we cannot expect this kind of safety. Politicians, used-car salesmen, agency administrators, bosses, and others performing institutional roles are not your friends, and when you forget this, you are likely to be misled.

In fact, the same person may act differently toward you depending on what role she is playing. For example, your boss may also be your friend. If you really mess up on the job she may need to fire you, even if you both try to remain friends outside of the workplace.

The following table gives a sense of the kinds of relationships that tend to fit into different categories:

PRIVATE Relationships	PUBLIC Relationships
Family	Politicians, Public Officials, Police
Close Friends	Teachers
Oneself	Bosses, Co-workers, Employees
	Strangers
	Bankers, Store Owners

People who have not internalized this distinction between public and private relationships are much easier for the powerful to manipulate and control. That's why understanding this distinction is so critical.

"Don't Call Me Mr. Jones"

Haley Grossman[2]

It was very funny. . . . One county official started off the meeting with, "Well, I just want you to treat me like family." At the end he was saying things like "Don't call me Mr. Jones. Call me Anthony."

So afterwards we had some really good discussions about why he was doing all that.

He's trying to confuse us between public and personal. We're here to try to get public business done and act professionally. He's here trying to make this personal because he doesn't want us to hold him accountable. He's hoping that he can confuse us and have us leave saying, "Aw, he's such a nice guy." And he was a very personable guy.

But [there is a real danger that] we'll get distracted . . . and we won't notice that he's double-talking us here and saying that he'll do one thing but really not.

Characteristics of Public and Private Relationships

In "private" spaces, people tend to encounter others who are mostly like themselves. Private relationships are often inherited—few people, for example, can choose their families. And they are relatively permanent. One might want to disown a sibling or a parent, for example, but we rarely do. Similarly, once we decide people are our "friends," we become much more likely to tolerate their imperfections (and to expect imperfections to be tolerated in ourselves). In private, we have the right to expect to be relatively safe in a range of different ways, to be able to speak honestly about our feelings and fears and needs.

In the public, we often encounter people who are very different from us. Political philosopher Hannah Arendt goes so far as to say that we are most fully human in the public realm because we deepen our humanity by acting with a broad diversity of others who are different from us. But if we disagree or have conflict with people in the public, we are much more likely to vote with our feet rather than try to work things out. If we are "stuck" with them (on the job or in politics, for example), our engagements with them are likely to be guarded, since public relationships are usually less safe than private ones.[3]

Part of the reason for this lack of safety is that public relationships are much more likely to be instrumental. In public we work with people because we have something we need to accomplish or deal with. As a result, these relationships can be quite fluid, with old acquaintances fading away while new ones emerge (although we may also work with some people that we have public relationships with for decades).

Participation in the public sphere can certainly be enjoyable for its own sake. Arendt reminded us that there is even a word for this—"public happiness"—something that was once considered as essential to a human life as food, shelter, friendships, and jobs. Today, however, we generally do not think about public happiness as a reason to enter public life.

The table below summarizes these key characteristics of public and private relationships:

PRIVATE	PUBLIC
Safe	Unsafe
Sameness	Diversity
Given/Permanent	Fluid/Temporary
Intimate	Guarded
Restricted to small number of intimates	Open to a large number of acquaintances
Exists for itself	Has a purpose

Putting on a Mask

I say that there is no "Mike Gecan, individual" in the public arena. That person doesn't exist. I don't think of myself that way. I don't believe that journalists, corporate leaders, or political figures relate and respond to the singular, wonderful me. No, they relate to me, to the extent that they do, often grudgingly, because they understand the "corporate me"—the "me" that has relationships with leaders.

—Michael Gecan, *Going Public*

One effective way to distinguish between public and private is to think of the public as a place where people take on "roles" or "wear masks." When people hang out with friends, they can at least imagine that they are just "being themselves." But when Marie, for example, enters the public space as a leader with Wider Opportunities for Women (WOW) she puts on her WOW mask. And those she encounters in that space are also wearing masks—politicians, agency directors, business owners, and the like.[4]

The point is not that Marie as an individual disappears entirely. As the political philosopher Hannah Arendt points out, one's voice always "sounds through" this public mask, each person acting out their role in their own unique way. Marie does not play her role in WOW the same way that other leaders do.[5]

When WOW criticizes people for their actions, then, it is not critiquing them as fathers or mothers or sisters or brothers—those aspects of the life of targets are irrelevant to their public responsibilities (although if someone's mother can be convinced to pressure her son in his public role, well, that's generally fair game). WOW confronts people whose *public* actions in their *public* roles have hurt the organization's constituency. So when a public official complains that she is a "nice person" and that nasty organizing groups shouldn't make her life difficult, she is simply trying to confuse the situation (and she knows it). She is trying inappropriately to take off her public mask even as she retains her public power. Let's put it another way: *if powerful public officials don't want to be criticized for their public actions, then they shouldn't take on public roles.* People in public, then, take on a particular kinds of dramatic "roles."

This is common to teachers and politicians and bosses and workers. In these contexts, to one extent or another, all of us present a particular kind of "face" to the world. When you are "playing" a teacher or a car salesman, you are not simply being your unique self. Instead you are using your particular skills and insights to play that role as best you can, given the specific demands of the moment. The point is not that one must necessarily be dishonest in public—in fact, persistent dishonesty can destroy public relationships even quicker than private ones.

PRIVATE	PUBLIC
Just be yourself	Play your role
Spontaneous	Planned

"You're Not a Friend!"

Harry Boyte[6]

Beatrice Cortez [the president of Communities Organized for Public Service (COPS), a faith-based community organizing group] frequently tells a story about her daughter to illustrate how children can quickly pick up the... [difference between public and private relationships]. During her tenure as president of the organization, Cortez had a COPS phone in her house. One day the mayor, Henry Cisneros—whom she had known for years—called up on the line.

"My daughter answered and at first didn't know who it was.
" 'Who should I say is calling?' she asked.
" Cisneros said, 'Tell her it's a special friend.'
"Then she recognized his voice," Cortez said.
"She said, 'On this line, you're not a friend, I know who you are. You're the mayor!'
"I told her, 'You've got that right, honey!' "

The Divergent Aims of Private and Public Relationships

The reasons we develop private and public relationships are quite different. In the private, we want to be accepted. We expect some level of loyalty, regardless of how problematic our actions may be at any moment. And we have a need to be liked or loved by our family and friends. In return, we are loyal ourselves. We often give without much expectation of getting anything in return. In private, we tend to trust other people, sometimes to a fault—we're not constantly watching our backs.

A key aspect of public relationships, in contrast, is *accountability*. In public, it's important to hold people accountable for doing what they said they would do. Because public relationships are based on self-interest instead of basic loyalty, there is a much greater chance that if you are not paying attention, someone you are dealing with in public will do something underhanded. In public we should expect to be held accountable for what we say or do, and hold others accountable in the same way.

Because public relationships are instrumental, what are most important to understand are the self-interests of the different people involved. What motivates us and others?

The table below summarizes the benefits and aims of public and private relationships:

Private Relationships	Public Relationships
Need to be liked	Call for respect
Expect loyalty	Expect to be held accountable
Altruistic self-giving	Quid pro quo/self-interest

Restaurant Intimacy

Waiters and waitresses know quite well the power of fake private relationships. In fact, there is clear evidence that patrons who are touched lightly during a meal will give a larger tip than those who are not. Of course, at a restaurant one is paying, in a sense, for a kind of manufactured intimacy. But much of the impact of the strategies used by waitstaff is quite invisible to patrons. Patrons "feel" more personally connected, and this activates their "private" tendencies.

The Dangers of Mixing Up Private and Public Relationships

You're looking for love
In all the wrong places.
        —Marc Almond, "Looking for Love in All the Wrong Places"

While we usually learn how to act in the private realm in our families, "most of us" Liners explains, "never really learn to accept the rules of the public arena. So we worry about whether people will like us. We refrain from criticizing what we know to be wrong because we apply the rules of our private relationships to the public realm." Because few of us were taught how to swim in the seas of power, we recoil from fostering conflict, or saying potentially rude things, or embarrassing other people. We try to treat others in the public like we would treat our friends. And we often respond in ways appropriate for the private realm if they offer to be friends. As the song notes, above, we "look for love in all the wrong places."

Today, this distinction between public and private is a key concept that organizers teach novices during trainings. They discuss how others often pull our strings by misappropriating the language of friendship. Public figures, organizers stress, are not your friends. In their public roles, they are not even each other's friends. For example, at home two married US senators will have a "private" relationship. But on the Senate floor their relationship will be "public." This is something that politicians and powerful people generally understand quite well. It's why very conservative and very liberal senators can say terrible things about each other's views on the airwaves and then go play an amiable game of golf. And the fact is that a personal relationship with and between the powerful can be useful tools in a range of ways as long as the individuals engaged understand when they are playing different roles. (Extreme political polarization can make this distinction between public and private relations difficult to maintain, however, something one can see in the American Senate and other spaces in U.S. politics today.)

When someone powerful starts treating you like a friend in the public arena, they are trying to manipulate you, *and they know it.* As Liners notes, "Politicians famously blur the line between public and private. That's what kissing babies is all about. It's why they like to be called Jimmy and Billy and Teddy. They want you to think of them as part of the family. (Then you would feel just awful if they lost their job—and you would hate to see them embarrassed, even if they did make a mistake.)" A car saleswoman who asks you to buy a car because it will get her a bonus—"help me out, here"—is playing on your lack of public sensibility. She is playing on your emotions. In fact, she may just be lying to you, something she probably wouldn't do with her mother or her husband. She knows it's just business. The truth is, she won't take it personally if you don't buy the car—how could she? She hardly knows you and you hardly know her. "We trust more than we should," Liners says, "then feel betrayed when others show no loyalty to us."

The conception of "private" and "public" in community organizing is designed to help people limit their responsibilities by distinguishing between public colleagues and intimate friends. One organizer noted, for example, that he used to try to treat everyone in his organization like they were friends. He ended up totally exhausting himself and actually damaged his relationships with people who really were his intimates—like his family. Learning to distinguish between "private" and "public" relationships helped him let go of relationships with people in his organization who weren't living up to their responsibilities. He was able to stop just being loyal and instead hold participants accountable, leaving more time to concentrate on leaders he could depend upon.

Private and Public and the Morality of Action

The public/private distinction also provides useful guidelines for what is an appropriate "public" action in community organizing. In general, people's authentically private lives should be off limits. An ethical organizing group would never target someone's children, for example. But this guideline can be tricky. Again, people will often try to use the shield of privacy to inappropriately relieve themselves of responsibility for their actions.

A recent effort to target a notorious slumlord with many inner-city properties provides a good example. Bad landlords rarely live in the area where their properties are rotting from disrepair. This one was no exception. She lived in the suburbs among well-groomed lawns and quiet streets, in what she believed was her purely private space. But CHANGE didn't agree. Leaders left leaflets with her suburban neighbors with pictures of her properties and a description of how her lack of upkeep was affecting residents and their neighborhoods. This forced the landlord to acknowledge her public actions to her neighbors—something that she would otherwise have liked to keep hidden. With this action, CHANGE was arguing that what she wished to keep private was actually public. Not surprisingly, this landlord quickly made a deal with CHANGE.

Another moment came during a fight between a coalition of CHANGE and other organizations and the local school board. The board president, who was opposing us, declared at a public meeting that anyone could come to his house any time they wanted. His door was always open for discussion. At the time Aaron raised the possibility that this opened him up to a very effective action where the coalition could come in force to his house and present its collective demands. From Aaron's perspective, the school board member had tried to use his offer as an example of how he was really a "personable" kind of guy, to resist our efforts. The visit to the school board member's house never happened, however. The board president had younger kids and there was legitimate disagreement about whether this would overstep ethical bounds.

While the public/private distinction can be a useful tool, then, in truth the world is too complex to be easily split. Many people you meet and interact with do not fall easily on one side or another. The role of a teacher is a good example. Teachers and students both have a set of public responsibilities and should be held accountable for whether they accomplish them. At the same time there are private aspects of the teacher–student relationship as well. To some extent, it is important for a teacher to be loyal to her students, and to balance accountability with a more personal kind of caring. This kind of complexity is especially important in what we call the "civic" realm.

"Outing" and the Right to Privacy

Rinku Sen[7]

There is an ongoing debate about whether using certain pieces of information constitutes a violation of a target's privacy.

Perhaps the most contentious issue arises in the fight for sexual liberation. On occasion someone with a secret history of homosexuality or cross-dressing, for example, emerges as an important target or as opposition in a sexual-rights campaign. Is it acceptable to out that person to expose his or her hypocrisy? Or to threaten exposure as a tactic?

There is a wide range of thought on this question. Certainly, the guarantee of privacy around nonabusive sexual behavior should be the cornerstone of a free society and not given up lightly. And exposing someone's sexual behavior might reinforce the message that it is immoral. However, if such people have the power to deny rights to others while protecting themselves, what of the rights of that larger group?

Ultimately an organization has to make such decisions on a case-by-case basis. My only caution is that revelation has far-reaching consequences and should not be done without wide agreement among members.

Between Private and Public: The Civic Realm

We all need a safe place to dream together how our world can be.
—Rosa Martha Zarate, organizer

Most aspects of life represent a complex admixture of both private and public components. There are few "purely" private or public spaces. Like all of the concepts we discuss in this book, at best distinctions between public and private provide what Harry Boyte calls "flexible guidelines for 'appropriate behavior' in different realms."

Organizers often downplay the messy overlap of these distinctions in the real world, however, laying out the public/private divide in quite absolute terms. Why? Their reasons are quite pragmatic, as usual. Most Americans—especially committed church members—are deeply programmed to treat everyone politely. So trainings for new organizing leaders intentionally leave little wiggle room for participants to start falling back into their old patterns.[8]

We believe, however, that the starkness of this distinction in a world in which such clarity is often hard to find can be confusing. For that reason, we complicate this dichotomy with what we call the "civic" realm, which we use to describe transitional spaces *between* the extremes of public and private. Sara Evans and Boyte discuss something quite similar that they call "free spaces." In simple terms, the "civic" is where we learn to transition *between* "private" and public roles. Some common characteristics of the civic include:

- It is somewhat but not completely safe.
- Members can generally but not entirely trust each other.
- It generally only includes people with some common cause or shared interest that holds them together.

Organizing groups are good examples of such civic spaces. They give participants opportunities to interact at different levels of pre - public performance. The relative safety of civic spaces allows participants to try out different ideas and ways of being; at the same time, different levels of risk introduce actors to the kinds of sanctions and problems these different actions can lead to. In civic spaces, people may not have to constantly watch each other to make sure everyone is doing what they should; yet a failure to hold others accountable for their actions can also to lead to the failure of any but the most deeply shared, communal efforts. Settings range from fairly informal brainstorming sessions to highly structured board meetings. Opportunities are also provided for practicing how to act when you emerge fully into the public realm to contest the actions of the opposition. Role plays, for example, allow leaders try out different ways of responding to powerful individuals—often played by an organizer who has wide experience with how the opposition is likely to think.[9]

After this kind of preparation, a leader is ready to step out of the civic and into the power realm of the public, leaving relative safety behind.

Community organizing groups are unusual in our society, however. We desperately need more civic spaces like these in America that can provide participants with skills for engaging in public action.

The Personal Is the Political

As we noted in Chapter 3, "the personal is the political" was a core tenet of the second-wave women's movement, a conviction that contemporary organizing is deeply indebted to. Too frequently the abstract ideal embraced by organizers is not met. Too often the private lacks safety and becomes a realm of oppression and violence. The idea that the personal is the political grew in part within what were called "consciousness-raising" groups, where women came together to discuss their lives and discovered commonalities of oppression that had previously been hidden, making them available as issues for public action. Carol Hanish emphasized in an important early essay on consciousness raising that "the reason I participate in these meetings is not to solve any personal problem. One of the first things we discover in these groups is that personal problems are political problems. There are no personal solutions at this time. There is only collective action for a collective solution."[10]

While the term "consciousness-raising" group was largely used to describe contexts mostly dominated by white, middle-class women, many people throughout history, including the low-income leaders of the Welfare Rights Movement have "carved out . . . social spaces insulated from control and surveillance from above" where they could "formulate patterns of resistance." These informal, generally transient spaces have always made up a core component of what we are calling the "civic" more generally.[11]

Through dialogue in civic spaces like these, women and others continue to work together, transforming their personal pain and challenges into shared public issues.[12]

Evolving Understandings of Public and Private

The specific meanings of "public" and "private" used in organizing, today, drew from earlier understandings which were adapted to serve the particular needs of the organizing context. As you read this book it is important to remember that all of the social concepts that we describe were similarly created for particular purposes at particular times, and they have continued to evolve over time to reflect new realities. As with "public" and "private," key questions to ask in the case of all the concepts we present in this book are: what does each help us to understand? and what important aspects of our world, society, or experiences may they also obscure?

Notes

1. Of course, "public" and "private" are constructed differently in different cultures. This model was developed for a generalized "American" context, but even here there are many different cultures. The organizing argument is that this particular model is especially useful in American politics. How it would work in different countries or in neighborhoods with very distinct cultural characteristics in the U.S. is something to explore in more detail.

2. Haley Grossman, cited in Kristin Layng Szakos and Joe Szakos, *We Make Change: Community Organizers Talk about What They Do—And Why,* 1st ed. (Nashville, TN: Vanderbilt University Press, 2007), 163.

3. In *Associations and Democracy* (Princeton, NJ: Princeton University Press, 2000) Mark E. Warren talks about the tension between "voice" and "exit" in the political realm. The often idealistic American ideal of public spaces where everyone comes together to engage with each other around common problems is hard to create because people are likely to "exit" such groups when they face conflict and disagreement.

4. The best and most comprehensive discussion of the relationship between roles (or masks) and the public can be found in Richard Sennett's *Fall of Public Man* (New York: Faber and Faber, 1977), chapter 2.

5. Hannah Arendt, *On Revolution* (New York: Viking Press, 1965), 106.

6. Harry Boyte, *CommonWealth: A Return to Citizen Politics* (New York: Free Press, 1989), 98.

7. Rinku Sen, *Stir It Up: Lessons in Community Organizing and Advocacy* (San Francisco, CA: Jossey-Bass, 2003).

8. Boyte, *Commonwealth,* 63.

9. Sara M. Evans and Harry Boyte, *Free Spaces: The Sources of Democratic Change in America* (New York: Harper & Row, 1986).

10. Carol Hanish, "The Personal Is the Political," in *Notes from the Second Year: Women's Liberation,* ed. Shulamith Firestone and Anne Koedt (New York: Radical Feminism, 1970), http://www.carolhanisch.org/CHwritings/PIP.html (accessed February 10, 2010).

11. James C. Scott, *Domination and the Arts of Resistance: Hidden Transcripts* (New Haven, CT: Yale University Press, 1990), 118–119.

12. One characteristic of the private and public distinction agreed upon by nearly all feminists is that these concepts and spaces are "gendered" in our society, the private having traditionally been a "women's" space and the public a space for and dominated by men.

CHAPTER 10

One-on-One Interviews

The single most important element in the interview is the interviewer's capacity to listen. Listening is an art, requiring discipline and training. [It is] the art of asking the right questions about children, about the neighborhood, about work, encouraging the person interviewed to speak about what he feels is important.

Often the person interviewed, in articulating his concerns, is for the first time making clear to himself what those concerns are.

—Industrial Areas Foundation, *Organizing for Family and Congregation*

During the first half of the twentieth century, American culture was often grounded in tight-knit ethnic and religious groups, with many associated clubs and organizations. Cities in the United States were rich in community. It was in this context that Saul Alinsky developed his strategy of organizing existing organizations. He searched out respected "native leaders" whose opinions and directions others were willing to follow. The core challenge Alinsky faced during these early years was the history of conflict between these groups, and much of his work involved breaking down barriers of suspicion enough to allow community networks and institutions to come together to address common challenges.

Near the end of his life, however, Alinsky saw that the mutualism of the 1940s and 1950s was dissolving. "To organize a community you must understand," he wrote in 1971, "that in a highly mobile, urbanized society the word 'community' " has taken on a new meaning In fact, Alinsky was no longer sure exactly "what the community is now." As a result, he began to explore ways to alter his approach to organizing, including creating block clubs that could provide the kind of local organization that was slipping away.[1]

Today, especially in our urban areas, the challenge of social isolation has only gotten worse. Violence, police intrusion, and deep poverty in inner-city areas have fostered distrust. Inner-city community organizations are usually directed by middle-class staff who don't live in the areas they serve. Even in more privileged areas, people have retreated into their houses behind manicured lawns.

Of course, many people today in all communities do belong to different organizations. But volunteering with Habitat for Humanity, participating in a 12-step group for some addiction, or joining a bowling league rarely produce robust collectives that can be brought together into a power organization. Other organized groups, like criminal gangs, may be robust but seem of limited relevance to organizing.

Churches represent the most important exception to this trend, but even here connections between congregation members can be tenuous. And churches that serve poor people tend to focus on "faith, not works."

Today, then, the key challenge facing those seeking power through solidarity is less about overcoming barriers between communities and more about helping to develop communities in the first place. Speaking about segregated central city neighborhoods, for example, Angela Davis notes that "it is extremely important not to assume that there are 'communities of color' out there fully formed, conscious of themselves, just waiting for vanguard organizers to mobilize them into action. . . . [W]e have to think about organizing as *producing* the communities, as generating community, as building communities of struggle."[2]

The fact that there are few formal civic organizations does not mean that poor areas are completely disorganized, however. Challenging conditions in many of these neighborhoods, for example, have generated cultures of avoidance. They exhibit patterns that Alinsky called "organized apathy," even if it looks different than it did during his heyday. Alinsky argued that "all organizing is reorganizing," and this is still the case even in areas that seem disorganized.

A central strategy that community organizers use to foster community in our new world of weaker communities is the one-on-one interview. It was developed by Edward Chambers, Ernesto Cortes, and other key organizers in the Industrial Areas Foundation (IAF) in the years after Alinsky's death. One-on-one interviews are a tool for rebuilding webs of relationships and trust. At the same time they help create organizations that are more democratic and responsive to members than older, mostly hierarchical and usually patriarchal ones.

A one-on-one has four aims. An interviewer seeks to

1. uncover self-interests,
2. develop a relationship,
3. evaluate leadership potential, and
4. recruit for the organization.

As we describe below, understanding people's self-interests allows leaders to see where they might fit into their organization. Furthermore, when leaders complete a large number of one-on-ones, this process helps them understand the kinds of issues their community is most likely to be concerned with. The relationships that one-on-ones develop provide a basis for collaboration and mutual respect, while laying a foundation for trust. They also give leaders permission to call upon respondents later on when they need support and participation during key moments of issue campaigns. Finally, one-on-ones provide opportunities to assess people's potential for leadership and to recruit them into the organization.

(1) Self-Interests and Stories

Those new to organizing are often uncomfortable with the field's focus on self-interest. "Social action shouldn't only focus on being selfish," they'll sometimes complain, "social justice comes from caring about the interests of *others*!" When newcomers say things like this, however, they show their lack of understanding about what organizers *mean* by self-interest.

In trainings, organizers often make a distinction between the following three kinds of motivations:

- Selfishness
- Self-interest
- Selflessness

Selfish people ask "what's in it for me?" They may get involved in organizing because they think a campaign could increase their property values, or because they want to feed their ego, or because they hope the reputation they gain through participation may attract more customers. Selfishness is a very problematic motivation from the perspective of organizing. Those focused only on their own needs and desires are not well equipped to strategize about how to support the community as a whole. And if your only reason for participating is what *you* get out of it, you are unlikely to stick around when not much is happening, are likely to balk at doing the everyday grunt work involved in keeping an organization strong, and will probably drop out when the going gets rough.

Selfless people might seem more useful. But the problem with selfless folks is that they don't really know who they are or what they really care about. They are the kind of people who, when asked what movie you want to see, say "whatever you want, dear." After a while this gets kind of annoying. A selfless person is there to serve, not to act, not to assert themselves in the public sphere. Perhaps most problematic, selflessness is a pretty weak motivation when it comes to the long term. After a while, for most people, doing for others and never for oneself is quite draining. Selfless people are likely to come to a couple of meetings because they feel it is something they *should* be doing, but then fade out. And if a person doesn't know what they care about, what is to keep them in *your* organization rather than someone else's? In the end, then, like the selfish, the selfless aren't really that reliable.

If self-interest isn't selfishness, and it isn't selflessness, what is it?

Self-interests encompass all of those aspects of people that motivate them to act. As Michael Jacoby Brown argues, from an organizing perspective, "self-interest includes our whole selves, our stories and memories and the relationships we have with close friends and family. It involves all that makes us tick and why." Another term that organizers use for self-interest is "passion." When you understand someone's self-interests, you know what makes them angry, what elicits their deep sympathy, and what is likely to generate commitment over the long term. A core self-interest is not simply about what someone wants to get, but about "who" someone is or wants to be.[3]

It would be more straightforward (if less interesting) if we could just go up to people and ask them what their self-interests are. But few of us have been asked to really think about our vision of ourselves as citizens, and even fewer have ever learned much about how power operates in the public world. So most of us have trouble articulating what our self-interests are.

As a result, we have to get at people's self-interests in a more roundabout way. We need to have a broader conversation, listening to the stories they tell about important moments in their lives and watching for the issues that really seem to get them engaged. The kinds of personal issues and feelings that generate passions relevant to organizing are as diverse as are people in the world.

- If your sister was killed by a drunk driver, you may be interested in participating in campaigns to help addicts or toughen DUI penalties.
- If you have spent years trying to get better services for your disabled child, issues related to improving education may really get you excited.

- If you have always felt powerless, the opportunity to simply participate in anything that will let you feel like you can make a positive change in the world may really engage you.
- If you walk by children playing at a local homeless shelter every day after work, you may find you have developed a deep concern for the plight of poor families.

The Complexity of Real Lives

Michael Gecan[4]

The trouble with many of us, and with our culture as a whole, is that we don't take the time to "relate," to connect publicly and formally but meaningfully with others. . . . We don't take the time to meet one to one with others, to hear their interests and dreams and fears, to understand *why* people do what they do or don't do what they don't do. . . .

When you develop the habit of individual meetings, you stop thinking of people as "the poor" or "the rich" or "the establishment" or even "the enemy." You don't size up another person to see if you can make a sale. . . .

No, you sit and listen, you probe and challenge. You try to gauge whether or not you and the other can build the kind of public relationship that is mutual and respectful and capable of withstanding the tension that all healthy relating tends to generate over time. . . .

Done well, individual meetings allow people to break out of the kinds of relational ruts that limit us all. The person who walks in the door of the congregation [or the organization] is no longer just a congregant or a client. And the person who works on the parish staff ceases being just a one-dimensional provider.

We see more of the many facets of people who have come to think of themselves as invisible or voiceless not just because the powers that be fail to see them and hear them, but because those who claim to care about their concerns also fail to relate to them and with them. And they see more facets of you. . . .

Our democracy was founded and forged by women and men who were profoundly relational. It may be that the very habit of building public relationships is part of the human constitution of vital democracy.

(2) Creating a Relationship

Why are "relationships" so important to effective power organizing?
One of the key mottos of organizing is the following:

> People don't come to a meeting because they saw a flyer. People come to a meeting because someone they know invited them.

This is a powerful truth of human motivation. In the most basic sense, it is much easier to go to a new place with new people if there is someone there that you "know." Being invited also makes a person feel more important—it seems like it actually matters if they show up or not. Finally, you can't be accountable to a flyer or a public service announcement. You can only be accountable to another human being. If someone calls you up and invites you and you say yes, then you are accountable to that person for your actions. (And it helps if you remind people of these commitments. Fred Ross even said that "reminding is the essence of organizing.")[5]

Second, people feel part of organizations not only because they care in the abstract about issues, but also because they feel connected to the individuals in that organization. Within an organizing group, leaders do one-on-ones among themselves to strengthen their ties and help them understand the underlying motivations of the people around the table. The more relationships you have with people in an organization, the more you will feel a part of it and personally responsible for its success or failure.

Third, when you have a relationship with someone, you gain permission to engage with them around their self-interests or "passions." If a random person calls you up and says "I know your brother is in jail and I know you care about sentencing laws, so why don't you come to our rally," you might even be offended. But it's appropriate for someone who has had a personal conversation with you, and to whom you have made some commitment, however small, to at least call you up and talk with you.

Fourth, once you do a significant number of one-on-ones, the group you are a part of starts seeming less like an abstract collective and more like what it is, a collection of unique individuals drawn together for a range of diverse reasons and convictions. You start to understand your organization's challenges and internal tensions in more complex terms.

As someone once said to Aaron:

It's not the idea, it's the people.

This is a pretty profound statement, when you think about it. No matter how great your idea is, how "right" you are, you won't get anywhere if you can't get other people together around it. If you don't know your "people," then you won't be able to understand which ideas will and won't "go," or how to get people to understand the "truth" of ideas you hold dear.

Finally, as we discuss below, doing one-on-ones helps you understand what your "constituency" cares about. Through the one-on-one process, you learn what issues will really draw people together in collective action. One-on-ones are much more effective than surveys (which organizing groups also do) because one-on-ones push people to go beyond their surface or knee-jerk reactions to what motivates them at the core.

The capacity of the one-on-one to create significant relationships can be experienced even in fairly artificial contexts. In our classes, we always have students do one-on-ones with each other. They play out each step, making an appointment and then representing themselves as members of an organization during the interview. When we ask whether they feel like they gained a relationship with each other, most of them say they were surprised at how connected they now felt with their partner. In fact, in Aaron's last class he had a very quiet group. Early in the semester, when he came into the room almost no one was talking with each other. In the class period after they completed their one-on-ones, everyone was chatting with each other so much it was hard to shut them up. The one-on-ones altered the culture of the classroom. Students were actually a little upset that he hadn't required them to interview each other earlier.

(3) Judge Leadership Potential, and (4) Recruit

Relational meetings are NOT an indiscriminate search for information. You're looking for something very specific—talent, passion, vision, and energy. . . . You don't just meet with anyone. You're looking for leaders—people with a following; people who can relate well to others; people who have passion rooted in anger (cold anger, not rage); people who will stand for the whole, not just their particular issue or their race or ethnic group.

—Fair Immigration Reform "10 Rules for One-on-Ones/Relational Meetings"

The quote, above, is a classic statement describing how organizers tend to view the recruitment aspect of one-on-ones. As we note in the next chapter, our (Aaron and Marie's) vision of leadership tends to be broader than standard statements like this one tend to acknowledge. Nonetheless, with limited time you have to be selective about who you will interview. You are going to seek out people who, at least on the surface, seem to have the potential for contributing in some way to your organization, have knowledge that is important for the organization to know, or are in a position that makes them important to some campaign you're engaged in.

If you decide an interviewee is someone you want to recruit, you should conclude your interview with what people in the fund-raising biz call an "ask." You want to get recruits involved as quickly as possible. The ask could be an invitation to a meeting or an action, or even a request for help in some basic task the organization needs to complete ("can you come help us stuff envelopes on Thursday night?"). It is through participation, which involves becoming comfortable with other members and the culture of the organization, that people become reliable participants and leaders.

At the same time, you want to evaluate whether this person is worth the "trouble" of recruiting and drawing in to your organization. Are they passionate enough about anything to keep them engaged over the long term? Is this someone who seems reliable? Is this someone who is likely to be disruptive in meetings? Remember that "public" relationships are, in the ideal, driven by self-interest, the need for respect, and a willingness to hold others accountable and to be held accountable oneself. Some people may be useful to call on periodically for participation in an action, but may not fit well as a consistent leader within the organization.

Be careful about making such decisions too quickly, however. It is really impossible to know for certain how someone will act in an organization unless you have actually worked with them. Characteristics like race and gender can also bias our perspectives without us even knowing it. Sometimes the people who look great turn out to be "terrible," and the people who look terrible turn out to be great (although often in ways you may not have predicted before). And, finally, the fact that someone does not seem likely to "fit" well with your organizational culture may say as much about your organization as it does about them. It is only by welcoming diversity that an organizing group will be able to generate the kind of collective solidarity necessary to attain significant power.

The Four Goals of One-on-Ones: A Recap

1. Uncover self-interests.
2. Develop a relationship.
3. Evaluate potential for leadership.
4. Recruit for the organization.

Personal but Public

Relational meetings are the glue that brings diverse collectives together and allows them to embrace the tension of living in-between the two worlds [of public and private].

—Edward Chambers, *Roots for Radicals*

A one-on-one interview is a "public" but "personal" interview with another individual.

The interview is personal in the sense that it often gets into quite intimate stories about someone's life. Of course, it is always up to the person being interviewed what they are willing to share. But people in our society are rarely asked to talk about personal issues they care about. We are seldom asked to share our stories, and are often quite willing to do so when asked. As an anthropologist once said at one of David Liners' trainings, "Most people have a lot more to say than other people are willing to listen to."

Regardless of how personal it may get, however, a one-on-one interview remains public. As an interviewer, your goal is not to generate an intimate friendship (although this may also be an eventual result). Instead, you are trying to link this person into a larger group, giving them and the organization more power to make the kinds of changes they would very much like to see in society. You seek a "public," not a "private" relationship with this person.

One-on-ones are generally set up in a relatively formal manner. You don't just start chatting with someone without warning. Instead, you ask someone to meet you in a particular place at a particular time so that you can talk with them, get to know them, and help them understand your organization. This formality is important because it sets the stage for what is going on. From the beginning the person knows that you are approaching them in the *role* of a leader or organizer and not as a private individual who just wants to chat.

Organizers generally argue, not surprisingly, that when conducted in good faith one-on-ones are not designed to manipulate people. If an organization is going to be strong for the long term, it doesn't have time to constantly pressure people to participate. From a purely pragmatic standpoint, people who are not willing to be held accountable, who are not reliable over time, are simply not going to be good leaders. Again, the "public" and "private" distinction is crucial, here. Yes, organizers and leaders try to twist people's arms in order to get them to significant actions where numbers are critical. To this extent they can be used to manipulate. But more than this organizers and leaders don't have time to do.

Conducting an Effective One-on-One Interview

While a one-on-one is an interview, it should feel more like a conversation. The interview should be fairly informal. At points you may feel it is helpful to share some of your own experiences, although you should make sure the conversation stays focused on the respondent (about 80/20 is a common rule of thumb).

You shouldn't take notes while you are chatting, but once the interview is over and you are back in your car or walking home, you should pull out your little notebook (Don't have one? Get one.) and jot down the important points that came up. You don't want to get mixed up about who said what after you've done a lot of one-on-ones.

A common guideline is to use open-ended instead of closed-ended questions. An open-ended question is designed to elicit a story or an explanation, while a closed-ended question can be satisfied with a "yes" or "no," or some discrete piece of information. "How old are you?" or "Did you like the public meeting" are closed-ended questions. Closed-ended questions actually tend to *stop* the conversation. Your respondent might answer, say, "44 years old" or "yes." Then she will likely wait politely for another question, interrupting the flow of the dialogue.

Unlike closed-ended questions, open-ended questions, like "how do you think unemployment is affecting your community?" or "what was it like to move to Milwaukee from the South?" draw out stories instead of shutting them down. But open-ended questions, alone, aren't enough to make a good conversational interview. If you just ask someone a bunch of premade open-ended questions, you aren't going to have much of a conversation. *You* will end up driving the discussion instead of developing a dialogic partnership. Instead of coming to listen to what your partner wants to say, you will have determined what the important topics are ahead of time.

It is entirely appropriate, however, to ask new open-ended questions when the flow of the conversation opens a space to do so. For example, if someone has children but this issue doesn't come up naturally in the conversation, you may want to ask them "how did it change your life to be a parent?" You may discover that, once prompted, children's health or something of the sort is a key passion of theirs. More generally (as the Fair Immigration Reform group's one-on-one guidelines note), "when probing, the most radical thing you can do is ask the person 'Why?' 'Why teach?' 'Why do you do social justice work?' . . . You must be prepared to interrupt with brief, tight questions like these."[6]

Seek to be fully present and attentive with your interviewee. This might be more difficult to do than you imagine! Your mind might wander, or you might need to fight the urge to jump in and start sharing your own anecdotes.

Finally, organizers generally recommend that one-on-ones last no more than 30–45 minutes. It's hard to sustain a real connection for longer than that. You can always set another meeting with them if you want. And limiting the time you spend on each interview will let you do more one-on-ones. It's better to leave people wanting more than to wear them out ("I'm not going to do that again . . . "). You can tell them you have to get to your next appointment.

Why One-on-One?

Sometimes people ask why organizers conduct relational interviews with one person at a time. It seems pretty inefficient. Why not just meet with people in groups?

In fact, the "house meeting" process, developed by Fred Ross, is a central tool used by community organizers, especially in areas without strong existing organizations. House meetings allow people in a community to come together and talk about their common concerns. They start to build spaces where what James Scott calls "hidden transcripts of resistance" can slowly be developed. House meetings can provide the basis for the development of a larger organization, when organizers tie together the different communities created in different meetings.[7]

When you see people operate in a group, you learn very different things about their capacities than you do one to one. But only face-to-face engagement will give you an opportunity to truly begin to develop a relational bond. Further, as Edward Chambers notes, stories that "reveal the underpinnings of someone's public action or inaction . . . don't rest on the surface to be picked up in casual chatter. Only concerted and intentional encounters will bring them to light."[8]

By creating webs of connection and respect between core leaders and less active members of the organization, organizations increasingly gain capacity to mobilize members for action. In many current neo-Alinsky organizing groups, people become leaders not because they are elected to positions, but because they have a large number of relationships they can draw on, a large number of people who will respond when called upon.

(Note that only interviewing the most prominent members of an organization won't give you the results you need. The "usual suspects" are often already buried in other volunteer work and may not have time to actually do any work when you need them.)

Using One-on-Ones to Choose Issues and Frame a Campaign

Will our people really give a damn about that?
—Gale Cincotta, *Women Activists: Challenging the Abuse of Power*

Imagine a group of 10 leaders coming together in a church basement to try to figure out which of the many community challenges their congregation of 1,000 members should engage with. By themselves, they don't really represent the congregation very well. If they just decide on an issue to pursue based on their own preferences, then it may turn out that few of the rest of their fellows will really commit to it. While you can try to educate others about the importance of one problem or another, in the end you can't *make* them participate. Ultimately, you will gain long-term commitment only when they can link the issue to core aspects of their personal story, to their self-interests and passions.

But what if each of these 10 leaders has completed 10 one-on-one interviews with congregation members? Together, then, they have some sense of what 10 percent of the congregation cares about.

As part of an "issue-cutting" session, discussed in Chapter 13, an organizer will often take these leaders through an exercise where each reports on the different passions that came up in his or her interviews. The organizer or one of the leaders will place similar self-interests near each other on a chalkboard or piece of newsprint. After this exercise, leaders can often stand back and see the clusters of interest areas emerging.

This exercise requires leaders to let go to some extent of the concerns that really engage *them*. If your pet problem doesn't arise in the discussion, then you may need to go to some other group if you want to organize around it.

Leaders in this position must take on aspects of an *organizer's* role. The job of an organizer is to organize people to act for the concrete changes *they* want, as long as they fit within the ethical framework of values of the organization. An organizer, in the ideal, is not supposed to care about the specifics of an issue. The organizer's job is to help people develop *power* as an organization around multiple issues, whatever these issues might be. The passion that drives a classic organizer usually doesn't emerge out of a specific issue area, but from broader concerns about the powerlessness of so many people in America today.

Again, don't overdo it. Choosing an issue is a complex balancing act. No issue is perfect. Too much democracy can kill an organization with limited resources as quickly as too little. Sitting around forever and chatting and getting everyone's unique perspective on everything can lead an organization to fall apart because it never *does* anything.

Barack Obama: A Genius for Listening

James T. Kloppenberg[9]

Trying to mobilize a group of fifty people, a novice [organizer] will elicit responses from a handful, then immediately transform their stray comments into his or her own statement of priorities and strategies. The group responds, not surprisingly, by rejecting the organizer's recommendations

By contrast, a master takes the time to listen to many comments, rephrases questions, and waits until the individuals in the group begin to see for themselves what they have in common. A skilled organizer then patiently allows the animating principles and the plan of action to emerge from the group itself.

That strategy obviously takes more time. It also takes more intelligence, both analytical and emotional. Groups can tell when they are being manipulated, and they know when they are being heard.

According to [organizer Mike Kruglik, when Barack Obama was an organizer in Chicago he] . . . showed an exceptional willingness to listen to what people were saying. He did not rush from their concerns to his. He did not shift the focus from one issue to another until they were ready . . . .

How did Obama, lacking any experience as an organizer, learn the ropes so fast? In [organizer Greg] Galuzzo's words, "nobody teaches a jazz musician jazz. This man was gifted."

Notes

1. Saul Alinsky, *Rules for Radicals* (New York: Vintage, 1971), 120, 184–185.
2. Cited in, "Incite! Women of Color against Violence," *The Revolution Will Not Be Funded: Beyond the Non-profit Industrial Complex* (Cambridge, MA: South End Press, 2007), 161.
3. Michael Jacoby Brown, *Building Powerful Community Organizations: A Personal Guide to Creating Groups That Can Solve Problems and Change the World* (Arlington, MA: Long Haul Press, 2006), 200.
4. Michael Gecan, *Going Public* (Boston, MA: Beacon Press, 2002), 21, 24–25, 31–32.
5. Fred Ross Sr., *Axioms for Organizers* (San Francisco, CA: Neighbor to Neighbor Education Fund, 1989), 2.
6. Fair Immigration Reform Movement, "10 Rules for One-on-Ones/Relational Meetings," http://www.fairimmigration.org/learn/black-brown–beyond/bbb-10-rules-for-one-on-ones.html, accessed September 1, 2010. Edward T. D. Chambers and Michael A. Cowan, *Roots for Radicals: Organizing for Power, Action, and Justice* (New York: Continuum, 2003), 50.
7. James C. Scott, *Domination and the Arts of Resistance: Hidden Transcripts* (New Haven, CT: Yale University Press, 1990).
8. Chambers and Cowan, *Roots for Radicals,* 51.
9. James T. Kloppenberg, *Reading Obama: Dreams, Hope, and the American Political Tradition* (Princeton, NJ: Princeton University Press, 2010), 28–29.

CHAPTER 11

Leadership

Organizers build community by developing leadership. They help leaders enhance their skills, articulate their values, and formulate their commitments, and then they work to develop a relationship of mutual responsibility and accountability between a constituency and its leaders.

—Marshall Ganz, "Organizing"

The central job of an organizer is to develop leaders. Let us say that again: *the central job of an organizer is to develop leaders.* In standard forms of community organizing, organizers are not themselves leaders. Organizers provide the institutional supports—training, provocation, ideas for tactics, advice during negotiations, and more—that help leaders to succeed. But indigenous leaders are the ones who make the final decisions and who, given limited funding for staff, do most of the actual work of the organization.

In this section we explore the idea of "leadership" in community organizing. In general, we embrace a broad and inclusive vision of who counts as a "leader." And we touch on some of the tensions and contradictions that inevitably face organizers and leaders in community organizing.

Leadership and Democracy

Visions of egalitarian democracy are always in tension with conceptions of strong leadership. In fact, "fear of leadership is a basic justification for democratic forms of government." But the truth is that any effort to foster effective democracy without leaders "is a conspicuous distortion of historical experience." As Matthew Trachman notes, while "skepticism toward leadership" may safeguard groups "against the dependence of hero worship, it also leaves them ill-equipped to understand the pervasiveness of leadership in American life. More important, it impedes any effort to develop forms of leadership that might foster a more democratic politics in America."[1]

Alinsky had no interest in utopian ideas about a world without strong leaders. He was deeply supportive of democracy, but argued that democracy must find a way to integrate leadership, not denigrate it. In a mass power organization made up of incredibly busy, sometimes desperately struggling people, it is realistic to expect only a small percentage of members to participate on a regular basis. From the perspective of community organizing, then, building a strong and authentic leadership is critical. This is why *finding, nurturing, and training new leaders is the central task of a community organizer.*

What Makes an Effective Leader in Community Organizing?

Books on community organizing tend to describe "good" leaders in two ways. First, they argue that leaders are people who "have followers." Then they give a list of characteristics and skills that good leaders in organizing groups generally have.

Leaders Have Followers

Real leaders, community organizers often emphasize, have *followers*. For example, the writers of the widely used Midwest Academy organizing textbook state that "the importance of understanding that leaders have followers can't be overemphasized.... People who can motivate and move others are basically in tune with the community or constituency.... A person who comes to every meeting and has a strong opinion on every subject but who never can bring another individual is likely to be out of sync with the community."[2]

If leaders are those who have followers, then leader training in organizing should focus, at least in part, on strategies that help people gain followers. This is why, in many community organizing groups, the first practical skill new members learn is how to conduct one-on-one interviews. The one-on-one process is designed to help leaders generate new relationships and secure understandings of the motivations of each person interviewed. When you have a relationship with someone, they are much more willing to respond when you contact them about an opportunity to participate. And once you understand people's passions and desires, you are in a much better position to understand which issues and activities they are most likely to be willing to come out for.

A leader who has conducted many one-on-ones develops relationships with a broad group of people that she can turn out for actions. An action related to educational reform? She can target those who really care about that issue and she knows them well enough that they will be less resistant when she calls them up and challenges them to participate. A campaign to improve pay for foster parents? The same leader knows a different, perhaps overlapping group of people for whom child abuse is a central issue. Thus, in the parlance of community organizing, she has "followers."

More broadly, a group of leaders who has completed a large number of one-on-ones has a good sense of the kinds of issues their communities are most interested in, and this knowledge guides their selection of new campaigns. The one-on-one process roots leaders in the hopes and dreams of their constituents and allows them to bring these with them into their dialogues with other leaders.

The Characteristics and Skills of a Good Leader

Along with the requirement that a leader have followers, organizing books generally give a fairly long list of the characteristics and skills a good leader should have. The Midwest Academy textbook, for example, states that good leaders exhibit

- commitment,
- honesty,
- positive outlook,
- confidence/self-assurance,
- trust in people, and
- mistrust of unaccountable institutions.

The same authors argue that key leadership skills in organizing include

- listening,
- diplomacy,
- recruitment,
- personal organization, and
- goal setting.

We don't know about you, but for us reading this list is a bit overwhelming. Each of us is confident in some of the areas listed, but others point to areas that we are not sure we will ever adequately exhibit. Aaron, for example, is not always the best listener. As much as he tries, he often gets impatient with what feels like too much "process." Marie loves group process, but probably gets low marks on personal organization if the condition of her desk and filing cabinets are any indication.

Of course, the Midwest Academy authors understand that everyone brings different capabilities with them to organizing. This list is meant to represent a set of aspirations. And certainly it is useful to have a broad sense of the different components of leadership that are important in organizing.

At the same time, however, we worry that this way of framing effective leadership often makes people feel inadequate. Inadvertently, it tends to focus people on what they lack, not on what they are most equipped to contribute. At the same time, we also worry that this list perpetuates a traditional and somewhat exclusive view of what a good leader is.

Complicating Leadership

On "leadership" day in Aaron's class, the first thing students do is push all the tables and chairs against the walls. Then they start to separate themselves from each other based on leadership characteristics.

First, in one direction, students stand in a line that runs from those who see themselves as "front of the room" leaders to those who hate speaking in public. Then, they move sideways based on how they see themselves more or less as "salespersons." Finally, from those close to them at this point, the "orderly," "anal" people and the "flexible," "messy" people separate themselves in small groups.

It ends up looking kind of like the picture below:

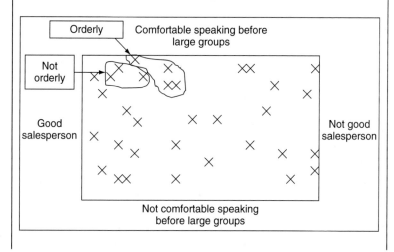

At this point each group has a discussion and writes down the pluses and minuses of their group as leaders.

There is nothing magical about the criteria Aaron uses. Another set would probably work as well. And the groups that result are not homogeneous—usually a few have trouble coming up with a common vision of themselves as leaders. But most of the groups can lay out a pretty detailed description of their leadership styles.

Here are a couple of the leadership types that emerged in previous classes:

The "Loud" Leaders

The "front of the room"/"good salesperson" groups generally present first. Their members are often quite loud, cracking jokes as they talk about how they are good at getting people engaged and getting decisions made, although they usually acknowledge that they sometimes talk over others. Their self-confidence is on display.

The "Quiet" Leaders

The presentations from the "back of the room" groups are, not surprisingly, much more restrained and quieter. Members often state that this was a challenging exercise for them, since they never really thought of themselves as leaders before. Some groups in the "orderly"/"back of the room" groups tell their peers how they are the ones who often actually get things done in groups. They make sure the materials are ready, get rooms scheduled, etc. And presenters from the "salesperson"/"back of the room" corner speak about how they talk one on one with different members, making sure things stay on track.

Students on the "quiet" side of the room usually reveal how much they can resent the way students on the "loud" side often talk over and ignore them. The "quiet" groups talk about how their contributions often seem unappreciated or ignored. What the "quiet" people tell us is that they are interested in helping and participating and leading, in their own ways. When they aren't respected, they often leave.

Learning to Value Themselves and Others

The "quiet" students are, sometimes for the first time, able to voice the ways they really *are* leaders—describing how they often get things done, support action in the background, strengthen a group's web of relationships, and more. If they aren't given recognition and if their ideas aren't acknowledged, they tell the "front of the room" types, then they will leave, and the loud leaders will be left talking to each other.

The "front of the room" groups end up somewhat chastened by this experience—although they generally have too much self-confidence to be bothered that much—as they hear about what other less charismatic folks think about them. Aaron emphasizes that the "loud" students do have much to contribute, and leavens the exercise with humor (assigning himself to the "loud" group, for example). But he and the "quiet" students help the "loud" students see how their easy assumption of roles in the spotlight can shut others down. In fact, a key discovery in this exercise is how much of a "problem" those who have the characteristics *traditionally* assigned to leaders can be to a group if they aren't well controlled.

After this discussion, the dynamics of Aaron's course often change. The "quiet" students are usually more willing to participate, often with the support of other quiet students. The "loud" students are somewhat more conscious of the ways they can shut others down.

A More Inclusive Approach to Leadership

80% of success is showing up.

—Woody Allen

If the central problem for community organizing groups is finding enough leaders, then it makes sense to frame leadership as widely as is possible to capture as many potentially useful people as you can. Openness to a range of personalities and skill sets also sets a tone for the rest of the organization. It models the idea that everyone has some capacity for democratic citizenship. It is certainly true that there are people whose individual foibles can actually harm an organization: they may talk too much and dominate conversations, or they may be unrelentingly negative, or they may develop destructive relationships with other members. Most of the time, however, a good organizer in collaboration with a good senior leadership team can find ways to leverage most people's individual skills and capacities.

In 1974, Richard Rothstein wrote that "members of real organizations have marriages or affairs, jobs and children; and problems with each. They may join an organization because, in the long run it *might* alleviate some of those problems, but in the meantime those problems occupy most of their time and energy. In real organizations, leaders are not just those with the best policy and action proposals (although that helps) but often those who are more willing and able than most to ignore their everyday lives."[3]

While Rothstein made a good point, his blunt call for leaders to ignore their lives illustrates a problem with many early organizing efforts. Today, good organizers understand that they need to support the participation of many leaders by meeting at times least likely to conflict with work or family obligations, providing on-site child care, refreshments, and so on. Good organizers assume that a person's self-interest drives their engagement, and this is likely to be based on his or her personal life.

In the end, an organization will be most successful when it makes the most of those it has, *of who actually shows up*—the people who come to meetings on a reliable basis. Many successful organizing groups shift the question from "who is a leader?" to "what kind of a leader can each person be?" They focus on what people do *well* instead of what they are less skilled at. Different people can bring different capabilities to the table: some may be able to write well, or do research, or cook, or do accounting. These are potential resources that no organizing group can afford to lose.

Organizations like these still encourage people to conduct one-on-ones. But their relatively flexible stance on leadership also accepts that some people aren't that social. Some leaders are unlikely to do many one-on-one interviews.

There is a real danger with this inclusive approach to leadership, however. If you have too many leaders who have not done sufficient one-on-ones, or who are not otherwise rooted in the organization's key constituencies, your leadership teams can become disconnected from the desires and beliefs of those the organization is supposed to serve and mobilize. Ultimately, leaders' relationships with their constituencies are what justify their assertions that they represent the voice of the community. A group without these connections really becomes an "advocate," speaking *for* a community instead of authentically representing a community's perspective.

Many Leaders, Not Few

Nicholas von Hoffman[4]

A big organization demands a variety of leadership talents:

- money raising leadership,
- oratorical leadership,

- tactical leadership,
- leadership for routine,
- leadership that can measure community sentiment,
- [leadership] that knows when to move and when to stay put . . .
- [And, we would add, leadership with a deep capacity to develop relationships with others.]

It is just unrealistic to expect a big organization to produce more than a few all-purpose leaders who can perform most of the various leadership tasks exceptionally well.

The Importance of a Leadership *Team*

You never know what is going to happen when you start organizing. Alinsky used to say that "the action is in the reaction." You act collectively to get a target to react—but you cannot control *how* it will react. A single charismatic leader, or even a small group of homogeneous leaders, may not be able to generate the kind of ongoing creativity necessary to respond to the unpredictable realities of the political world.

In his book on Cesar Chavez and the United Farm Workers (UFW) union's fight against grape growers in the 1960s, for example, Marshall Ganz argues that the union's leadership diversity was a key asset in its fight against grape growers and other unions. The different perspectives of many different leaders gave the UFW "access to [a range of] information, diverse networks, and tactical experience" as well as different "repertoires" of collective action drawn from union, "community, electoral, and issue organizing" traditions.[5]

A diverse group of leaders can also access different constituencies. In the UFW, for example, leaders from many different walks of life were able to draw religious congregations, college students, members of sympathetic unions, and participants in urban movements, like the militant Brown Berets, from across the state and even the nation. As a result, the UFW was not dependent only on embattled and impoverished farm workers. This broad constituency meant they were much more difficult to intimidate or defeat.

Finally, an enormous number of tasks need to be completed amidst any ongoing community organizing effort. Campaigns need to be guided and supported, fund-raising must continue, and core administrative tasks have to be addressed. If only a few people are responsible for getting these done, an organization is likely to face burnout. It may not be able to sustain action over the long term.

The Complexity of the "Iron Rule": "Do Not Do for Others What They Can Do for Themselves"

[Working in a] manical frenzy [does not] inspire people to get involved. It inspires them to see the maniac and say, oh good, you do the work for me, and see you later.

—Ellen Bravo, *Stir it Up!*

Doing It "For" People—If you think you can do it *for* people, you've stopped understanding what it means to be an organizer

Be Ready—A good organizer delegates responsibility, but is always ready to jump in and do the job himself if necessary.

—Fred Ross, *Axioms for Organizers*

Alinsky's "iron rule," "do not do for others what they can do for themselves," is quite simple in formulation, but can be quite challenging to put into practice. It is often difficult to know ahead of time what people can "do for themselves." Organizers and senior leaders are always in an experimental mode, constantly feeling out what different people can and cannot be depended upon to accomplish. They must struggle with the twin dangers of either doing too much for people and disempowering them, or depending too much on those who cannot or will not complete a critical task, putting the success of the entire group in danger.

There is a counterintuitive aspect of the iron rule that we will return to in Chapter 14 when we discuss effective tactics and strategies. A task that involves more people is generally better than one that involves only a few, even if it could be accomplished by a few. You want to keep your leaders involved in the work of the organization. If you do not, they are likely to find other activities to take up their time, and may be unavailable during critical direct actions.

It is the job of organizers and senior leaders to constantly push members into positions where they are "stretched," where they can gain increasing confidence in their ability to accomplish tasks they may not have originally thought they would be able to manage.

- The quiet youth minister learns that he can, in fact, confront a bank president in public.
- The unassuming househusband learns that an ability to organize a household can develop into the capacity to successfully coordinate a large public meeting.
- The high school dropout learns that she can present research, understand and present complex data about lead poisoning, and answer difficult questions in front of top city administrators.

In all of these cases, organizers and other leaders must have faith, even in the face of failure, in the capacity of ordinary people to surprise themselves (and others) as public citizens.

They Ain't Doing for Themselves

Ernesto Cortes, **Dry Bones Rattling**[6]

[At a meeting with a bank president to get him to pressure the mayor to support Cortes' organization]

My leaders freeze, and they don't do anything. I believe in the Iron Rule of organizing: never do anything for anybody they ain't doing for themselves. *But they ain't doing for themselves!* They're collapsing; they're folding. Our people are downstairs waiting with no instruction, no word and they don't know what to do.

I decide I've got to do something, so 1 move my chair over to Mr. Frost, and he's got a blood vessel that's exposed, and I focus on it and I look at it. I just keep moving. He moves away, and I move closer with the chair.

Then finally he says something, and I say, "Mr. Frost, that's a bunch of balderdash. You're the most arrogant man I've ever met." . . .

We have a priest there and Mr. Frost says, "Father, you better teach your people some manners and some values."

And finally the priest says, "Well, Mr. Frost, I don't know about that, but you know, you're apathetic and I think that's much worse."

Egalitarian Democracy and the Inevitability of Leadership

As we noted in Chapter 3, Ella Baker, who mentored the Student Nonviolent Coordinating Committee (SNCC) during the 1960s, famously declared that "strong people don't need strong leaders." To some extent, community organizers agree with this statement. They don't like dictators or authoritarian commanders either. But many organizers do think that there is a place for fairly strong leaders who are deeply rooted in the desires, beliefs, and culture of their followers. For basic pragmatic reasons, organizers in the Alinsky tradition are generally more supportive of hierarchy than Baker was.[7]

Part of the difference between the organizing approach to leadership and the nonhierarchical vision held by Baker, the "associationists" of the second-wave women's movement (also discussed in Chapter 3), and many others revolve around questions of *scale*. In fact, democrats from the time of the Ancient Greeks, at least, have struggled with the inability of large groups to operate effectively as "flat" democracies. Baker and the second-wave associationists generally focused on small, face-to-face groups where people could work together in relative equality through dialogue. This was especially evident in second-wave antirape and battered women's groups, which almost invariably lost their egalitarian "sisterhood" once they grew beyond a limited size. Baker was similarly able to maintain her mostly antihierarchical vision only because she was largely uninterested in mass movements. Beyond a certain size, as political scientist Jane Mansbridge's work has shown in detail, hierarchy is almost always necessary for the coherent operation of any institution or group. As Mansbridge notes, without strong leaders—broadly understood—groups cannot generate "the power necessary to protect against oppression or [to] influence collective decisions on the large scale."[8]

Organizers seek to develop organizations that can mobilize enough "people" power to counteract the often overwhelming financial and institutional power of their opposition. As a result, they cannot operate without clear leadership and hierarchy.

More generally, even on a small scale, almost no one still believes that groups can operate effectively without systems of accountability and some kind of process to identify leadership. Jo Freeman's famous essay "The Tyranny of Structurelessness" was a key turning point. As Chapter 3 notes, following wide-ranging discussions around its ideas, second-wave organizations increasingly gave up the idea that they could operate effectively in any *pure* form of egalitarian "sisterhood." As Freeman pointed out, there are always differences of power in groups. If you don't acknowledge them and try to manage them, they will simply simmer and fester in the background. There are no groups without leaders of some kind or another.[9]

The Danger of the All-Purpose Leader

Nicholas von Hoffman[10]

When you do find the all-purpose leader, you would do well to beware of him. More often than not his domination leads to organizational despotism.

Strong Leaders

[The Industrial Areas Foundation trainings] always emphasized how movements are rotten with charismatic leaders, etc. I remember this friend of mine turned to me and said, "That's nonsense. We want a movement. I would love to have Martin Luther King here right now."
—Barack Obama, "Organizing in the 1990s"

Most groups need not only a large and diverse group of leaders but also a core leadership team, a group of strong leaders who can provide guidance and stability to the organization. These leaders often play a somewhat different role than other less senior leaders. Senior leaders are generally elected in some fashion to formal positions within the organization. These leaders often act as spokespersons for the group in key negotiations. They also make final decisions on key aspects of a group's work, for example, which campaigns will be pursued, how the group will advertise itself, etc.

Sometimes groups have particularly charismatic leaders who help maintain group cohesion in hard times and can present the organization's perspective eloquently to a wider public. They provide what social movement scholars call a collective "frame" within which group members and others can make sense of the world. Rod Bush describes this perhaps best in a discussion of Malcom X: "The secret of Malcom X's leadership was that he was able to give back to people in a highly refined and clarified form ideas and insights that were rooted in their *own* experiences. Malcom X was not a man on a pedestal who bedazzled people with oratorical brilliance and held the status of a remote deity. Malcom X was most of all a man of the people, a man who deeply and profoundly loved his people." Like Malcom X, or Martin Luther King, Jr., the best charismatic leaders in organizing are those who are the most connected to their constituents, who spend a great deal of time listening to what the common people have to say. Instead of trying to exalt their own ego, or assert their own idiosyncratic desires, they reframe the myriad hopes and fears of their people into a coherent, shared vision.[11]

The power of such leaders should not be overstated, however. At their best, organizing groups generally take the form of what Aldon Morris, in his research on the Civil Rights Movement, calls "formal, non-bureaucratic" organizations. While there are formal roles within such organizations (like the president of the organization, pastor of a church, or chairperson of a committee), much of what happens can seem ad hoc. The real action in an organizing group usually happens in a range of committees where participation is fairly fluid and open. Key contributions are often made by participants without any assigned role, and decisions are usually made through open dialogue, voting, or consensus. New leaders are sometimes given key roles in public meetings and engagements with "targets" after careful role playing and vetting of statements. Members are often pushed to the edge of their comfort zones in an effort to grow the number of experienced actors.

Strong leaders are often an important resource for organizing groups. They become destructive when they shift to domination. When an organization seizes up into a sclerotic, immobile command structure, its organic link to the community is degraded. It loses its fluid capacity for constantly elevating new leaders into key roles and, as a result, its grassroots character declines. Lacking multiple layers of emerging leaders, such organizations become dependent on particular individuals. And when these supreme commanders get bored and go somewhere else (or die, or get into titanic fights with each other over control), the organization generally dissolves.

Even with the best charismatic leaders, there is great danger of becoming too dependent on a single person. In the case of both Malcom X and Martin Luther King, their organizations foundered when they were gone. Does this mean we would have been better off without either of these individuals? Would we have been able to accomplish as much without figures like these to help us make our dreams into concrete realities? How strong is *too* strong for a leader?

This is not a question we can answer. You will need to answer it for yourself. Just because something is dangerous does not mean it is not also, at the same time, necessary. The question of leadership within social action groups is fraught with uncertainty and imperfect choices. And this is true with so much of community organizing. In an unpredictable world, organizers and leaders who are honest with themselves will find that are no absolute rules to follow, no certain paths to take.

Notes

1. Kenneth Patrick Ruscio, *The Leadership Dilemma in Modern Democracy* (Northampton, MA: Edward Elgar, 2004), ix. Dahl cited in John Kane, "The Ethical Paradox of Democratic Leadership," *Taiwan Journal of Democracy* 3, no. 2 (2007): 34. Matthew L. Trachman, "Rethinking Leadership: Presidential Leadership and the 'Spirit of the Game' of Democracy" (PhD, York University), 2.
2. Kimberley A. Bobo et al., *Organizing for Social Change: Midwest Academy Manual for Activists,* 3rd ed. (Santa Ana, CA: Seven Locks Press, 2001), 119.
3. Richard Rothstein, *What is an Organizer?* (Chicago: Midwest Academy, 1974), 3.
4. Nicholas von Hoffman, *Finding and Making Leaders* (Chicago, IL: Industrial Areas Foundation, 1963), 11.
5. Marshall Ganz, *Why David Sometimes Wins: Leadership, Organization, and Strategy in the California Farm Worker Movement* (Oxford; New York: Oxford University Press, 2009), 199.

6. Ernesto Cortes cited in Mary Beth Rogers, *Cold Anger: A Story of Faith and Power Politics* (Denton, TX: University of North Texas Press, 1990), 114–115.

7. Barbara Ransby, *Ella Baker and the Black Freedom Movement: A Radical Democratic Vision* (Durham, NC: University of North Carolina Press, 2005), 217. At the same time, however, it is important to acknowledge that Baker was no theoretical purist, herself. Despite her discomfort with strong leadership, for example, Baker strongly supported Fred Shuttlesworth, the key local leader in Birmingham, Alabama. Even though others saw Shuttlesworth as "an authoritarian preacher rather than an inclusive democrat," Baker felt that his "zeal and charisma" were "talents applied in the service of the collective interests of the disenfranchised rather than self-aggrandizing gestures on the part of a single individual." Baker was willing to support him despite her general discomfort with strong leadership because she thought "he tried to act in accordance with the wishes of the 'masses', even if he did not always poll them" directly. Ransby, *Ella Baker,* 188.

8. On the challenge of scale for democracy, see Robert Alan Dahl and Edward R. Tufte, *Size and Democracy* (Stanford, CA: Stanford University Press, 1973); Robert Alan Dahl, *On Democracy* (New Haven, CT: Yale University Press, 1998). Jane Mansbridge, "A Paradox of Size," in *From the Ground Up*, ed. George Bonnello (Boston, MA: South End Press, 1992), 172. There are limited exceptions, of course. We discussed the anti – Vietnam War movement, for example, which had little discernible structure. But, as we noted, this lack of structure also meant that the movement had little or no capacity for focused, strategic action, part of what limited its capacity. A better example might be the AIDS activist group ACT UP, although chapters seem have remained fairly small. See chapter 3 of Aaron Schutz, *Social Class and Social Action: The Failure of Progressive Democracy* (New York: Palgrave Macmillan, 2010) for a much more detailed discussion of this issue.

9. Jo Freeman, "The Tyranny of Structurelessness," *The Second Wave* 2, no. 1 (1972–1973): 20.

10. Von Hoffman, *Finding and Making Leaders*, 11.

11. Roderick Bush, *We Are Not What We Seem: Black Nationalism and Class Struggle in the American Century* (New York: New York University Press, 2000), 185.

CHAPTER 12

Power and Targets

Ordinary people have little direct experience of exercising power in public life.

—Ed Chambers, *Roots for Radicals*

Power only respects itself. . . . This means that the power arena has its own rules. Those in power only respect others who know the rules.

—PICO, Power Training

What is "power"? Who has it? How do you get it? These are central questions for community organizing because *the central goal of community organizing is the generation of power*. "Wait a minute," you might respond. "Power? But what about democracy, citizenship, community?" Yes, all of these represent goals of organizing. But without power, the tradition of organizing argues, none of the other goals are really achievable. Without power, there is no democracy. Without power, citizenship is a mirage. And without power, you cannot protect your community from the persecution of others who do have power.

The public realm is the realm of power. Because most people never get the chance to act in public, they never learn how power works or how to use power if they ever get any. As a result, a key area of training in organizing involves helping leaders understand this slippery concept of power.

It is important to emphasize that community organizers see "power" as a fairly neutral concept. Those who have power can use it for good or ill. Without power of different kinds, our society would grind to a halt. Power exists. The job of community organizing is to generate power for those who don't currently have much, and to take power away from those who misuse it. As Edward Chambers notes, "There is a difference between strength and bullying. Power can afford to be practical, flexible, wise, patient. Power can administer justice."[1]

Saul Alinsky defined "power" simply as "the ability to act." Many current organizations follow him in this definition, usually adding some explanation to give it a more coherent sense. In this same tradition, for example, Alinsky-trained organizer Ernesto Cortes said that power is "two people with a plan." In the end, however, we believe that Alinsky's definition is too vague to be that useful. Who *can't* act? Act to do what?

Instead, in this chapter, we provide two different definitions of power: one for organizing groups and one for the opposition. In our terms:

> Power for organizing groups is
> "*the capacity to incite a response.*"
> Power for the opposition (or what organizers call "targets") is
> "*the capacity to command.*"[2]

Power is attained by organizing groups and targets in different ways as well. Power for organizing groups generally emerges out of "organized people." Power for targets usually comes from some combination of organized money and institutional position.

Before we can examine these definitions in more detail, however, we first need to explain how community organizers characterize the opposition they encounter during organizing campaigns: what they call a "target."

What Is a "Target"?

A key term in the neo-Alinsky community organizing toolbox is "target."

A *target* is "*the group or person who can make the change you want.*"

A *secondary* target is "*a POWERFUL group or person that can influence the target.*"

In other words, the "target" is the concrete embodiment of your opposition. Instead of railing against the "system," you figure out exactly who to pressure. Fundamentally, in this model, if you don't know what (or preferably who) your target is, then you can't really act in a coherent way. For example:

- In our state, there are severe "caps" on the amount of additional tax dollars our local school districts can raise. In our city, the district is already desperately short of funds. Therefore, if you want to start a new program that will cost a lot of money, the targets will likely have to be the state legislature and the governor (depending on who disagrees with you), not the school board.

- In our city, there is an unwritten tradition that gives complete power over the awarding of licenses and decisions over zoning to the city council person in a particular district. If the city threatens to withdraw the occupancy permit for an important homeless program, the specific council member from that district is your target.
- In some states decision about tuition increases are made by the statewide board of regents, not the local university presidents. Therefore, the key regent or regents that oppose you are your targets, not the chancellor.

Determining the right target is critical. If you address all your attention to the wrong target, you won't get what you want, and you will make your group look incompetent.

You don't want to hold a large rally outside the chancellor's office at your university demanding a tuition reduction, and have her come out and tell you that you've got the wrong person—the regents make these decisions. You don't want to bring the city sanitation director to a large public meeting to demand an increase in garbage pickups if the local city council person is actually the one who makes this decision.

Similarly, you don't want to get this kind of response and realize that you don't actually *know* whether they have the power to make the change you want. They may just be trying to confuse you by denying responsibility for something that they do, in fact, have power over. As Alinsky notes, the "constant shifting of responsibility from one jurisdiction to another [is a continual challenge]—individuals and bureaus one after another disclaim responsibility for particular conditions, attributing the authority for any change to some other force."[3]

Screwups like these can completely demoralize your organization, especially if they happen in front of large groups of your members. If you misidentify your target, you basically need to start over again, engaging with a completely different person with a completely different set of self-interests.

This kind of misplaced action happens all the time. Groups get mad about some issue or another and decide to protest in front of someone's office without doing any homework, only to find out that the person they are attacking has nothing to do with their concern. By the time they figure this out, they've wasted whatever collective energy they may have been able to muster, the mobilization dissolves, and nothing is accomplished.

Secondary Targets

A secondary target is *a powerful individual or group that can put pressure on your target.* An organizing group often chooses to focus on a secondary target instead of the primary target if it can't figure out how to get much direct leverage on the primary target. For example:

- The mayor of your city may be the person who actually decides whether or not you can get more police patrols in your neighborhood. But your council person may be a good friend of the mayor and easier to pressure. The mayor may give in to you if you can get the council person on your side.
- The school board of your school district may have the power to decide whether to allow condom distribution in schools. But the superintendent of the district may be somewhat sympathetic to you, and if you can bring her publicly onto your side her support may provide "cover" for a number of key school board members who otherwise wouldn't have the courage to support you.
- The president of a large, multistate bank may be the person who decides whether the bank will provide more small business loans to low-income applicants. You may not be able to figure out a way to put pressure on the president, directly. But what if you can get the city council to pass a resolution reprimanding the bank for its loan history? And what if the city currently uses the bank for its deposits? The threat of losing these deposits and the bad public relations from the censure may be enough at least to bring the bank president to the table.
- The county board of supervisors makes decisions about the location of hospitals and clinics, but what if a hospital in an adjacent county wants to reduce its emergency room costs by serving fewer residents from your county? The hospital from the other county may be able to put pressure on your board of supervisors to increase hospital funding.

It is important to make sure everyone in your organization understands that the secondary target is not the primary target. Otherwise, they may think they have won when the secondary target comes over to your side. Secondary targets may be important, but they cannot, by themselves, get what you want done.

Your Constituency

The constituency for a particular organizing campaign is made up of those people you are trying to organize. It includes all of the members of your organization as well as others who are particularly affected by an issue. For example, the constituency of a campaign to remove a liquor store from a block in your neighborhood would likely include residents in the area who don't like the clientele as well as other business owners. The constituency for an effort to get the local park cleaned up more regularly would include people who use the park and others who live in the local area and might use it if it were clean.

A common mistake made by people learning about organizing is to confuse their constituency and their target. For example, in an exercise in one of our classes, one group "targeted" local homeowners in their effort to get rid of the liquor store instead of the liquor store owner, and another group decided to "target" people in the area around the park for a neighborhood cleanup instead of the local parks department.

In the first case, students confused the people they were organizing with the person they needed to put pressure on. Organizing residents around the liquor store may be a necessary precursor to a campaign against the liquor store owner, but it will not, by itself, get rid of the store.

In the second case, the group confused organizing with the "by your own bootstraps" approach. Holding a neighborhood cleanup may build a sense of togetherness among residents. And it does get the park cleaned up (once). But this activity implicitly accepts that the city department that is supposed to clean the park cannot be forced to do so. From an organizing perspective, this is not very empowering. An organizer would argue that few of the real problems in any oppressed neighborhood can be solved without putting pressure on the outside agencies that are doing the oppressing. Forcing the parks department to clean up a park may not seem like a big accomplishment, but it represents an initial lesson for your constituency about the power they can generate with solidarity and careful planning. It can be a first step in building power for the organization to address other issues like police harassment, the lack of grocery stores in the area with healthy food, the lack of transportation to jobs in other communities, and many other issues.

The goal of organizing is *to take power from the powerful*. If an organizing group doesn't do this it may be accomplishing useful tasks, but it isn't engaged in community organizing as we define it here.

A Campaign to Fund Sports Programs in the Public Schools

Imagine that you are a leader in a local action group that wants to get school sports re-funded in your district. The first thing you need to do is find out who makes that funding decision. And this involves figuring out not only how power works in your district but also the different ways that sports teams might get funded within that system.

For example, the superintendent might have the power to shift some funds to the sports teams. In other districts, the school board might need to decide. And the amount of money involved would be important, too. The smaller the amount of money, the lower on the totem pole the decision will probably be made. Generally you want to go for the weakest link, the target that will be easiest to influence.

Figuring out the target is crucial, because once you figure out who makes the decision you want, you can start figuring out what might influence the person or institution that makes the decision. To act, you need to understand what motivates your target: its interests, fears, powers, etc.

Make It Personal

Abstractions are not going to get feet marching. You must name who is responsible for [the problem] or those who are will slither out of reach with bromides like, "There is enough blame to go around."
—Nicholas von Hoffman, *Radical: A Portrait of Saul Alinsky*

Targeting individuals prevents the real decision makers from hiding behind the protective walls of institutions. Any campaign can have multiple targets, and it is a sign of sophistication if we can manage such a scene.

If a group is looking for a vote from its city council, for example, it should target each individual member. We would not treat the entire city council as a single target because each person has different attitudes, constituencies, and interests that we need to take into account in designing tactics.
—Rinku Sen, *Stir It Up: Lessons in Community Organizing and Advocacy*

In most cases it is best to target a single person rather than a group or institution. You want to generate enough outrage among your members to keep them engaged in a long-term campaign. And it's easier to get pissed off at an individual.

It's hard to get mad at the state legislature or the city council, for example. They are too abstract and undefined. It is easier to generate outrage at the council president who is unjustly blocking your important legislation. "President Johnson doesn't care about people suffering from addiction in our city!"

You might say, well, it's not really fair to target individuals. They may just be doing their jobs. And they may be your friends. For most organizers, however, this answer is part of the problem, part of how we misunderstand the workings of power in the public sphere. As we noted in Chapter 9, when people choose to take on institutional roles, they insert themselves into the public space and take on a set of responsibilities to the public. From an organizing perspective, they need to be held accountable for their public actions. It's not personal. Or, at least, it's not supposed to be.

Power for Targets: The Capacity to Command

In general, a target is someone or some group whose position allows them to decide what the institution does. A target can be a police chief, a mayor, a group of legislators, the undersecretary of the state health department, the president of a bank, the local board of historic preservation, and the like. Within more or less clearly prescribed limits, these people have the power to "command" an institutional response. In contrast with community organizing groups that have to deal with messy issues like internal democracy, they can generally "make" their institution do what they want.

Of course, this power is never absolute. Underlings can rebel (in fact that is what union organizing groups aim for).

And the power of your chosen target is not always clear-cut, however. For example, your group may want the local school board to change a policy—perhaps you want them to add an after-school program to a particular high school. If you have done your research (see below) you will know how many votes you need to get what you want. But with limited resources, you may try to "target" only a single important member in hopes that if this person comes over to your side, the other votes you need will as well. In this case, your target has *some* institutional power to command, but their importance also resides in their capacity to influence other members. (And again, sometimes you choose a "secondary target" who may have no direct power of command at all.)

Power for Organizing Groups: The Capacity to Incite a Response

Community organizing groups live in civil society, in the world outside of defined institutional spaces. They are trying to get more established actors to respond to the interests of ordinary people. While organizing groups often make demands, they do not have any direct way of *forcing* the opposition do what they want. In fact, campaigns for social change usually involve multiple rounds of organization action and opposition response. In the case of issues a target really doesn't want to address, this often involves a series of foot-dragging responses, including efforts to pass the buck, or to ignore, co-opt, split, or delegitimate the organizing group. While experienced leaders and organizers learn to predict what a target is likely to do, this is always an uncertain process.

Alinsky often stated that *"the real action is in the reaction of the opposition."* Organizing groups are always somewhat dependent upon the response of targets. As a result, organizing "actions" are often designed to unsettle targets in different ways, to get them to make a mistake, or respond too aggressively, or say something offensive that will draw media attention to the campaign, activate the organization's constituency, and more. In general, then, organizers and leaders must continually work to "realistically appraise and anticipate the probable reactions of the enemy." You have to learn to walk in the oppositions' "shoes," becoming able to "identify with them" in your "imagination and foresee reactions to [your] actions."[4]

This is also why Alinsky always recommended that organizing "actions" be designed to go *outside the experience of a target and make them live up to their own rules.* At one point, one of Alinsky's groups took 50 people into a bank where they took up all the tellers' time in changing nickels into dollars and back. This tactic essentially shut the bank down for that day. While the bank was likely prepared for standard forms of protest like a picket, it wasn't prepared for this creative strategy that actually used its own procedures against it. As a result, the bank quickly gave in to the organization's demands.

This same approach likely wouldn't have worked so well even a few months later, however. The opposition is constantly learning how to respond to new tactics. They quickly develop new strategies for dealing with new efforts to put pressure on them. Thus, organizing groups are constantly exploring new and unexpected ways to get "outside" the experience of the particular opposition they are facing. We discuss tactics in more detail in Chapter 14.

"The Real Action Is in the Reaction" A Thoughtless Answer Ignites a Constituency

Walter Haggstrom[5]

In one city, people representing a small neighborhood went to a district sanitation inspector to appeal for better street cleaning. During the course of the discussion, the supervisor mentioned that there was no point in putting additional equipment into such neighborhoods, since the residents didn't care whether their streets were clean or dirty. When the story of this insult was widely reported (the organizer helping the report along), a large number of people wanted to do something to change street-cleaning practices, which they had never before clearly understood to be discriminatory.

They planned a series of actions, including sweeping their own streets while newspaper reporters recorded the event [attracted by the outcry created by the supervisor's statement]. Several times neighborhood residents carried the debris to the homes or businesses of politicians who were responsible. They picketed the district sanitation office.

The city had received national beautification awards and the mayor wanted to maintain its reputation. Various politicians feared that their reelection would eventually be jeopardized. As a result, the embarrassment was enough to end the discrimination.

The Status Quo and the Necessity of Conflict

[An] organizer understands that only in conflict situations do issues become clear with real interests no longer camouflaged; only in conflict situations does the rhetoric of the powerful lie exposed and the mobilization of a movement become possible.... The reactionary interests of those in power are best exposed when they resist popular movements making reasonable demands.

—Richard Rothstein, *What Is an Organizer?*

The status quo does not want to change. That's why it's the status quo. It represents a relatively stable balance of forces and interests. Efforts to change the status quo create "friction." They threaten the power of established authorities to make the decisions they want to make. If the status quo were ready to change, then there would be no need to organize. As Alinsky notes, "when there is agreement there is no issue; issues only arise when there is disagreement or controversy."[6]

Conflict, from an organizing perspective, is not only welcomed but encouraged. Conflict helps members of organizing groups clearly understand who they are targeting and why. And it is through conflict that members realize the power they can generate, showing them that they can, in fact, make the powerful do things that they don't want to do.

Conflict also contains the key tool for making targets come over to your side. In organizing campaigns, conflict creates "a situation where external opponents" learn that it is "less costly to their own interests and goals to accept the demands of the community organization than to continue the conflict."[7]

Polarize and Personalize!

> Pick the target, freeze it, personalize it, and polarize it . . .
>
> A leader may struggle toward a decision and weigh the merits and demerits of a situation which is 52 per cent positive and 48 per cent negative, but once the decision is reached he must assume that his cause is 100 per cent positive and the opposition 100 per cent negative. He can't toss forever in limbo, and avoid decision. He can't weigh arguments or reflect endlessly—he must decide and act.
>
> —Saul Alinsky, *Rules for Radicals*

Alinsky argued that in a public conflict, once a group has decided on its target it needs to then "polarize" the situation. Both sides are, to some extent, in a battle of public perception. For example, in a battle over whether the public health department will allocate more of its budget to treatment for addicts, the target, perhaps the commissioner, may try to show she is a caring person in an impossible situation, that she really can't find the money. At the same time, the organizing group is seeking to portray the target as someone who doesn't care about the scourge of addiction, someone whose priorities are simply in the wrong place.

Today, despite popular mythology, organizing groups do not usually pursue a "scorched earth" policy. The aim of a campaign is generally not to *destroy* a target but to increase pressure to the point where recognition and negotiation is in the target's best interest. If you attack a target too strenuously during one campaign, even if you "win," you may have poisoned the relationship with this person or group to the point that they are much less willing to deal with you in the future. Remember the motto "No permanent friends. No permanent enemies." You don't usually want to create permanent enemies.

There are times when the "scorched earth" approach may be relevant—especially when the goal is really to remove a particular person from their institutional position. And there are some present-day groups, like ACORN (or the remnants of ACORN), who tend to use a more antagonistic approach for reasons specific to their organizational model and structure.

Overcoming Middle-Class Politeness: The "Bucket of Shit" Approach

Richard Harmon[8]

[When a group is preparing to meet with a power figure,] some persons will be afraid: "Let's not make it personal, now." That's especially true among middle class people, who tend to be mainlined with massive doses of politeness. But the organizer can draw from the group the admission that institutions of power are made up of persons . . . and therefore, if the group really wants to get rid of its hurt, then it has to identify, . . . [for example, that Joe Cullerton, a city council member, is] the responsible decision-maker to negotiate with. This step is crucial in bringing people to the edge of personalizing the issue—naturally and easily out of their own experience and common sense. . . .

The organizer . . . knows that Cullerton's reaction to the group will teach them some basic lessons. . . .

What is the timetable for the response? Asking Cullerton for a timetable—"When do we get your answer?" or, "When will you act on what we want?"—is the single most effective way to cut through the problem of politeness. For if the organizer can keep the spokespersons focused on the specifics of the agenda, and on the timetable for an answer or an action from Cullerton, Cullerton will react. . . .

The spokespersons do not have to be impolite, just persistent. All they have to do is to keep repeating, "When do we get it?" until Cullerton either caves in and gives them a victory, or blows up and makes himself the enemy.

In middle class organizations, the heart of the educational process occurs when people discover they have real enemies who regard them as invisible. . . . That discovery is a rite of passage into the real world.

That is why the organizer prays, not for rain, but for defecation. When Cullerton throws the bucket of shit in the group's face, they are forced to start grappling with the real relations of power between themselves and Cullerton's institution. They discover quickly that issues are always personalized—that Cullerton the person made a decision, Cullerton the person insulted them. And they have to decide whether they're willing to fight for what they want from him.

Reciprocity and Recognition

In an action, you act as if the enemy is 100 percent wrong, but you know that he may only be 60 percent wrong, and this is why you leave him some dignity. You have to have some humor about it. You have to exercise some restraints. . . . All's fair in love and war. But this is not about war. We're talking about politics. Ultimately, it's about making a deal both sides can live with.

—Ernesto Cortes, *Cold Anger*

In most cases, "winning" against a target involves negotiation and compromise (which is why it's generally a good idea to start by asking for more than you actually need). What organizing power generally achieves, then, is recognition as a force to be reckoned with, as a group with the power to apply meaningful sanctions to people who do not treat it well. Michael Gecan frames it this way: "Without power there's no real recognition. They don't even see you. They never learn your name. Without recognition, there's no reciprocity; there's not even a 'you' to respond to. And without reciprocity there's no real relationship of respect. Without power, you can only be a supplicant, a serf, a victim, or a wishful thinker who soon begins to whine." Anyone can speak, but mostly nobody that matters pays attention to what unorganized people say. Thus, power in organizing is, in part, a tool for generating real "reciprocity" in Gecan's sense.

As David Liners emphasizes, an important moment comes when "the target has agreed to do the right thing." At this point, it "is immediately time to 'de-polarize.' Now we're back in the world of negotiation. This is also the time to 'de-personalize.' Now, it is no longer 'us' (the outsiders) demanding justice from 'them' (the people in control of things). Now it is 'all of us' working together as partners."

"They Go by Their Guts"

***Dolores Huerta,* Dolores Huerta Reader**[9]

Luckily farm workers many times—because they don't go to school they go by their guts—they know what's right and they know what's wrong and they aren't afraid to take action. . . .

[As we worked to create the United Farm Workers (UFW) union,] I had to unlearn about being rational. . . . Because when you are dealing with a big social fight and trying to make changes, the people that you are dealing with are not going to be rational and they are not going to change things on the basis of justice—they respond to only one thing and that is economic power. So somehow you have to hurt them in the pocketbook where they have their heart and their nerves and then they feel the pain.

Otherwise they can give you a thousand arguments on why something can't be done.

Two Forms of Power: Organized People and Organized Money

What good is money if it can't inspire terror in your fellow man?
—Mr. Burns, *The Simpsons*

Power corresponds to the human ability not just to act but to act in concert. Power is never the property of an individual; it belongs to a group and remains in existence only so long as the group keeps together.
—Hannah Arendt, *On Violence*

We live by the Golden Rule. Those who have the gold make the rules.
—Buzzie Bavasi

Organizers often argue that there are two key forms of power in the public realm:

- organized people and
- organized money.

We add a third:

- institutional position.

Organizing groups generally don't have a lot of money. As a result they generally depend on organized people. The more people they can get together for actions, the more capacity they have to get a target to pay attention to them.

The core power of targets who are institutional leaders is grounded in their ability to dictate the actions of their institution and their ability to direct the organized money held by that institution. Sometimes, however, the key power resource of a target may be mostly financial, like an important donor to a politician whose mind an organization is trying to change, or the Chamber of Commerce, which is running ads against your issue.

Building a Reputation for Power

Day Creamer and Heather Booth[10]

A few people in our society have power. Our task is to build a movement which can change that fact. This means organizing around specific demands which can be won, and which in the process will alter power relations, thus building our power base as women. Winning in one situation will give us the ability to move beyond that victory to greater challenges and the accumulation of more power. We feel one of our movement's worst enemies is its lack of visible successes—to give us faith that we can win. Such small, tangible successes also help to make our vision concrete.

At the same time, in the struggle for concrete victories women will gain both a sense of our power and the meaning of power in society. As women, one of the major obstacles we must confront is the belief that we have no power and there is nothing we can do about it. Most of us have never had any influence over policies which affect our lives; and we have never experienced a situation where that might be different. Our challenge is to prove that wrong by building organizations which, in fact, win.

Power as Reputation: Why Mobilizing Doesn't Generate Power

Power is not only what you have, but what an opponent thinks you have.

—Saul Alinsky, *Rules for Radicals*

Finally we said we'd go to [the] governor's office [in our fight for child care funding] and just sit there and wait. It would be the first time we were prepared to be arrested. . . . [His aides] spent the whole day trying to decide whether to arrest us or not. . . .

[The next morning the governor's chief of staff stepped over sleeping bags and bodies to agree to a meeting.] The legislature found the money, no one went to a waiting list, and they didn't touch that program again for a long time. . . . [After two years of organizing, this was the action] that got us recognized as trouble—don't mess with those women!

—Deeda Seed, *Stir It Up!*

In Chapter 2, we noted that "mobilizing" is not the same as organizing. The need to generate power is a key reason why. A central component of power for organizing groups is their reputation. A mobilizing group, because it disappears after a particular campaign, cannot carry a reputation. A similar group of people may assemble themselves later on, but they will have less power because they cannot depend upon people's memories of an earlier win.

In contrast, an organizing group has a name. Let's call ours CHANGE. When the CHANGE groups starts, it has no reputation. Nobody has any reason to pay attention to it. Then it conducts its first campaign. It chooses something small because it doesn't have the power to win something big. For example, after some conflict it manages to get the local city council person to agree to have a street where lots of children play blocked off to traffic. Now the group has a reputation, albeit a small one. The media may write a small interior page story about their accomplishment; the city council member may speak to her colleagues about them. A "buzz" about the group begins.

The group's increased power can be concretely shown by the fact that the next time CHANGE calls, the city council person it worked with is likely to actually call back. Leaders gain skills in social action through their participation in the campaign. New members join because CHANGE has shown it can actually win. If it is an organization of organizations, new organizations indicate interest in joining. All of these developments add to the power of the group.

CHANGE then moves fairly quickly to a second campaign. This time CHANGE picks something more challenging. An issue presents itself: the mayor announces that she is closing an important firehouse in a low-income area of the city. Again, through carefully managed conflict, CHANGE wins a victory—it saves the firehouse, although it loses the emergency medical truck and team as part of a compromise. And this win again builds the group's reputation. More members flock to the organization. CHANGE is now not only on the city council's but also on the mayor's radar. When CHANGE speaks on an issue, the powerful are likely to at least listen and take their opinion into account. The combination of the group's reputation, its new members, and the skill developed by its leaders through participation in two campaigns all increase the power of the group.

In fact, when CHANGE gains a sufficiently robust reputation, powerful people will actually start to call it up *before* they take controversial actions that might impact the group's constituency. Its leaders may be included on planning task forces and the like (sometimes as an effort to co-opt the group). And some actions may never be taken because of a fear that CHANGE might respond. This is when a group has truly gained a position of power in its arena of action.

CHANGE can never simply rest on its laurels, however, or allow itself to become too comfortable with its new place at the institutional power table. Its reputation, ability to attract new members, and capacity to keep continuing members engaged will only be maintained by continual engagements in new conflicts. And, hopefully, each of these conflicts will also add to the growing power of the organization.

While this example presents the development of power in an organizing group as a fairly simple, stepwise process. In fact, as with everything in the messy world, the reality is more complex and often less celebratory. This is especially true in terms of a group's reputation.

Whenever an organizing group wins a campaign, a struggle begins over who will take "credit" for the win. The powerful people who initially opposed the change immediately turn around and trumpet their responsiveness to the public. And because the opposition usually has more influence with the media, they are often successful in reducing the "reputational power" that the organizing group will gain from the win. In fact, this issue of "credit" is a crucial challenge for organizing groups, and a failure to be able to effectively gain credit in the public sphere is a key factor in keeping organizing groups from increasing their power over time.

Recently, for example, an organizing group won a multiyear campaign for regulations that would force road-building contractors using state funds to hire more people of color. The state officials who had initially opposed this plan then had a 20-minute professional video made celebrating their many efforts to diversify the construction workforce that was played on local TV stations. The video mentioned the organizing group only once in passing. Who do you think garnered the most public credit for this change?

Researching Power

Tom Gaudette[11]

Gaudette: Once I can figure out who's in power (What's their mother's name? What church do they go to? All that stuff) then there's something I can do. Without that, they're still the enemy and I'm [just] righteous. How do you win? I've got to know something about [the powerful people in a community], how they think, which I can use in [a campaign]. . . .

Interviewer: How do you walk into a community and figure out the power structure?

Gaudette: You of all people! Read the newspaper. The first place I go is—"What newspaper do you read?" [In one area where I was setting up a new organization, they] had a neighborhood newspaper. There were two women. I said, "Can I go back five years?" They gave me newspapers.

And I said, "What names show up? What organizations keep jumping at you? What activities are going on? What businessmen? Who takes out ads?" Just go through the paper. And after [going through] about three or four years—bingo! I've got a list of about 100 people I've got to see right away.

As you begin to [meet with] them, you begin to get a reputation:

"I was asked to come in here by these churches, in fact they gave me this kind of money in my name at so-and-so bank to come in here and build an organization. It's a community organization where people can participate in the life of the community, and whatever's going on they deal with. These are some of the things I've heard about. I've heard about the real estate, I've heard about the schools ... "

And their reaction is what you're looking for ...

You go around and interview. What you're studying is the power structure. And it's amazing, people in power, how they refer you to their friends. . . .

What they're saying is, "You've got to prove that I'm important."

And it's always a biggie: "Mr. So-and-so, Charlie your friend said I should come over and see you."

"What's Charlie up to now?"

"Well, I'm trying to build an organization."

"Oh, you're the guy. I've heard about you. Oh, it's my turn"

You find friends in all of these places. You find assholes: "The commie, you're a commie." . . .

This began to create the web. Who knows who?

Power Analysis

In the interview above, Tom Gaudette—a famous organizer who worked with Alinsky—talked about how he approached power analysis when starting a new organization. By doing one-on-one interviews with many different important people, he started to trace out the web of relationships in that community. He also began to figure out what the different people in the community cared about. This process gave him some of the information he needed to start planning campaigns for change. It revealed who was likely to be willing to support him and who might oppose him on different issues. By understanding who was related to whom, he began to understand how different groups were likely to line up—who had a self-interest in supporting (or not supporting) whom.

This initial process described by Gaudette, however, provides only a very rough and broad-based map. As organizations get more specific about cutting specific "issues" to work on, they increasingly need to drill down and collect much more specific information about the powerful individuals who might be important to a campaign around this issue. And this involves an increasingly detailed power analysis process. In this sense, knowledge is power. The more you know about what makes a target react, the better equipped you are to influence it.

Power analysis involves understanding the following key issues:

1. Who or what group has the ability to make the change you want? The answer to this question will give you your "target."

2. Who has influence on the actions of this person or group? The answer to this question will give you possible secondary targets.
3. What are the different self-interests of each potential target? The answer to this question will help you understand what kinds of actions are most likely to influence your target to change their minds.

In essence, power analysis is largely a process of understanding the lines of command authority relevant to your issue, as well as the self-interest of those who hold the power to command.

Ernesto Cortes points out that the root of self-interest indicates that a self only exists because it is in relation to others. Remember that self-interest includes much more than personal greed. For community organizers, self-interest includes issues a person cares about, the people they are most likely to listen to, how they feel about their reputation, which groups they belong to and value, and more. Self-interest includes every issue that is likely to be important to a person. For example, if I have a brother in jail for drug possession, then issues related to alcohol and other drug abuse are likely to be things I care about and may provide an avenue for influencing me.

Suppose, for example, your organization wants to explore the possibility of getting a new after-school program at a local high school. The first power analysis task is to figure out who the target for such a campaign would be. Who has the institutional power to make this happen? Let's say you figure out that this is something the school board could make happen.

Then you need to find out everything you can about the school board. First, you need to know who is already in support of the after-school program. If most of the school board opposes your program, then you may decide to stop, there, and look for another issue to work on (unless you believe you can generate the power necessary to change the minds of so many people). But if you find out that you only need to "flip" a couple of members to get majority support this starts to look like a potentially doable campaign.

Now you need to figure out which school board members you should focus on as targets. Which ones are you most likely to be able to flip? Who isn't as deeply opposed to the program, and who might you have some special leverage on? Who has the most influence on others you need to flip?

Once you have figured out your key targets or, hopefully, target, it's time to do research to figure out everything you can about the target. Who donated to their campaign? What percentage did they win their last campaign by? What is their voting pattern? Who knows them and can tell you about them? Who are their friends and enemies on and off the board? What other interests do they have? What is their job outside the school board (most school boards are not full-time jobs)?

How do you do this research? You look at newspapers. You read Web sites. You look at public campaign reports. But most importantly, you talk to people who can give you a good sense of the lay of the land.

You may discover all kinds of interesting things. For example, if you are congregation-based organization, you may discover that your target (or your target's mother) belongs to one of your churches, giving you a potential lever of influence. You may find that you have a large number of members in one board member's district, giving you more potential clout. You may discover that a key donor to a board member's campaign could be convinced to support the after-school program (in which case, you might focus on the donor as a secondary target).

All of this information can then be used to map out the key interests of each board member of interest, helping you figure out specific actions that are most likely to lead each to change their minds.

Power and Self-Interest

Walter Haggstrom[12]

Organizers . . . have to develop a systematic theoretical analysis of the opponent . . . and think through much more carefully alternative possible lines of action, given an understanding of [the] alternative reactions that may occur. . . .

- Does a public agency fear public scrutiny? An organization of the poor can draw public attention to it.
- Does a city councilman need a thousand additional votes? An organization of the poor can affect many more than that number.
- Does a department store need a positive image? A margin of profit? A mass organization may be able to affect the one by bringing employment discrimination into the open, and the other by a combination of picket lines and boycotts.
- Does a social agency need to pretend that it is meeting needs? A people's organization can demonstrate unmet needs by helping 10 times as many people with legitimate need to apply for help as the agency has openings.
- Does a school claim that parents in a neighborhood are not interested in education? The parents can seek public funds to sponsor their own school, picket and boycott the existing school, [making] it clear that their interest in education is as intense as their opposition to the existing school.

- Do a variety of people and organizations want to avoid the fray, to stay neutral? The organization can focus public attention on their neutrality, force them to examine the issues, force them to take sides.

Notes

1. Mary Beth Rogers, *Cold Anger: A Story of Faith and Power Politics* (Denton, TX: University of North Texas Press, 1990), 48.
2. For a much more sophisticated discussion of power in the context of community organizing, see the Web site developed by John Gaventa and colleagues, www.powercube.net, accessed September 1, 2010.
3. Saul Alinsky, *Rules for Radicals* (New York: Vintage, 1971), 131.
4. Alinsky, *Rules for Radicals*, 74, italics added.
5. Warren Haggstrom, "The Organizer," unpublished paper (1965), 8–9. This passage has been edited in minor ways; the original text was a draft.
6. Alinsky, *Rules for Radicals*, 116.
7. Donald C. Reitzes and Dietrich C. Reitzes, *The Alinsky Legacy: Alive and Kicking* (Greenwich, CT: Jai Press, 1987), 37.
8. Richard Harmon, "Making an Offer We Can't Refuse," unpublished paper (1973), 6–9, italics added.
9. Mario T. García, *A Dolores Huerta Reader* (Albuquerque, MN: University of New Mexico Press, 2008), 146.
10. Day Creamer and Heather Booth, "Action Committee for Decent Childcare: Organizing for Power," in *Radical Feminism: A Documentary Reader*, ed. Barbara A. Crow (New York: New York University Press, 2000), 408–409.
11. Tom Gaudette, "From Tom Gaudette: Good Stories and Hard Wisdom," in *After Alinsky: Community Organizing in Illinois*, ed. Peg Knopfle (Springfield, IL: University of Illinois-Springfield, 1990), 116–117. Some minor textual alterations have been made to make it easier to read.
12. Haggstrom, "The Organizer," 28.

CHAPTER 13

"Cutting an Issue"

Problems vs. Issues

We live surrounded by "problems":

- racism,
- drug addiction,
- pollution,
- joblessness,
- failing schools,
- and more.

"Problems" are vague and overwhelming. They seem impossible to solve. They make you want to crawl into bed and pull the covers over your head.

Organizers are pragmatists. They know that we can't simply wave a wand and solve world hunger. But just because we can't fix *everything* doesn't mean we can't do *anything*. And a core challenge in organizing is to figure out what we *can* do, given the power that we have, to make our world a better place.

You may not know how to eliminate "drug addiction," but your group could start a campaign to get the county government to allocate one million dollars for drug treatment. You can't eliminate racism, but you might be able to mandate automatic video cameras in police cars to cut racial profiling and harassment. Completely stopping all pollution is impossible, but maybe you can stop the electric utility from putting a coal power plant in your neighborhood. And while nobody knows how to completely turn around our school system, we do know that smaller class sizes help students learn better. In this way, organizers "cut issues" out of broader problems.

The key characteristic of an "issue" is that it is *discrete and specific* instead of vague and overwhelming.

Beyond this, however, a range of criteria help organizers distinguish between better and worse issues to focus on in particular situations.

A Good "Issue" *Always* Includes a Solution

Go to power *with* a decision, not *for* a decision.
—Ed Chambers, *Roots for Radicals*

Before we go into these criteria, it is important to stress that, in organizing, an "issue" always includes a *solution* to the challenge you have identified. You don't go to the chancellor of your university and ask her to reduce parking fees unless you know exactly how much of a reduction you want. Otherwise, even if you win, she is likely to cut rates a couple of cents and call it good (and maybe raise fees somewhere else to make up the cash). You need to know what you want to see happen before you go to the superintendent of your local public schools and ask her to "do something" about falling reading scores. The superintendent may end up ordering a few new textbooks when you really wanted smaller class sizes, or she may institute a new reading program that conflicts with your philosophy about how children learn to read. Or—most likely—she may form a "task force" to explore the problem that never ends up doing anything at all.

When you don't know what you want, what the solution should look like, you give your opposition the power to define the solution themselves. It is hard to demand a change when even you don't know how (or sometimes even *if*) it can be made to happen.

When we say "solution," we mean *everything* that goes into solving a problem. For example, in cases where your solution will cost money, a key question is about where this money will come from. Students often raise the parking fee issue in our classes. It seems obvious to them that the fees are too high. But when we point out that on our campus the upkeep for parking structures is paid directly out of the income raised by fees, they start to see that the issue isn't that simple. If they want to lower the fees, they need to be able to explain where the money to maintain the parking will come from. In fact, in class we often convince students that there really isn't any way to reduce parking fees. "Lower fees," we tell them, "only mean less parking."

Then we turn around and explain how we may have snookered them. Maybe we are just lying—maybe the administration is siphoning money out of the parking fee account to pay for their pet projects. They won't know until they check. Or maybe the parking office spends too much on overhead. Or maybe other campuses in the state system fund their parking system in a different way that we could copy.

Too often, ad hoc groups of activists don't do their homework before they start agitating for changes. As a result, they come off as uninformed and not really serious before the opposition, the media, and even their own potential constituency. Too many campaigns are lost when they have hardly begun because activists start making broad knee-jerk demands before they have figured out what they really want and how what they want can be accomplished.

One final point in this vein: because organizing almost always involves a process of negotiation, organizing groups almost always ask for *more* than they would be willing to settle for. You might ask for three million dollars for drug treatment when you think one million would actually be reasonable. If you start with one million, you are likely to end up with a few hundred thousand. In fact, if you are lucky you might actually *get* the whole three million (at this point, you will be kicking yourself for not asking for five million).

If you haven't fully defined a solution, then, from an organizing perspective, you aren't done "cutting" your issue.

A Question of Framing: Simple and Clear

Another key consideration is how you present your issue to the public. This is not about the issue itself, but about how you get the message out about it.

Sometimes the issues organizing groups address involve fairly intricate legislative changes or complicated programs with many different components. An effective organizing group will distill these intricacies down into a message that foregrounds the most important aspect of the change it is seeking. For example, CHANGE in Milwaukee recently won a battle for the Milwaukee Opportunities for Restoring Employment (MORE) ordinance. This new law now requires developers contracted by the city to hire more Milwaukee residents and to pay them prevailing wages (much higher wages than they otherwise would pay), among other provisions. The actual ordinance was quite complex and the formal text of the legislation—like that of most legislation—was more likely to put people to sleep than incite them to action. Imagine a flyer like this:

Example #1

Support the MORE Ordinance!
What will it do for you?
This:

Prior to submitting a proposed term sheet for a project, the commissioner of city development, in consultation with the emerging business enterprise administration or such other entity as may be designated by the city from time to time, shall determine the appropriate level of participation of unemployed and underemployed residents of the city for the project to reflect the job or trade categories required for the project and the pool of available certified and qualified workers within each job or trade category. The total appropriate level of participation shall be presumed to be 40 percent, unless the commissioner determines there is sufficient reason to impose a lesser requirement.

A better approach might be the following:

Example #2

**MORE jobs. MORE pay. MORE business.
Milwakee Taxes Should Create Jobs for *Milwaukee* Residents**

We demand:

- Milwaukee residents first in line for new jobs.
- Milwaukee businesses first in line for city contracts.
- High-paying jobs.

**Support the MORE Ordinance
(See www.CHANGEMilwaukee.org for more information)**

Or a more target-focused message:

Example #3

Need a Job?

Alderman Hinker Thinks You Don't Deserve One.
"We don't have enough good workers in Milwaukee"
Come to a rally at Hinker's office on Monday.
Show him just how capable we are!

Even our second and third examples aren't perfect. But organizers and leaders are rarely expert marketers. They do the best they can with the time and skills they have.[1]

In any case, the point of clarity is not to misinform your leaders or the public (although the opposition often tries to do this). In the case of the MORE ordinance, CHANGE's core leaders were educated about the nitty-gritty details of the ordinance. The actual text of the ordinance was given out at rallies and linked to on the CHANGE Web site. Detailed summaries were created for people who wanted more information but weren't ready or able to make sense of the legalese of the ordinance.

But, of course, there is always some "spin" in simplification. You want to frame your issue in ways that will excite (example #2) or piss off (example #3) your constituency. The MORE ordinance, for example, affected private development projects (new buildings for private uses) supported by the city. Because there was constant negotiation about the specific details of the ordinance, it was never really clear how many jobs it would create for Milwaukee residents, or whether these jobs would actually reach those most desperately in need of employment but lacking in actual skills. It was not a perfect issue by any stretch of the imagination. But our messaging didn't deal with these issues.

Nonetheless, to the extent possible, you should craft your core message so it will engage and activate your constituency.

What Makes a Good Issue?

There are many schools of thought about the correct criteria for choosing an issue. Some groups have 10 or 20 different criteria. The widely used "Organizing for Social Change" textbook put out by Midwest Academy lists 16. In our experience, however, it is difficult to keep all these criteria in your head. Organizing groups should ideally come up with their own lists of criteria based on the values of their organization. For example, Rinku Sen describes the criteria used by the Center for Third World Organizing that define ways the proposed issues highlight race, gender, and class inequalities. Here is a short list of criteria commonly mentioned:

- Build the power of your organization
- Be winnable
- Be deeply felt (a "gut" issue)
- Resonate widely
- Be tangible
- Unify your constituency

When you start trying to "cut" issues, you will quickly find that these criteria are often in conflict with each other. An issue that is winnable, for example, is often not one that is deeply or widely felt. Your organization may have the power to get a new stop sign at a dangerous intersection, for example. But only a few people are likely to care much about this. Similarly, an issue that resonates widely may not be very winnable. Many people may care about putting automatic video cameras in cop cars to reduce police harassment, but your organization may not be powerful enough (yet) to actually make it happen.

A Good Issue Builds the Power of Your Organization

> Organizations have organized on some very strange issues. . . . Some examples of these issues: shopping carts, bells on ice cream trucks, toilet paper at the school. None of these are earth shaking, but they were won, a constituency was built and the organization moved on to bigger issues.
>
> —Shel Trapp, *Basics of Organizing*

A good issue builds the power of your organization. *If it doesn't build power, it isn't a good issue.* It's as simple as that.

People who are new to organizing usually have trouble internalizing this criterion. It's easy to understand, for example, that a good issue is something an organization can "win." It's more difficult to understand that organizations generally *avoid* easy wins, and instead intentionally *seek out* issues that are difficult to win.

Remember that the core components of power for organizing groups are *organized people* and *organized money.* And an organization's power is maintained over time through its *reputation for effective action* ("Don't mess with us or you'll regret it!").

An issue that builds power, therefore, is one that will accomplish at least some of the following:

- Expand membership
- Improve members' leadership skills
- Increase financial resources
- Develop productive relationships with powerful people
- Educate the public and your constituency about the vital importance of the problems you are focusing on

Issues accomplish this by generating controversy and outrage, which draw attention to your efforts and actions. Good issues provide opportunities for leaders to learn by doing as they participate in the many tasks of an ongoing campaign. Good issues "stretch" the capacity of your organization to take on larger and larger challenges, thereby also building up your reputation.

The organizer David Liners tells a cautionary tale about a time when his organization chose as an issue—the goal of getting $5 million per year set aside in the state budget to provide drug and alcohol treatment for low-income people in Milwaukee County.

> The President of the organization and I went to speak with a State Senator about the matter. The Senator said he had an idea, and asked us to just keep

quiet about it. If we raised a ruckus about it, then others might notice and it would likely get cut.

The stealth strategy worked. The money appeared in the state budget (and has been in the budget every year for the past 10 years).

Unfortunately, the issue did absolutely nothing to build the power of our organization—most members of the organization didn't even know it happened. Those who did felt no part in it.

It is a nice thing that thousands of people have gotten drug and alcohol treatment, but as an organizer, I feel I failed on that issue. My job is to build the organization.

Avoid Easy Wins

"Avoid easy wins": This simple motto (or mantra) can help novice organizers remember that good issues always build power. In three simple words, it encapsulates most of the core characteristics that make issues "power builders." And it directly confronts the tendency of most novice organizers and leaders to focus on winning instead of on power.

Why are "easy wins" so problematic?

- An easy win is not controversial—so it doesn't generate much publicity and attention for your group.
- An easy win doesn't force your leaders to do much work—so they don't learn much.
- An easy win doesn't draw a broad mass of members into actions—so you don't do much recruiting or mobilizing.
- An easy win doesn't enhance your reputation for winning—because you don't overcome any real opposition.
- An easy win usually only involves a couple of core leaders—so it doesn't foster broad democratic participation.
- An easy win is never as easy as it looks—it almost always sucks up leaders' energy and attention (often more than you think) that could have been put to better use.

So:

"Avoid Easy Wins"

A Good Issue Is Winnable

Organizers have no time or patience for noble causes we can't win. Most of the people we set out to organize are accustomed to being overpowered by the forces of the status quo. If we are going to change the dynamics of power, we have to get some momentum on our side. We have to get a few issues in the "win" column.

—David Liners, Personal Communication

You want to make sure that the issue you choose is something your organization can win.

How do you know if you can win? It's pretty easy, at least in theory; you just need to figure out whether your organization is powerful enough to get the opposition to do what you want.

A block watch may have enough power to get a stop sign at the end of their street. The same group likely won't have the power to get the residency permit pulled from a disruptive nightclub. A neighborhood-wide organization of a few hundred people can likely get rid of the nightclub, but probably won't be able to get the superintendent of schools fired because he's incompetent.

At the same time, it's not really that simple. Every issue is unique. Every issue depends on the specifics of the interests of the people involved on all sides (there are usually more than two). Remember that *power* in organizing is about *people*: what they want, what they care about, what they are worried about, who they know, and so on.

Even something as apparently simple as a new stop sign may prove to be more (or less) contentious than you had thought. Let's say that the local city council person makes the final decision on all stop signs in your neighborhood. What if the city council member drives to work on your street and doesn't want to stop? Well, then, an annoying little block watch group probably won't convince her to mess up her commute. But what if a small child was just hit by a car at this intersection and sent to the hospital? Now the situation is fundamentally different. Before the kid got hurt, a threat to go to the media about a missing stop sign would have been laughable. Now it's a real threat. She doesn't want these people on TV complaining about how she doesn't care about children. *Now* it may be worth it to mess up her commute.

What about the nightclub? Again let's assume that the city council person gets to decide about residency permits. And let's assume that this nightclub has been irritating people in the neighborhood for a couple of years—playing loud music late into the night, its customers vomiting on sidewalks and cars, throwing cigarette butts and bottles on lawns, and getting into fights. At this point, it's not entirely illogical to assume that there is some reason why the city council person hasn't *already* done something about this problem. And that reason could be all kinds of things: maybe the nightclub owner makes a large election contribution; maybe the owner is a friend, or a relative, or a friend of a relative; maybe the owner is connected to other powerful people who could make the council person's life difficult if she tries to yank the permit. And, even worse, what if it turns out that the nightclub is in one council member's district on one side of the street, while most of the irritated residents (your members) live in another district on the other side. In this case, why should the council person with the nightclub care about what your people think?

In both of these cases, "power" is more than simply the number of people you can produce for some action. To know what is "winnable" requires that you understand the web of relationships and interests that surround a particular issue. As you do your homework to understand these—conducting one-on-ones, reading newspapers, digging up government documents, and the like—the substance of your "issue" may change as well. Maybe you can accomplish what you want with a stop sign on a different intersection that won't mess with the council person's commute. Maybe speed bumps would be more palatable. For the nightclub issue, it may turn out that you just can't generate the kind of power necessary to target the council person. But you might turn up issues in your research that could allow you to target the building inspector's office instead if there are possible issues with zoning—perhaps the regulations don't allow such large crowds in the space. Or there may be a secondary target that you could focus on: a large donor who does live in your organization's primary district, or maybe the council person's father-in-law goes to one of your churches, or . . .

Above, we talked about the problem with an "easy win." The reverse is also sometimes true. Some organizers argue that, at rare moments, picking an issue you are likely to lose can actually be productive for your organization. Again, it is critical to remember that winnability is only *one* criterion for a good issue among others, and that *building the power of the organization* is the most important. Those new to organizing generally have trouble keeping this in mind. With a laser beam – like focus on winning, all the other criteria tend to fall far into the background.

Once, for example, a group in Texas tried to stop their city from passing a tax to build a new sports stadium. Their organizer didn't think it was winnable, but the organization's leaders were convinced they could do it. So they put a lot of effort into defeating it. They failed, just like their organizer thought they would. But in some ways this loss was enormously important for the future of the organization. Leaders who had been very successful in the past gained a better understanding of their limitations. The loss taught them about how to "cut issues" more realistically. Many new leaders were trained through this effort. And the organization learned many things about how the city power structure worked.[2]

David Liners reports that "after initial wins, it is not unusual for an organization to strategically choose an issue that will not necessarily win on the first try. Sometimes, a losing effort can be part of a larger strategy. Some efforts take two or three attempts. (I [Liners] have been involved lately in the effort to win the possibility for felons to be able to vote once they are out of prison. We didn't make it in this session of the legislature, but feel we created enough awareness and enough support that maybe next time we can finally push it over the top.)" Other times, an unwinnable effort can help you gauge the identity, power and whereabouts of your adversaries. Mary Steeg of Working Partnerships for Women argues that "it's OK to lose if your goal is to organize and come back after the loss."[3]

Many organizations, however, simply do not have the capacity to come back after a major loss, and many have dissolved after an outcome like this as exhausted leaders bail out in disappointment. As Rinku Sen notes, "coming back after a loss requires leaders who are more politically sophisticated and experienced than they were before the fight and a membership that is more educated and committed to standing up for the original and similar issues."[4]

For our purposes, it is most important to understand that within the tradition of organizing the key aim of "winning" is the increased power of your organization to win bigger and even more important wins in the future.

Fighting for Cable TV

A local organizer in our city was trying to organize a housing complex a few years ago. The complex had a range of problems: drug dealers, plumbing and heat issues, and so on.

When she went around and talked to residents, however, she found that those issues weren't the ones that were most compelling to them. What was?

Cable television. They wanted to have cable access in their apartments.

Now, she knew she could probably get them cable TV without much work. But she saw this as an opportunity to get them engaged in collective empowerment, helping them develop the capacity to make even larger changes. So she brought them together in a complex-wide meeting where they strategized about ways they could convince the complex's owner to allow the building to be "cabled." She used this issue to teach them basic skills about organizing. They wrote letters and went to a meeting with the owner's property manager.

And they won.

At the celebration, she asked, "well what other problems do you want to solve?"

A Good Issue Is Deeply Felt

> Just because you think it is an issue does not make it an issue. Just because you think it is not an issue does not mean it is not an issue.
>
> —Shel Trapp, *Basics of Organizing*

The job of an organizer and local leaders is to find out what a particular community really cares about. It's not about what *you* want.

Yes, you can try to educate people about the importance of particular issues. But, in the end, you can't make people care about something they don't care about. Your best bet is to use what people do care about as the base for issue development. Cable television, as in the story we told above, may not seem important to you, but if it's important to your constituents, then it's a legitimate issue. Again, "*does it build the power of an organization?*" is the key question. If your people don't really care about an issue, they won't put their full energy into the fight, they'll shy away from controversial tactics, and they won't feel as triumphant and empowered if they win.

You want an issue that hits people in the "gut," that elicits a depth of emotion likely to keep them engaged over the inevitable roller-coaster ride of a campaign. ("We're winning! Oh no, we're losing . . . Oh, wow, now we're winning again!").

How do organizations discover what their constituencies care about? They ask them. As we noted, the one-on-one process is, for many organizations, the central tool for figuring this out. But organizations also survey members, or go door to door in a neighborhood to ask people to tell them what is bothering them. One way or another, however, a group needs to know what really grabs its membership and potential membership.

Just Put Out a Mousetrap!

Barbara Trent[5]

You go into towns and get to know people and ask, "So what's the problem?" Then they'll say we got rats in the alleys, we've got this or we've got that. It may seem like, oh my God, put out a mousetrap!

But you start with people's issues because your goal is not to transform them into you. Your role is to empower them into who they want to be. If this is the issue they want to resolve, you help them learn the methods to do that.

Who's in charge of vermin control? Who is on the town council? Where are the pressure points? How do you get it dealt with? Then

> they give you the next problem, and you help them analyze how to address and resolve it. And people win.
>
> You don't *give* people anything. You facilitate people in finding the taste of blood, the taste of success. Then you get into bigger and bigger issues.

Balancing Interest and Reality

You can go too far with this process of judging interest. An organizing group must always balance the "deeply felt" criteria with all of the other criteria of a good issue. Unless the organization is fairly small, it simply isn't feasible to fully educate all the members about the pluses and minuses of different issues. Leaders, informed by the information they have about the desires and hopes of their constituency, must decide on the specific issue they will go after.

And, in fact, it is important to acknowledge that the depth of feeling generated by a particular issue is at least partly a result of how it is framed for an organization's constituency. We gave one example of this already when we talked about the MORE ordinance. The time CHANGE started working on a campaign to get better dental care for kids in schools is another. Now, dental care doesn't necessarily sound that exciting—we don't tend to think about this as a critical health problem. But what if we put it this way:

> Too many of our children hide their faces from friends, embarrassed by their rotting teeth. Too many of our children aren't listening in class because of their pain. We hear horror stories about parents pulling their kids' teeth with pliers on the kitchen table. Too many families despair because they cannot find a dentist to help their children feel better.

It might be possible to get a large number of people to care about this. In this way, it may even be possible to link dental care with two problem areas people *do* tend to care a lot about: health care and education. Nonetheless, we probably need to accept that dental care will always be a difficult sell as a "gut" issue to a wide constituency.

In this case, however, the dental issue came to the fore because it was a logical next step for an issue group that had been working for a couple of years on school health problems. The group had just won $4 million for school nurses, and wanted to keep the momentum going. In their research, it turned out that dental care was ripe for addressing given the political climate of the state. It seemed like the biggest health issue the group was capable of going after right then. And if the group won, it would build a strong reputation across the state that would set them up for successfully tackling other health issues. So this group of leaders needed to balance the competing criteria for deciding on their issues. In the end, they took the risk that they would be able to excite their constituency about dental care.

A Good Issue Resonates Widely

The stop sign issue discussed earlier might really grab a small group of residents who live around that intersection. But unless there is some specific reason—like lots of people getting injured there—most people in the rest of the city or even the rest of the neighborhood aren't likely to care much about it. Conducting a campaign around the stop sign may really weld that block club together, then, but it is unlikely to draw many new members beyond that group.

Now, sometimes training existing leaders and strengthening their links to your organization may be a good enough reason to pursue a particular issue. And it's also often a good idea to have small groups in your organization working on local issues at the same time as the entire organization is pursuing broader issues. It can keep people engaged and excited and strengthen the organization's capacity.

But for the organization as a whole, you generally want to pick issues that are likely to attract new members. If most of the power of community organizing groups is generated by organized people, building more power means increasing your membership. And this requires issues that resonate beyond your current group.

A Good Issue Is Tangible

A simple way to think about this criterion is to ask the following questions:

- How will you know if you win?
- How will you hold your opposition accountable for making good on your demands?

Organizing groups tend to avoid issues like "increasing public confidence in the police" or "creating a better environment for children" or even "increasing achievement in the schools." Issues like these are too fuzzy to easily measure. What exactly "counts" as "confidence" or "satisfaction"? (You can be sure that the opposition will come up with a measurement that makes them look good.)

What you want are issues that are easy to measure:

- Instead of "increasing public confidence in the police," you can campaign for automatic video cameras in police cars.
  (How many video cameras were installed?)
- Instead of "creating a better environment for children," you can fight to turn a vacant lot into a park with a play structure.
  (Did you get the park?)

In each case, you can explain to people fairly easily what you have won. And you can keep track of whether your target is meeting the obligations of its agreement with you after you win. Are the video cameras in the police cars or not? Did you get the park or not? Are the class sizes smaller or not?

Even these issues could be refined from the perspective of "tangibility." How do you know that the cameras in the police cars are actually turned on? If they aren't, they won't do much good, will they? The simpler the "ask," the easier it will be to hold the opposition accountable for actually doing what they agree to. Remember, winning is only the first step. Then you need the capacity to monitor what targets are actually doing over the long term. Otherwise what you win today will likely be taken away tomorrow.

The Danger of Fuzzy Issue Areas

Education is a good example of an area where cutting a solid, "tangible" issue can be quite difficult. "Fuzzy" issues are pretty common in education. It's very difficult to know what "counts" as better education, or, more broadly, how to intervene in dysfunctional school systems. Achievement tests are usually terrible measures of learning, and when you focus on them schools just end up teaching to the test—making education worse, not better. There are so many disagreements about what counts as "good" pedagogy or effective school structure that it's very difficult to come up with an effective intervention. The small schools initiative that was so popular in the last few years has actually proved pretty ineffective on a broad scale, for example. Furthermore, you can't just hold a protest in front of a school and demand that teachers teach better. What does that *mean,* exactly? And is confronting people a good way to make them more committed to your children?[6]

Community organizing groups actually avoided education as an action area until fairly recently for just these reasons. While CHANGE has an education committee, it has struggled to find good issues to work on. Its turn to the "school health" area was part of an effort to identify issues that would be very "tangible" and clear. It just makes logical sense that unhealthy kids won't learn as well, and the plight of sick children is a clear "gut" issue for most people. CHANGE has also worked in the past on reducing class size, one of the few simple, "tangible," and easily understandable ways to address the achievement issue.

Tangible Issues

David Liners, Unpublished Paper

A good issue has to result in something you can see or touch or measure.

"Changing attitudes" is not an issue. In part, that is because you are never really sure if you changed attitudes, or if people are just faking it better.

As a result of a win on an issue, you want to be able to point to very specific accomplishments like:

- Five hundred people were able to purchase homes because of the change in lending practices by the banks—which we got them to change . . .
- The gas station on the corner doesn't sell drug paraphernalia anymore.
- There are 40 schools in Milwaukee that were able to reduce the size of their 1st and 2nd grade classes because of the budget amendment we got put in.
- That playground over there used to be unusable, and now there are kids out there every day.
- After the festival, the County had collected 200 pounds of aluminum cans that last year would have gone into the regular garbage . . .
- Mr. Johnson, who was wrongly fired, got his job back.

Even if your goals are lofty, you need some tangible victories along the way. Sometimes, it can be as simple as getting an article in the newspaper about your cause, or getting some powerful ally to publicly commit to supporting your effort.

A Good Issue Unifies Your Constituency

Every community organizing group serves a particular constituency, both members and potential members. The broader your constituency, the more power you can command. This is why Alinsky didn't like single-issue organizations. Multiple-issue organizations can attract people with a wide range of passions, generating more people power. But as a group's membership widens, its diversity necessarily increases as well. And this diversity of opinions and beliefs ends up narrowing the topics a group can safely address without fracturing.

Faith-based community organizations (FBCOs) are a good example. As we explained earlier, FBCOs bring together a range of Christian and often non-Christian denominations. Unlike more right-wing coalitions, FBCOs embrace a diversity of religious traditions, with often quite different interpretations of the Bible, Koran, etc. Because they do not share any formal dogma, they are held together more tenuously by common values for equality and justice. This means that they can work together on fairly noncontroversial issues, like fighting for treatment instead of prison for nonviolent drug offenders or public service jobs programs.

Other issues, however, are anathema to FBCOs. Abortion, gay rights, and school vouchers, for example, are no-no's. (Interestingly enough, these are the very issues that often hold right-wing groups together.) On these and other issues, member congregations agree to disagree. They may even find each other facing off at demonstrations—in our group, for example, some Unitarians marching for pro-choice and Catholics on the antiabortion side. To be a member of an FBCO, a congregation has to accept these disagreements as a usually unspoken background to their work together on other issues of social justice. No one is arguing that these are unimportant problems—only that CHANGE is not the appropriate place to deal with them.

A Divisive Issue You Can't Avoid

The challenge of divisive issues is not always dealt with so easily. Sometimes a problem area cannot simply be ignored.

The most salient example in America, today, is probably immigration. Concerns about the unfairness of our immigration system are of deep and abiding importance to key ethnic and racial groups. Discrimination against undocumented immigrants is the central challenge facing many Latinos in our city. Many lack documentation or have friends or family who do. Attitudes about immigration also affect the lives of Latino Americans with no personal connection to undocumented immigrants, since anyone who looks or sounds Latino may face frequent questions about the legitimacy of their own citizenship. As a result, ignoring immigration in CHANGE would be tantamount to ignoring the existence of Latinos in our coalition. Not only would this lead to a hemorrhage of Latino members, it would raise questions about the extent to which our organization really values equality and multicultural coalition building. Because the south side of our city is primarily Latino, CHANGE would become a representative only of the north.

At the same time, however, the organization has taken steps to reduce the potential for friction. The immigration committee works hard to educate the rest of the organization about the unfairness and injustice of America's treatment of immigrants. In presentations in different member churches and at issue committee meetings, immigration committee leaders explain the issue and answer questions. Individual immigrants give testimony about their experiences. The effort, here, is not simply to transmit information but also to give this otherwise abstract issue a human face. When necessary, presenters focus in on areas of discrimination most likely to build solidarity across potential disagreement. For example, the practice of transporting people awaiting trial prior to deportation far from their families and detaining them for many months instead of allowing them to continue to work until a determination has been made is often something that even those opposed to other immigration reforms can agree is unjust.

In general, however, there are more than enough issues in the world that you can address that will not split your coalition.

Notes

1. Okay, well we'll fess up. CHANGE didn't do very effective messaging on this. For example: "The 'Milwaukee Opportunities for Restoring Employment' (MORE) Ordinance is an essential tool for bringing economic recovery to Milwaukee's Main Street. Essentially the MORE Ordinance extends the City's Resident Preference Program (RPP) and Emerging Business Enterprise Program (EBE) provisions to private development projects seeking financial assistance from Milwaukee's taxpayers." Part of the problem, however, was that no one was really sure how many jobs the ordinance would create. So at least CHANGE didn't lie.
2. This story is told in Mark R. Warren, *Dry Bones Rattling: Community Building to Revitalize American Democracy* (Princeton, NJ: Princeton University Press, 2001).
3. Rinku Sen, *Stir It Up: Lessons in Community Organizing and Advocacy* (San Francisco, CA: Jossey-Bass, 2003), 58.
4. Ibid.
5. Barbara Trent cited in Marie Cieri and Claire Peeps, *Activists Speak Out: Reflections on the Pursuit of Change in America* (New York, NY: Palgrave, 2000), 20.
6. For examples of efforts to use organizing to change relationships between communities and schools, see Dennis Shirley, *Community Organizing for Urban School Reform* (Austin, TX: University of Texas Press, 1997).

CHAPTER 14

Tactics and Strategy

I n the previous chapter we discussed how organizers figure out *what* to fight for by "cutting an issue." This chapter is about the next step: *how* to fight for the issues you cut.

Again, as in cutting an issue, an organizer's key concern about tactics and strategy is making sure that they increase *the power of her organization*. This means, counterintuitively, that the *easiest* way to win is not always the *best* way to win. A general rule is that you want your actions *to expand your organization's membership* and *increase the capacity and savvy of your leaders*. These goals are almost as important (sometimes more important) than how effectively an action puts pressure on a target.

What Do We Mean by "Tactics" or "Actions"?

For the purposes of this book, we use the terms "tactic" and "action" inter-changeably. A tactic or action is defined as *anything that puts pressure on a target*. There are many things that community organizers do, then, that don't count as tactics. Collecting research, for example, is critical for any successful campaign, but it doesn't count as a tactic. If what you are doing won't influence your target in some direct way, then, for us, it isn't a tactic.

It is important to emphasize that community organizing groups rarely attack people or institutions without provocation. There is usually an effort to negotiate in good faith before they shift to a more confrontational atti-tude (you might sit down to ask a bank president to lend more money in the central city, for example). In this chapter, we will not refer to these pre-confrontational or pre-pressure engagements as "tactics." Only after a target refuses to act or takes some other action that indicates that they won't be cooperative does an organization move toward "action." Of course, some-times you know beforehand that it isn't really worth your time to sit down and chat. In these cases, you may move pretty quickly to bring more focused "pressure."

Put more simply, "actions" and "tactics" come *after* you've said "pretty please." You start thinking about tactics when you decide you need to move forward and impress upon the target the fact that you have some "power."

Fart Perfume

Ken Galdston[1]

We often used ridicule as a gimmick and humor. In this case Joanne Wilhelmy, the chair of the [pollution] committee, confronted [the Union Carbide board member] and asked if he knew what it was like to live with this smell. And she then took out a bottle of trick perfume that smelled like a fart.

And on the front page of the Chicago Daily News the next day was a photo of Joanne holding a bottle up to this guy's nose. He had his eyes closed and his face scrunched up and his arms crossed. It was the height of Alinsky's ideas about putting pressure on people who were indirectly, in some ways, connected with our issue or were on the board of a corporation like Union Carbide, and getting them to respond.

And we won that fight—forced them to put in a scrubber that cleaned up the smell and made the neighborhood livable. The leaders were very excited and proud of their win. It made a big difference in what it was like to live there.

Challenges Are Good

There is a tendency in our culture to think of problems as bad things. We want a world where we get everything we want. But community organizers see things differently. The emergence of a good challenge, a good fight, is one of the most productive things that can happen to a community organizing group.

Why?

First, community organizing groups *exist only when they are acting.* Unlike other kinds of organizations, like churches, a people's power organization tends to dissolve when nothing is going on. People will go to mass every week even if they don't have any particular task to accomplish. Few people will keep coming to community organizing meetings if there isn't some good reason why they need to be there. And the best way to keep leaders engaged is engage them in an ongoing campaign. A year without a battle is a year when the organization is falling apart.

The point is not that we love fighting, exactly (although it doesn't hurt if you enjoy confrontation to some extent if you are an organizer). Instead, the fact is that our society is rife with incredible oppression and inequality. Children go hungry, receive substandard educations, can't get their cavities treated . . . People of color are thrown into prison to rot for years, can't escape crappy neighborhoods, aren't allowed to buy houses because of the color of their skin . . . And on and on.

If you aren't fighting against these problems, then what *are* you doing? If your organization isn't actively involved in trying to do something, then how do you prevent people from falling into hopelessness and immobility? If you don't consistently demand some of your participants' time, how will you prevent them from filling up their lives with other important activities, so that they are not available when you finally get your act together?

You Can't Just "Get" the Media

Often when we discuss tactics with our students they come up with examples that include, somewhere, a line that says something like "and then we'll get the media to. . . ." This reminds us of the famous cartoon where a physicist writes a complex formula on the chalkboard, and in the middle he includes a key step that says "and then a miracle occurs . . ."

You cannot "get" the media (or anyone else, for that matter) to do anything. The media is going to do what it wants to do. And unless you are doing something very creative, or are closely linked to an issue the public/media is already interested in (like an emerging story about political corruption) or a shocking event (a child is hit by a car at an intersection without a stop sign), the media is unlikely to show up. Just because you hold a "press conference" doesn't mean that the press is actually interested in hearing what you have to say.

There are a wide range of strategies for seducing different forms of media to pay attention to what you are doing. One key approach is to develop personal relationships with key reporters. Another is to link your actions to a narrative (story or unfolding event) that is already generating buzz. Another is to make sure that your action is so impressive that the media simply needs to cover it (if you shut down a major highway, for example). Sometimes you are just lucky to be at the right place, with the right issue, at the right time. But learning to work with the media is a complex arena, and we have neither the space nor the expertise to discuss it in detail, here. Furthermore, it is a field that is currently in a state of rapid change in the face of new media, declining finances in the newspaper industry, and the like.

The key take-home message right now is that influencing the media, like influencing anyone else, requires you to understand and address the self-interest of reporters. Just because *you* think your action or issue is important (who doesn't?), won't mean the media will think it's worthy of their time. In fact, it is likely that *most* of the marches in the United States have occurred without any mention in a mainline venue.

Some of the vignettes we give in this chapter (and in earlier chapters) talk about how media coverage helped them win, or at least helped make sure their action made an impact. Just remember that there is usually a story *behind* the story, a process by which a particular organization was able to convince some part of the media to pay attention to them in the first place.

Criteria for Good Tactic

As with issues, organizers have a set of criteria for what makes a more or less effective tactic. And, again, different organizers will frame these criteria in divergent ways. Some will identify only a few; others will discuss 10 or more. Here, we list the seven that we think will be most helpful.

A good tactic

1. puts pressure on a target,
2. includes a specific demand,
3. is outside the experience of the target,
4. is within the experience of your own members,
5. gets large numbers of people involved,
6. educates your members and develops leaders, and
7. is fun, engaging, or educational!

A Good Tactic Puts Pressure on a Target

This criterion basically repeats our core definition of what a "tactic" is in the first place. But it's important enough to repeat. If your action is not designed, in some way, to put pressure on a target or a secondary target, then you are probably wasting your time.

The Problem with Petitions

Don Keating[2]

Petitions don't get results: people do.... Petitions can be used as excuses to get people talking to people, but they don't bring many people into the organization. Those who sign usually stay at home. About all a petition does is make shut-ins feel involved.

Taking a petition is what you do when you ... don't know how to organize. ... Petitions don't achieve very much in bringing about changes because signatures on pages just don't carry very much clout and they certainly don't offer much in organizing mileage. ...

[When a group of leaders were talking with Paul Baker, a representative of the transit authority,] Baker was asked: "Approximately how many names do you need on a petition to get a bus [route]?"

Baker could have tried to use that as a red herring to encourage the people to busy themselves with petitions, but he blurted out his true feelings in a way that was a delight to the organizers. He told us what I always tell people: coming from him, it was better.

"A petition doesn't mean a thing. If your officers make a request on your behalf you get just as much action on that as if you had 10,000 names on a petition. Petitions mean very little.

"*You can get people to sign petitions to have their heads chopped off.* ... It's [too] easy to get people to sign something without knowing what's on it."

A Good Tactic Makes a Specific Demand

Kimberly Bobo and her colleagues argue that "the weakest tactic is one that is not aimed at anyone and makes no demand." They use the example of "a candle-light vigil to save the whales that doesn't call on anyone to do anything in particular." Unless you've got a whole lot of people behind you at such a vigil (and maybe even then), you're probably wasting your time.

In fact you may actually be reducing your ability to make change. You may be fooling all those people at the vigil into thinking that they *are* "doing" something useful to make change. So they don't need to do anything else.

What exactly are you trying to get out of a particular action? What, as fund-raisers often say, is the "ask"? The "ask" can be as large as a request that a target meet all of your organization's demands, and can be as small as an attempt just to get a meeting with the target.

Understanding what you are asking for doesn't mean that you will get it, of course. In fact, you may actually hope that you *don't* get what you are asking for. For example, if you request a meeting with an official and the official's representatives just blow you off in some insulting way, well, they've just activated your base. Nobody wants to be disrespected. (Remember Richard Harmon's story about the "bucket of shit.")

Knowing what you are asking for is also important for designing your action. A request for a meeting, for example, is going to require a different level of power, a different kind of demonstration, than a final request at a public meeting for five hundred million dollars of new loan guarantees for low-income housing. The former can happen fairly early in the campaign, and may not involve a huge number of members (if you are a new group, you may not even have that many members). The latter is something that you would need to build up to, an ask that would happen after you have already demonstrated sufficient power to make you think the target may actually give in. For example, the Industrial Areas Foundation's (IAF) East Brooklyn Congregations organizing group got Mayor Rudy Giuliani to come to a large public meeting and agree to provide funding to expand their Nehemiah Homes project (which has built over 2,100 units) only after an extended series of efforts to impress upon him the power and importance of their organization.

Act Differently

William Gamson[3]

[Social movements] can easily run afoul of . . . the ritualization of collective action. Feistiness and disruption may disappear altogether in actions that court arrest but could hardly be called unruly.

For example, some forms of civil disobedience [have] become scripted events in which demonstrators, police, and journalists play well-rehearsed and thoroughly predictable roles. Far from disrupting the system, the challenger-authority interaction is absorbed into its routine operation. Lacking the criteria of newsworthiness, the action is back-page, local news at best, essentially invisible to any larger audience whom the challengers hoped to move by example.

The most successful challengers . . . refuse . . . to follow a script that absorbe[s] . . . them into the routine functioning of the social control system.

A Good Tactic Is Outside the Experience of Your Target

In the simplest sense, you want to do something that the target isn't already ready to deal with. This is why traditional pickets, marches, and petitions are often less effective than you might expect. As Gamson notes, above, even seemingly impressive tactics like chaining people to the front doors of a bank or having a die-in in front of a polluting power plant can become somewhat old hat. If people are used to these actions, they are generally ready to deal with them (and the media won't be interested enough to cover them).

Bobo and her colleagues give the example of a group that had hundreds of members apply for postal service jobs with photocopies of applications. The target wasn't ready to deal with this tactic and made a mistake, rejecting all of the applications because they weren't "originals." This action made him look "so unfair and prejudiced" that it became much easier to paint him as obstructive and "wrong." Another example discussed in a previous chapter was Alinsky's tactic of having large crowds overwhelm a bank branch with requests to open accounts and change dollars into change. This tactic used the bank's own rules and regulations against it, making it hard for the bank management to respond.[4]

Guerrilla Housing Inspection Team

Gabriel Thompson[5]

Otilia had a brilliant idea: we could form a guerrilla housing inspection team. If the city couldn't be bothered to help tenants with emergency housing situations, then why not hold an event to challenge not only the landlord but the entire ineffectual code enforcement system that forced tenants to live in dangerous housing?

And why not invite the media?

Right then and there we formed the "People's Housing Unit." I went out and bought a few jumpsuits and created official inspection forms. With some handmade patches stitched onto the uniforms, we sent out a press release offering to give the media tours of the building.

The next day we found two newspaper reporters and four television camera crews lined up outside the building. They followed the tenants and inspection team as we went from apartment to apartment, cataloguing such violations as busted water pipes growing centers of mold, infestations of rats and cockroaches, and constant leaks and gaping holes in the bathrooms. As the inspections took place, tenant leaders spoke to the media about the need to beef up the city's code enforcement division and advocated for pending citywide legislation that would make the city's housing agency more effective in documenting and correcting violations.

Our event prompted rapid agency response: that very evening, city inspectors visited the building and did a thorough inspection of every unit, finding ninety violations. The city's housing agency issued a public apology (a first!) that was featured in a prominent newspaper the following day. The landlord, whose building was suddenly featured on many media outlets, stopped by our office and made a commitment to complete the work quickly—but we decided that given his previous inattention, we needed a court order to guarantee results. When we returned to court, we had a violation printout as evidence, and the judge ordered the landlord to make the repairs quickly or face severe financial penalties.

Two weeks later, many of the major hazards had been fixed.

A Good Tactic Is Something Your Members Think Is Reasonable

This criterion is crucial. You can't engage in a tactic that your members don't feel is ethical or that they are uncomfortable with in some way. If they are, you may end up creating negativity among your members while pursuing it.

For example, in an earlier module we talked about how Aaron had an idea for his organization to do an action at the house of a school board member who had said that anyone could come to his door to talk with him. Many members didn't feel this was ethical because the board member had younger children.

Bobo and her colleagues give an example of a labor coalition that planned to pray in a hotel lobby for four days. The leaders assumed, incorrectly, that praying and bringing religion in this way into the public sphere of confrontation was something that most of their organization members were comfortable with. But they weren't.[6]

You don't want to get into loud, shouting confrontations when you are working with a culture that is uncomfortable with this (e.g., some Native American tribes). Instead, you may want to hold silent vigils—perhaps in places where you obstruct the "business as usual" of your target. A Native American tribe in our city, for example, recently convinced the chancellor of a university to keep an agreement to hire a Native American professor by simply showing up unannounced at one of his lectures in full regalia and standing in a line on either side of the hall. They stayed completely silent, and simply turned around and left when the lecture ended. We are told that you could see the sweat beading on the chancellor's face. He quickly called up the group and agreed to meet their demands.

You need to take into account the culture, education, class, and other general characteristics of your group or groups to understand what fits within their culture and experience.

Of course, you don't just need to simply accept what people are "comfortable" with at any point in time. You can "stretch" people's comfort zones, helping them learn slowly to accept a wider range of kinds of tactics. They may not be willing to be arrested in defense of their own interests today. But next year they may become willing to.

A Good Issue Involves a Lot of People

Issues often come up that a relatively small number of participants could achieve without much effort. This is especially true after an organization has gained a reputation for power. But just because you can win without working too hard doesn't mean you should.

Again, organizing groups want to get a large number of people involved in campaigns and individual tactics. It is through the act of involvement that new members become a real part of your organization, and that your current members feel like they are a continuing part of the struggle.

Charles Dobson cites an important study by the League of Women Voters in 1999 that found that people perceived a lack of time as the key barrier preventing them from participating in community efforts. If you can't keep your key leaders involved in organizing activity, then, they are likely to stop carving out time for your group. And when you need them you will find that they no longer have time for you—they've replaced the time they used to spend on organizing with coaching a little league team, or delivering meals to shut-ins, or whatever. This is another reason to keep a broad range of people active and involved.[7]

A parent organizing group in California once got the state to investigate problems in their local low-income school district when the president of the group wrote a letter to the state superintendent. So this tactic worked. But it didn't get people involved. It didn't build her organization.

Another approach would have been to ask a whole bunch of the organization's members to write letters to the state. This, at least, would get more people involved and educate them about the specific laws the district seems to be violating. But even this approach keeps members fairly isolated from the realities of power on the state level. They send their letters and then they're done.

It would make more sense to have these letter writers get on a bus and go on a trip to the state capital to collectively present their demands to the superintendent, perhaps visit their local representatives, and maybe even make a presentation or give testimony.

The latter would involve a lot of work. But even if it didn't ultimately accomplish more in concrete issue terms than the president did when she wrote her letter, it would be a much more productive strategy for the organization. The bus trip to the capital *builds the power of the organization.* The single letter written by the president of the organization really doesn't.

The take-home message is that you want to prioritize tactics that make real demands upon a wide range of your members, *sometimes even if you don't strictly need their participation to "win."* And, as we noted in the previous chapter, you want to prioritize *issues* that will involve tactics that require extensive member participation to win.

A Good Tactic Educates

Education in community organizing groups doesn't happen in classrooms and workshops as much as it does through *acting.*

Community organizing groups do often hold training sessions around particular concepts and skills. You want to make sure your leaders share a common "language" about organizing. And you don't want to engage with an issue unless your members understand why the organization has chosen it.

More generally, however, organizers believe that we learn to fight power by fighting power. We learn about the ways powerful people can try to trick and use us when we are tricked and used. We learn about the complexities of creating effective tactics by creating tactics (which sometimes succeed and sometimes don't work so well). We discover how it feels to be in a collective struggle only when we actually engage in collective struggle.

But learning is not automatic. Your tactics actually need to be designed to help your members learn. This will happen in at least three ways.

First, you should find ways to involve a range of members in planning and carrying off a tactic. Each person who is participating will end up learning about how tactics work. These are people you can look to the next time you need to act.

In the "cable TV" example we gave earlier, for instance, we told about a time when an organizer engaged her group—people who lived in a particular housing complex—in tactics that were actually more involved than were actually necessary to get cable TV. She encouraged them to sit down and write letters together, and to carefully prepare for a confrontation with the building manager—creating signs, role-playing responses to different things the manager might say, practicing their statements. In this case, these tactics were more about educating the members of the group than putting pressure on the manager (although they surely did that, as well). This was a somewhat manipulative example, something that most organizers wouldn't try, either for basic ethical reasons, or simply because it might backfire if the members realized they were not being given the straight story. But it is a good example of the educational role of actions.

Second, you should make tactics themselves educational. The presentations that leaders give at rallies can help educate people about your issue. The materials you hand out can educate people. The structure of the tactic itself can be educational as people see effective ways of engaging with people in power.

Third, you must always include an evaluation after any action is concluded.

Acting and Learning: Discovering How the Other Side Lives

Gale Cincotta[8]

[Concerned with the effect of higher energy costs on low- and middle-income families, National People's Action decided to "crash" an industry-sponsored cocktail party.]

We asked around for whoever had a suit or a dress. We gathered about seventy-five people together . . . went to the top of the Hancock Building, and walked in on Exxon International.

We freaked them out. We didn't really think about it until later, after we'd left peacefully but God, they're all so guilty they probably thought we were terrorists, out to kidnap them or something. Suddenly there we were in the middle of [all those executives,] and we had women, and blacks, and men with beards!

I think it's important for our people to see how these executives live. But it's just as important for them to see us, and to know that there's no place to hide—not even the top of the Hancock Building, where they think they're so high above the people.

They didn't even have a security cop, they were so sure of themselves. Next time they'll have one. Probably more than one.

Action Evaluations

You, young man, are just a pile of undigested actions.
> —Saul Alinsky, *The Democratic Promise*

You have to constantly take the time to ask, "What have we learned from this action?" The evaluation of an action is as important as the action itself.
> —Michael Jacoby Brown, *Building Powerful Community Organizations*

After every action, established organizing groups conduct an evaluation. They bring all the key leaders together to discuss what happened, why it happened, what went well, and what could have been done differently. The central goal of an evaluation is for leaders to learn from what they just experienced. Mike Silver says, "This is mainly a process of reality construction. The [organizer's] role is to elicit from as many participants as possible their subjective descriptions of what happened, and then to help tie the descriptions together into an objective reality that is mutually shared within the organization."[9]

An evaluation is especially important after a confrontational action. Leaders need to make sense of what the target may have said, and what the action did or did not accomplish.

A Good Tactic Is Fun!

This criterion isn't that complicated. If you want people to come back, you want them to have fun at your actions.

When we say "fun," we mean it pretty broadly. If people enjoy what happened, either because they learned something, or because they got to see a good spectacle, or because there was an opportunity to engage with their friends, etc., then it still fulfills this tactic. You should think about how a tactic will draw your people in, how you can make it memorable and enjoyable.

A New Stoplight

Mike Miller[10]

[In Kansas City,] the Paseo, a major north-south boulevard cut through the heart of the Black community. At one of its intersections, elderly residents on the east side wanted to cross the street to go west to a shopping area; students on the west side had to go east to school. The residents wanted a stoplight.

The city traffic department measured cross-street foot traffic and said the volume didn't merit a stoplight. The community organization said the particular needs of the elderly and young children did. The city was adamant and refused to budge

One late afternoon, thirty-five or so residents, some walking with canes, others holding the hands of young children, walked around the four crosswalks of the intersection, bringing rush-hour traffic to a halt. Young men ran up the line of cars and handed flyers to frustrated drivers. "If you don't want us back next week, call Traffic Engineer

Falon and tell him there should be a stoplight here." The flyer provided his phone number.

Two days after our action, we got a call from the traffic department: "Upon further examination, the department has concluded that the particular circumstances of the intersection require a stoplight."

The story usually brought a grin to the listeners. Creative nonviolent direct action made rush-hour motorists allies of the otherwise powerless neighbors around that street.

Start Small

You want to be careful not to escalate actions too quickly. You want to start small, with less aggressive tactics that build up slowly to more risky assertions of power. For example, you really don't want to start a campaign with a broad boycott or by chaining yourselves to the doors of city hall.

If you start too aggressively too quickly, you run the risk of alienating both your own members and others you would like to recruit support from. By starting small, you can slowly generate increasing irritation and anger as your participants see powerful people refuse to respond to what should seem like fairly reasonable demands.

Good early tactics also should be educational for your members and others, because you want to make sure everyone really understands the key points involved in your issue. You are trying to build broader support for more aggressive and elaborate actions if they become necessary. Letter-writing campaigns where people meet together in groups to write and learn more about the issue and press conferences where you present facts about your issue and make sure that large numbers of your members attend are good examples of educational tactics that are fairly low key.

Only when you feel that you have generated sufficient anger should you move to more significant expressions of power. But be careful. If you organize a boycott and you can't pull it off, then you may have just shot yourself in the foot. If you do something really radical, like getting large numbers of your members arrested for civil disobedience and don't get any response from the powerful, you may actually end up only showing how powerless you really are. You need to be very strategic in how you approach tactics like these. Sometimes you may decide that you don't have enough power to win the issue as you originally framed it and will need to compromise in order to preserve the sense that you are an effective social action organization. Remember, Alinsky often didn't actually carry out an action—the mere possibility that he *might* could be enough to bring a target to the table.

Creative Tactics

I ... encourage people to experiment. That is actually the lesson I would draw from the period of the 1960s and 1970s, when I was involved in what were essentially experimental modes of conventional civil rights organizing. Nobody knew whether they would work or not. Nobody knew where we were going. ...

Young people today have too much deference toward the older organizers, the veterans, and are much too careful in their desire to rely on role models. ...

The best way to figure out what might work is simply to do it. ... One must be willing to make mistakes. ... Mistakes help to produce the new modes of organizing.

—Angela Davis, *Angela Y. Davis Reader*

If you are going to operate "outside the experience of the target," it helps to be creative about tactics. Bobo and her colleagues give a list of the standard categories of tactics that we have altered slightly:

- petition drives
- letter writing
- manufactured media (in-house videos and Internet sites)
- turnout events (like rallies or pickets)
- visits with public officials
- public hearings
- accountability sessions
- citizen's investigations
- educational meetings and teach-ins
- civil disobedience and arrest
- legal disruptive tactics

In our experience, organizing groups tend not to be very creative about how they develop their tactics within (and beyond) these arenas. In meetings to develop tactics, people move very quickly to what is familiar: "let's do a petition" or "let's have a rally."

The best tactics are designed specifically around the unique circumstances of a particular issue. They take into account everything an organization has gathered about a target and the particular historical context of their issue to develop their tactics.

In his second book about organizing, *Rules for Radicals,* Alinsky intentionally gave fewer examples of tactics. He did this, he said, because he found out that too many organizers and leaders were using *Reveille* as a kind of source-book for tactic examples. They'd get in trouble and riffle through the book for an idea of what to do. The problem with this, Alinsky emphasized, was that each of the tactics he described in *Reveille* was designed specifically for the unique circumstances of a particular campaign. You can't simply transplant a tactic developed for one circumstance into another. Instead, he constantly stressed, organizers need to be creative about how they develop their tactics, incredibly sensitive to the unique specifics they are facing at any particular time.

So: Be creative!

A Crying Need for New Tactics

Lee Staples[11]

Public and private institutional decision-makers have learned how to deal with many of the "standard" direct-action techniques. It is critical that new tactics be developed along with the momentum to make them work.

Tactics such as squatting, street blocking, citizen's arrests, tearing down abandoned houses, pledges, subpoenaing opponents, creative use of e-mail and the Internet, "people's hearings," buying mainstream advertising, "billing" the city for services done by the organization, and a host of dramatic props now are regular features of the direct action repertoire of many [grassroots community organizations]. Yet, these ideas only scratch the surface.

There's a crying need to create and execute imaginative new tactics in all types of organizing being done at the present. This problem doesn't receive sufficient attention and becomes more serious with each passing day.

Don't Get Arrogant

To this day many think that "Alinsky tactics" are fraternity house stunts or public relations arpeggios. Tactics which are not integrated with and thematically connected with a large effort soon roll off without enduring effect and may even backfire.

—Nicholas von Hoffman, *Radical: A Portrait of Saul Alinsky*

Creativity is not the same as stupidity or arrogance.

Creativity for the sake of being creative is a path toward ruin.

Especially near the end, Alinsky got a touch of megalomania in his lectures and writings. Again, the fact is that he never really put any of the truly zany actions he talked about into effect. For example, he never did actually try, in his battle with the mayor of Chicago, to get his organization to take over all the stalls at O'Hare Airport in Chicago, for what he called a "shit in," so that no one else could go to the bathroom. It seems highly unlikely that he could have pulled it off, and it also probably would have hurt public support of his efforts (TV videos of embarrassed and "innocent" tourists and kids squatting over plant boxes to do their business come to mind).

At the same time, as von Hoffman notes, Alinsky had a unique (and not entirely earned) reputation for being able to carry off actions that would be impossible for others. Thus, Alinsky could mention (not exactly threaten) the possibility of holding a "shit in" to people who he knew would get this idea back to the mayor (who saw the airport as one of his shining gems). And it got the mayor to the table. If anyone else had brought it up, the concept would have simply brought peals of laughter and ridicule. As Alinsky often said, power is not what you have, but what the other side *thinks* you have. Power, as we noted earlier, is a product, in part, of reputation.

Getting arrogant about what you can actually accomplish will destroy your reputation for having any real capacity to do what you say. Recall, Alinsky's recommendation about flashy actions: "never make a threat you are not able to carry out and even if you can carry it out, don't do it."[12]

Strategic thinking, not creativity, is the key to effective actions. The least creative action that is carefully designed to target the specific self-interests of the opposition is a thousand times better than a wildly creative action that doesn't target much of anything.

Power over the long term emerges out of your reputation, and this means that a reputation for effectiveness is the coin of the realm. Don't squander it.

Stay Flexible: The Real Action Is in the Reaction

Everybody's got a plan—until they get hit.
                    —Joe Louis (sometimes attributed to Mike Tyson)

Reality is messy. Don't forget it. As Helmut von Moltke said, "no battle plan survives contact with the enemy." You cannot simply *make* powerful people do your bidding.[13]

As we noted before, "the real action is in the reaction." The best you can do is speculate about the *kinds* of things a particular target is likely to do in response to an action.

An experienced organizer with a deep understanding of the self-interests of the opposition can often predict with fair accuracy what a target is likely to do, however. In fact, we heard about one organizer who was so good at predicting what a target would say that his leaders actually wondered out loud if he was a plant from the opposition.

Just as organizing groups often use a fairly standard set of tactics, the opposition has a collection of fairly common responses to organizing action. Bobo and her colleagues list some good examples of "tricks the other side uses":

- "Let's negotiate."
- "You are invited to the 'stakeholders' meeting."
- "I can get you on the Governor's commission."
- "Go work it out among yourselves."
- "I'm the wrong person."
- "This could affect your funding."
- "You are reasonable but your allies aren't. Can't we just deal with you?"[14]

Lee Staples categorizes these "tricks" into what he calls the " 'The Seven D's of Defense': Deflecting, Delaying, Deceiving, Dividing, Denying, Discrediting, and Destroying."

- **Deflecting**: "Many times, targets will try *deflecting* the thrust of an organizing campaign.... Common tactics include sending an assistant or 'flunky' to deal with the Action Group, 'passing the buck' to another department, trying to change the subject or switch issues," and arguing that they don't have the authority to make a decision.

  - *Common organization response*: Do your homework *ahead of time* so you know for certain that you have chosen the correct target.

- **Delaying:** "The stall." "Opponents may use delaying tactics to slow the pace of a campaign, in order to 'ride out the storm' of protest.... They may be attempting to buy additional time to develop a more effective counterstrategy. Or, they may be testing the Action Group's resolve, trying to wear down its energies." Other delaying tactics include putting organization members on "study commissions" or "community councils," which take a long time to deliberate, destroying a campaign's momentum, and producing reports that are then mostly ignored.

  - *Common organization response*: Set a deadline for the target to act or respond, and lay out specific consequences for the target if the deadline is not met.

- **Deceiving:** "This category covers a range of tactics from tricks and sub-terfuges to outright lies.... In many cases, the target will attempt to bewilder and perplex members through a sea of 'red tape' that makes the processes unintelligible. An array of [nonexistent] bureaucratic rules and regulations are invoked. Simple solutions suddenly become impossible to implement.... Legal issues emerge out of the blue."

    - *Common organization response*: Research, research, research. Experts can be helpful, but leaders should feel like they really understand the issues. Only then will they feel empowered to stand up to the opposition as equals.

- **Dividing:** "Perhaps the most insidious type of countertactic is the old standard. 'Divide and conquer'. If an organization's power lies in the strength of its numbers, then anything that splits and separates its members and leaders will weaken it."

    - *Common organization response*: Good discipline, a broad understanding of the benefits of solidarity over the long term, and a constant open dialogue between leaders can help prevent "divide and conquer".

- **Denying:** A target can either avoid meeting with an organization (some-times with "I'm too busy") or flatly refuse to make any concessions at all (often with something like "I'd like to help you but . . . my hands are tied, we just don't have the money"). The target may even deny there is any problem at all worth dealing with.

    - *Common organization response*: Escalate tactics. Tactics to address a refusal often include tracking down the target in unexpected places— "home, church, club, golf course, board meeting," and the like. Blanket refusals to act generally mean that more pressure must be exerted to make it worth a target's while to consider negotiating.

- **Discrediting:** Efforts to *discredit* may include challenging an organiza-tion's research, the credibility of its leadership (often with accusations of corruption or incompetence), or an organization's legitimacy as a repre-sentative of the community (sometimes combined with the creation of an alternate, opposition-controlled group).

    - *Common organization response*: In response to discrediting, organi-zations generally take the moral high ground, presenting evidence supporting their purity while mobilizing large numbers of people as evidence of their authenticity.

- **Destroying:** "On some occasions, opponents will . . . attack both the organization and individual leaders or members, . . . frighten its constituents, or threaten its very existence." This may include arresting key leaders, threatening leaders' business interests, evictions, and in extreme cases even infiltration and violence. The opposition will often pressure institutions to stop funding an organizing group.

  - *Common organization response:* Any individual who is attacked needs to be supported, drawing in allies where possible, and organizations need to think ahead about how they will continue a campaign if their funding is threatened.[15]

Simply mentioning possible responses doesn't mean these responses will be effective. There are no guarantees in organizing. Sometimes—often, in fact—organizing groups are outmaneuvered and outgunned by the opposition. At best, in cases like these, organizations try to walk away with symbolic victories, attempting to maintain their reputation for effective action by hiding the fact that they negotiated most of what they wanted away. As we noted in Chapter 13, this happened to Alinsky in his fight with Kodak in Rochester, where FIGHT had to settle for a vague "agreement" after an extended campaign. Sometimes "saving face" is the best one can do.

Planning an Action

Actions are heavily choreographed and rehearsed, like a play. When we do an action . . . the interaction in that venue has to read like a drama. A good action has stages; people play roles, and everyone prepares and practices. . . .

We generally spend a great deal more time preparing for an action than actually doing it. . . . A group defines the tone of an action in the preparation stage, not in the target's office.

—Rinku Sen, *Stir It Up*

Good actions are carefully planned down to the smallest detail. When you can't control much, you control what you can. Something will almost inevitably go wrong. So you need to prepare what can be prepared to give you space to deal with the unexpected.

Every participant needs to know his or her part: spectator, speaker, facilitator, timekeeper, etc. If there will be preplanned testimonials or speeches, then these should be written up and practiced. There is little worse than having a key leader stand up and start in on a demand that the entire group has not agreed upon, or go rambling on far past the time you have allotted.

The entire action and each section should be timed. And there should be a clear reason for the inclusion of each component. ("That's the way we always do it" is *not* a justification.) Less is more when more doesn't contribute anything clearly significant.

Sometimes the little details are the most important. If people are going to wear T-shirts, where will they get them from? When will signs be made? Who will provide water for a march in hot weather? Do you need day care for children? Will you provide food? Who will set up the tables, and where will you get the tables from? If you will have literature available, how do you make sure it doesn't blow off your table? Who is going to get the person giving a testimonial who doesn't drive to the event?

Part of the planning for an event, especially one that involves a direct engagement with a target, involves preparing for the different things that can happen and the different responses you can get. Often this involves actual role plays, where leaders try out different ways of dealing with different events and where an experienced organizer or leader plays the part of the opposition. In a meeting to try to get the president of the local electrical utility to agree to put a pollution scrubber on the coal plant in your neighborhood, what will you do if she offers to put together a commission to "study" the problem? What will you do if she says the utility can't afford the scrubber, that it would lead to major increases in electricity costs? What will you do if she says she'll look at the problem and get back to you later? What will you do if she decides not to show up at your meeting, and you are standing there with hundred people and no target to address?

You can't prepare for every contingency, but the preparation process itself helps leaders gain experience in understanding how the opposition may try to manipulate them. Through a role play, they can grapple with a range of possible challenges in contrast with the actual event when they will only deal with what actually happens.

Strategy: Planning Ahead

In a football game, tactics represent individual plays, while strategy is about a series of plays or even one's approach to the entire game. In other words, strategy represents the overall plan of action for a campaign. In this section we focus on the "tactics" aspect of strategy, but strategy really includes everything that an organization does to prepare for and then pursue a campaign.

In our organizing courses, we generally strip down the idea of strategy to its basics. We ask students to imagine a couple of different ways a target might respond to a particular action, and then we ask them to imagine how they would react to these different responses. Like a chess player, strategy in this sense involves thinking multiple moves ahead—"if I do this, and then she does that, what will I do then?" We give them a diagram like the one in Figure 14.1 to help them think this way:

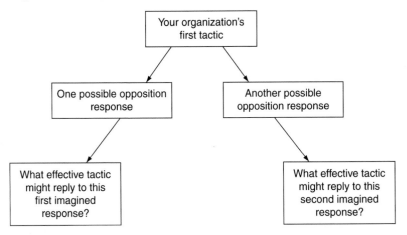

Figure 14.1 Anticipating opposition responses

The goal of this exercise is to give them practice in thinking like the opposition, considering the kinds of options the opposition has, and exploring what an organizing group might do in response. The truth is that many organizing groups get very focused on the specific action they are working on at the moment. They don't spend much time thinking creatively about the broader span of their campaign. Thinking about the longer term prepares leaders for an extended campaign and helps them anticipate the challenges they may face.

It's important in this exercise to try to put yourself in the shoes of your opposition. Instead of just making up any old response, really think about what a target's most likely responses are given your opposition's specific position, history, resources, and self-interests.

In their textbook for Midwest Academy's week-long community organizing training program (a program we recommend for readers as a good practical next step for learning about organizing), Bobo and her colleagues include their widely used "strategy chart," which goes beyond this very schematic approach to strategy and brings in a wide range of considerations central to any campaign:

- Goals
- Organizational considerations
- Constituents, allies, and opponents

- Targets
- Tactics[16]

In any event, it is important to remember that the lives of community organizations are structured around issue campaigns and not individual tactics, just as a football team is more interested in how many games it wins or loses than in whether a particular play comes off well. Thinking strategically over the broad span of a specific campaign, therefore, is critical for the long-term success of an organization.

Vision

[A] long term vision needs to be developed [in community organizing].
—Barack Obama, "Organizing in the 1990s"

We end this chapter and our discussion of key concepts in organizing with the question of "vision." In organizing terms, one's vision is about how one imagines all of one's campaigns coming together to produce a better society. And nearly all community organizers will acknowledge that while they may be good at thinking strategically about particular campaigns, they have never really figured out how to bring individual campaigns together into a broader vision of social change.

On the bus to a training early in the evolution of ACORN, Jay Hessey said to Gary Delgado that "The real question is whether we'll come out of this as a national organization or as three hundred local groups winning the hell out of stop signs." The recent demise of ACORN makes this question even more poignant. Certainly ACORN as an organization accomplished much more than simply winning stop signs. They achieved national successes in terms of living wage campaigns, against predatory lending practices, and more. Still, the question resonates. Did even ACORN, the most powerful national organizing group, have an adequate vision of how to get from where they were to the kind of society we would all like to see? We think most ACORN leaders would acknowledge that the answer was no.[17]

Developing a more comprehensive vision (or visions) remains a key and unfinished task in organizing today.

Notes

1. Ken Galdston cited in Kristin Layng Szakos and Joe Szakos, *We Make Change: Community Organizers Talk about What They Do–And Why* (Nashville, TN: Vanderbilt University Press, 2007), 159.

2. Donald R. Keating, *The Power to Make It Happen: Mass-Based Community Organizing: What It Is and How It Works* (Toronto, ON: Green Tree, 1975), 152, italics added.
3. William A. Gamson, *The Strategy of Social Protest* (Homewood, IL: Dorsey Press, 1975), 166–167.
4. Kimberley A. Bobo et. al., *Organizing for Social Change: Midwest Academy Manual for Activists,* 3rd ed. (Santa Ana, CA: Seven Locks Press, 2001).
5. Gabriel Thompson, *Calling All Radicals: How Grassroots Organizers Can Save Our Democracy* (New York: Nation Books, 2007), 5–6.
6. Bobo et al., *Community Organizing.*
7. Charles Dobson, *The Troublemaker's Teaparty: A Manual for Effective Citizen Action* (Gabriola Island, BC: New Society Publishers, 2003).
8. Gale Cincotta cited in Anne Witte Garland, *Women Activists: Challenging the Abuse of Power* (New York: The Feminist Press at the City University of New York, 1988), 51.
9. Mike Silver cited in Gary Delgado, *Organizing the Movement: The Roots and Growth of ACORN* (Philadelphia, PA: Temple University Press, 1986), 88.
10. Mike Miller, *A Community Organizer's Tale: People and Power in San Francisco* (Berkeley, CA: Heyday Books, 2009), 81–82.
11. Lee Staples, *Roots to Power,* 2nd ed. (Westport, CT: Praeger, 2004), 145.
12. Nicholas von Hoffman, *Radical: A Portrait of Saul Alinsky* (New York: Nation Books, 2010), 85.
13. Von Moltke cited in Joseph Cummins, *The War Chronicles, from Chariots to Flintlocks: New Perspectives on the Two Thousand Years of Bloodshed That Shaped the Modern World* (Beverly, MA: Fair Winds Press, 2008), 151.
14. Bobo et al., *Community Organizing.*
15. Staples, *Roots to Power,* 148–152.
16. Bobo, et al., *Community Organizing.* You can learn about the Midwest Academy's week-long training program at midwestacademy.com.
17. Hessey cited in Delgado, *Organizing the Movement,* 123.

PART V

Conclusion

CHAPTER 15

"Hope Is on the Ground"

Hope has never trickled down. It has always sprung up. That's what Jessie de la Cruz meant when she said, "I feel there's gonna be a change, but we're the ones gonna do it, not the government. With us, there's a saying, 'La esperanza muere ultima. Hope dies last.' You can't lose hope. If you lose hope, you lose everything."

—Studs Terkel

Low-income communities and communities of color can gain power to make lasting change through community organizing, but it will only happen if people feel that they are acting on their own felt problems. This book is designed to introduce people to the craft of community organizing, and to help insure that, while community organizing has had a rich and varied tradition in the United States, we continue to sustain it as a vibrant living practice today. We hope that more people will choose to get involved in existing organizing groups or start their own.

As we showed in our history chapter (Chapter 3), oppressed people in America have employed many different strategies to promote social change. Organizing, in particular, seeks to empower and provide tangible benefits to local neighborhoods and institutions. The benefits of community organizing are both local and national in scope. On the local level, low-income communities have successfully thwarted municipal plans to build highways through their neighborhoods and prevented companies from building toxic waste facilities. They have successfully forced parks and recreation departments to install more streetlights for basketball courts and local health departments to provide more services to the youth and elderly. Nationally, the hard-won benefits of organizing influence our lives every day. Organizing groups contributed to the creation of a federal minimum wage. Organizing helped pass laws requiring the government to enforce safety standards in consumer goods, to fund the work of community development corporations that develop safe, affordable housing, and that mandate environmental protections to ensure that everyone has clean water and air.

As these "wins" become an everyday part of our experience, it is easy to forget how they got here. If one looks closely at history, however, one discovers that the government almost always acts because some group or another forced it to do so, not because an authority figure decided to be nice to those living in regrettable circumstances.

The geographer Henri Lefebvre described hope as something that happens on the ground, in our lived experiences and in our lived spaces. It is within the context of everyday experiences where we actualize possibilities for social change, as "[i]t embraces the loci of passion, of action." In this sense, hope is not so much an abstract concept as it is a result of our rooted commitments and actions in the world. The importance of acting with a sense of hope that is grounded in a particular locale is central to traditional community organizing.[1]

We are all aware of the deep interconnectedness of local, state, national, and global circumstances. At first glance, it may seem futile to work on the local level when so many factors seem outside of local control. But sweeping national changes usually happen because people *started* organizing locally.

In this book we seek to help people "believe in the future of organizing," in part by introducing some of the specific tools and concepts that organizers employ. New political realities will no doubt bring new strategies. Instead of accepting what we write as some kind of dogma, we hope that the understanding of community organizing that readers gain from this book provides a springboard for the development of new forms of collective action. To succeed, we must press forward instead of holding back as we travel together into always-uncertain tomorrows.

Note

1. Henri Lefebvre, *Production of Space*, trans. D Nicholson-Smith (Oxford, UK: Blackwell, 1991).

PART VI

Appendix

Recommendations for Further Reading

"Nuts and Bolts": Introductions to the Practice of Community Organizing

Bobo, Kimberley A., Jackie Kendall, Steve Max, and Midwest Academy. *Organizing for Social Change: Midwest Academy Manual for Activists*. 3rd ed. Santa Ana, CA: Seven Locks Press, 2001. (Note: this is the textbook for the Midwest Academy training program listed below.)

Brown, Michael Jacoby. *Building Powerful Community Organizations: A Personal Guide to Creating Groups That Can Solve Problems and Change the World*. Arlington, MA: Long Haul Press, 2006.

Kahn, Si. *Creative Community Organizing: A Guide for Rabble-Rousers, Activists, and Quiet Lovers of Justice*. New York: Demos, 2010.

Sen, Rinku. *Stir It Up: Lessons in Community Organizing and Advocacy*. San Francisco, CA: Jossey-Bass, 2003.

Staples, Lee. *Roots to Power*. 2nd ed. Westport, CT: Praeger, 2004.

Books by Organizers about Organizing that Also Include Practice Suggestions

Gecan, Michael. *Going Public*. Boston, MA: Beacon Press, 2002.

Keating, Donald R. *The Power to Make It Happen: Mass-Based Community Organizing: What It Is and How It Works*. Toronto, ON: Green Tree, 1975.

Miller, Mike. *A Community Organizer's Tale: People and Power in San Francisco*. Berkeley, CA: Heyday Books, 2009.

Books on Congregation-Based Community Organizing

Chambers, Edward T. D. and Michael A. Cowan. *Roots for Radicals: Organizing for Power, Action, and Justice*. New York: Continuum, 2003.

Shirley, Dennis. *Community Organizing for Urban School Reform*. Austin, TX: University of Texas Press, 1997.

Swarts, Heidi J. *Organizing Urban America: Secular and Faith-Based Progressive Movements*. Minneapolis, MN: University of Minnesota Press, 2008.

Warren, Mark R. *Dry Bones Rattling: Community Building to Revitalize American Democracy*. Princeton, NJ: Princeton University Press, 2001.

Books on the Association of Community Organizations for Reform Now (ACORN)

Atlas, John. *Seeds of Change: The Story of ACORN, America's Most Controversial Antipoverty Community Organizing Group*. Nashville, TN: Vanderbilt University Press, 2010.

Delgado, Gary. *Organizing the Movement: The Roots and Growth of ACORN*. Philadelphia, PA: Temple University Press, 1986.

Fisher, Robert. *The People Shall Rule: ACORN, Community Organizing, and the Struggle for Economic Justice*. Nashville, TN: Vanderbilt University Press, 2009.

Swarts, Heidi J. *Organizing Urban America: Secular and Faith-Based Progressive Movements*. Minneapolis, MN: University of Minnesota Press, 2008.

Books by and About Saul Alinsky

Alinsky, Saul. *Rules for Radicals*. New York: Vintage, 1971.

Alinsky, Saul. *Reveille for Radicals*. New York: Vintage, 1946.

Horwitt, Sanford D. *Let them Call Me Rebel: Saul Alinsky: His Life and Legacy*. New York: Vintage, 1992.

von Hoffman, Nicholas. *Radical: A Portrait of Saul Alinsky*. New York: Nation Books, 2010.

Organizing Training Programs

Center for Third World Organizing (cwto.org)
Provides assorted training and support.

Midwest Academy (midwestacademy.com)
Among other offerings, Midwest Academy runs a standard five day residential training program a few times a year.

Direct Action and Research Training Program (DART) (thedartcenter.org)
DART has recently held a yearly competition to become a DART intern. Those chosen are trained and then hired for local DART organizations.

Local and national organizations also conduct training programs for leaders and organizers in their group or network.

Informative Websites and Online Writings

The Change Agency (thechangeagency.org)
Many resources to download.
Comm-Org: The Online Conference on Community Organizing (comm-org.wisc.edu)
Contains original writings, sample syllabi, organization lists, a listserv about organizing, and more. Probably the best site about organizing on the Web.
The Citizen's Handbook (vcn.bc.ca/citizens-handbook/)
A comprehensive online organizing manual.
Education Action (educationaction.org)
Aaron's website.
Shelterforce Magazine (shelterforce.org/)
Many stories on organizing.
TenantNet Organizing Collection(tenant.net/Organize/)
Includes a range of useful materials, including *Basics of Organizing* and *Dynamics of Organizing* by Shel Trapp.

Index